BODY

INTELLIGENCE

A NEW PARADIGM

Living a Heart-Centered Life
in a Mind-Centered World

Award-winning Author
JOHN L. MAYFIELD, D.C.

Publisher's Cataloging-in-Publication Data
provided by Five Rainbows Services

Names: Mayfield, John L.
Title: Body intelligence : a new paradigm / John L. Mayfield.
Description: Grass Valley, CA : Nubalance Publishing, 2016. | Includes
    bibliographical references and index.
Identifiers: LCCN 2015901889 | ISBN 978-0-9884937-4-2 (pbk.) | ISBN 978-0-
    9884937-3-5 (ebook)
Subjects: LCSH: Medicine, Chinese Traditional. | Change (Psychology)--
    Philosophy. | Spiritual life. | Quantum theory--Popular works. | Mind and
    body. | BISAC: BODY, MIND & SPIRIT / Inspiration & Personal Growth.
    | SELF-HELP / Personal Growth / General. | SCIENCE / Philosophy &
    Social Aspects.
Classification: LCC BF161 .M41 2016 (print) | LCC BF161 (ebook) | DDC
    158.1--dc23.

Although every effort was made to ensure that the information was correct at the
time of going to press, the author and publisher do not assume and thereby dis-
claim any liability to any party for any injury allegedly arising from any information or suggestions in this book. Readers are advised to consult with their health
care practitioners before beginning any new health regimen. The publisher has no
control over, and does not assume any responsibility for, third party websites or
their content, where portions of this book may appear.

Publisher: Nubalance Publishing Company, Grass Valley, CA
Editors: Nora Isaacs and Jim Gebbie
Book Doctor: Kim Tally
Proofreader: Kim Tally
Layout: Howie Severson
Cover Design: Kimberly Nelson-Coombs
Original Art: Judy Mayfield

CONTENTS

SECTION II: SPIRIT LIVING IN MATTER   105

SECTION III: TAPPING THE POWER OF THE BODYMIND   141

FIRST HABIT

Acknowledgments

This book has been a long time in the writing, and consequently I owe thanks to a great many people. First of all I want to acknowledge my family and friends, and especially all of my patients. Along with all of you I have lived, practiced and honed the principles discussed in this book. Working with you has been the crucible of fire that forged these principles into a more pure essence. You have helped me to turn this information into something cohesive and usable. Your contribution is invaluable.

After we thought the book was done, Kim Tally proofread it. She said "This is a great book, but all the chapters need to be stitched together like a patchwork quilt." Then over the next seven months she worked with me to clarify each concept until they were completely fleshed out and comprehensible. She is the "Book doctor" who left no stone unturned in helping me craft an impeccable piece of literature. The effort has made this book into a more cohesive and pleasurable read.

Right after my first book *Body Intelligence, How to Think outside Your Brain* came out I met Susan Schrier-Williams, an Alexander Method posture practitioner in my hometown area. Thank you, Susan. You taught me an understanding of posture that feels more like alchemy. With your simple and elegant understanding of posture, I knew immediately that I would have to completely rewrite every page in the book that dealt with posture. When the chapters on posture were brought up to this new awareness, they raised the bar for the rest of the book to be just as clear and concise. As every concept fleshed out into a more complete understanding, over time *Body Intelligence, A New Paradigm* morphed into an entirely new work.

I would like to honor the late Jeffrey Kauffman, M.D., who also held a secondary acupuncture degree from the Worsley Institute. He read my manuscript and gave so generously of his time by providing valuable insights into the five-element section.

I sincerely thank Wenda O'Reilly, Ph.D., of Bird Cage Press and her husband James O'Reilly, the developer of Traveler's Tales. Wenda has read my manuscripts many times over the years. The many changes she recommended helped this book (and me) to mature into something much finer than I ever could have imagined. She helped give the habits catchy names and suggested I reshuffle the information into smaller, more digestible chapters. As a result, the book became more enjoyable and accessible to all readers. Wenda has been my coach, mentor, critic, and, most of all, my dear friend.

Thank you, Kimberly Nelson-Coombs, for all the time and thoughtfulness that went into the brilliant cover design of this book, for your artistic suggestions, and for organizing the formatting of the book. Thank you to Howie Severson of Fortuitous Publishing for your impeccable formatting of this book for print, e-book and Kindle.

Nora Isaacs helped make changes, and recommendations that made *Body Intelligence* more fun to read. A very special thanks to Jim Gebbie for his nurturing manner and proficient editing, a wonderful person to work with.

I want to thank Kim Morris, Jennifer Crebbin, my brother Jim Mayfield, and my whole family for all their love and encouragement.

My wife's influence shows up all through this book. She is an incredible artist, a loving and generous partner, and my most fierce advocate. She is my first, last, and most exacting reader who has helped with each of the hundreds of edits, and lovingly stood with me through all the joys and difficulties of manifesting this work. Her wisdom and encouragement show up in every page. She made it all worth doing.

I also want to acknowledge how happy I am that *Body Intelligence, A New Paradigm* has matured into a book that takes the complexities and mysteries of our incredible body, mind, and spirit and presents them in a manner that is easy for everyone to fathom, enjoy and be able to implement into their lives. To this end I have dedicated my life.

Introduction

The Eloquence of Being Human

We are living in interesting times, which is both an ancient blessing and a curse. Collectively, we are waking up to the notion that *what we focus on is precisely what we create in our lives*. We are beginning to understand that we each manifest our own personal reality, our own unique world. Then we live in it.

When I graduated from Palmer College of Chiropractic—even armed with the incredible understanding of philosophy taught at Palmer and all the knowledge of western medical physiology—the mind still seemed as vast and totally mysterious as the fathomless, trackless ocean must have seemed to early explorers. At that time I could not imagine how one could *possibly* understand human consciousness—much less master it.

As I started working with "the five elements" of acupuncture theory, and practicing all the habits included in this book, the simple elegance of our body's functioning became clearer and clearer. Now it is so clear that most of what happens to us is predictable and easy to understand.

As individuals, we are the dreamers who have always dreamed our own unique world into being. We have always had the freedom to focus our attention on whatever we choose. The consequence of that focus is the world each of us has manifested into being. We have the free will to create our own personal reality within the context of what is going on around us.

All the chaos we have created in our lives comes from dividing our mind. Instead of single-mindedly focusing our precious attention on our plans and dreams—and letting our core values, beliefs and principles dictate our thoughts and actions—we let our mind wander about, focusing on all the problems of the world, our fears, and things we suspect will happen. As we bring our mind into harmony with the simple operating systems of our body, the chaos dissipates. We begin to manifest the desires of our heart. The once mysterious mind reveals that its consciousness is both elegant and simple. We attain peace of mind.

Because we are seven dimensional beings, with each organ existing on all dimensions, and because every organ and all our body's systems are interfacing instantaneously, all our operating systems are simple and non-ambiguous. Once we start bringing our consciousness into harmony with how each organ functions, all life starts making sense. Health and well being naturally follow.

This human body each of us gets to have, *and often take for granted*, is magnificent beyond all consideration. It is the finest gift any of us will ever receive. And every body is completely unique.

Since you create our own reality, I sincerely wish for you a life of fulfillment where your heart's desires come forward and single-mindedly become the dominant paradigm of your mind. Then the desires of your heart transform, from wishful thinking, to reality.

Renewal

What is called for
is not
a savage amputation
of your previous existence

No harsh excoriation
no cut
no evisceration

No —

The dawn of your
new life
is gentle
surrender

The sun rises
in the opening
of your hand

—Jock McKeen
As It Is In Heaven

St. Jude Children's Research Hospital

ALSAC · Danny Thomas, Founder

Finding cures. Saving children.

stjude.org

Kyani

208-529-9872

Kyani Science.Com

ACTIVATE YOUR BIGGER INTELLIGENCE

You have two consciousness operating systems, brain and heart. All through history people have let their brain do the thinking, with hellish consequences. As long as your brain is in charge, life is always difficult and peace of mind is simply not achievable. Believing that your brain is in charge of your consciousness is the cause of all the pain and suffering you experience.

As you read this book, you will learn how simple and easy it is to achieve peace of mind, fulfillment and contentment. You have an intelligence that is leagues beyond the mere functioning of your brain. In the first section of this book, you will learn how to access the incredible intelligence of your bodymind, where your heart is the Emperor, and each of your organs are like highly esteemed cabinet members that continuously lend their wisdom to your heart's decision-making process.

Your spirit and all your organs are communicating to you all of the time, but only your heart operates at high enough frequencies to access this incredible wisdom. Your heart—when it is in charge—translates all that wisdom and talent into a language your mind can understand.

The Chinese, in their centuries long exploration of the wisdom inherent in the body, distilled their discoveries into a body of knowledge called "the Five Elements." With this information, you will learn how simple it is to live longer, healthier and happier in the everyday pursuit of your plans and dreams. You will also learn how to live your life with a profound peace of mind you may have believed unattainable.

SECTION I – THE FIVE ELEMENTS

– CHAPTER 1 –

Transformation and Change

The system of the Five Elements (wood, fire, earth, metal, and water) extensively maps out the parts of consciousness generated by each organ. And each one of our body's organs is actually an energy system that functions on all our dimensions. When I began studying the five elements, which are the basis of Chinese physiology, I was moved to tears. Finally, here was a system that embraced my wholeness. It was like coming home. This highly evolved system embraces all our little oddities and eccentricities. I found myself so grateful for my body and for the blessings of this human experience.

This model of life will expand your awareness dramatically, as it has for me. "The Five Elements of classical acupuncture are the central foundation of a system of diagnosis that is one of the most precise and most wonderful ever devised," wrote Professor J. R. Worsley in his 1998 book, *Classical Five-Element Acupuncture: The Five Elements and the Officials.* Through his books and numerous worldwide organizations, Professor Worsley brought the "Five Elements" to the world outside Asia.

In the West, the first three years of *every* licensed physician's studies (whether they are doctors of medicine, chiropractic, acupuncture, osteopathy, naturopathy or any other licensed physician) are taken up with the same anatomy, physiology and pathology studies. We are all required to take the same basic science training in medical physiology.

The problem *is* medical physiology only recognizes the physical and mental dimensions, while we also function on etheric, emotional, attitudinal and dimensions that deal with our values and beliefs. The more you comprehend medical physiology, the less you actually know. In the end, the physician is left with a lot of information, yet a vast unknowingness. Every answer generates more unanswerable questions.

The understanding of the Five Elements organizes your body into simple, easier-to-understand components. By combining both medical and Five Element physiology, all the questions become answerable and life makes sense.

What Are the Five Elements?

The ancient Chinese, and later contributors like Lao Tzu and Confucius, developed a system of understanding the universe they called the Five Elements. The Chinese considered *transformation and change*—not atoms and cells—to be the building blocks of the material world, and used the Five Elements as a way to describe predictable patterns of change and interaction.

This system simplifies the unending complexities of the world and can be used to understand everything from the solar system to the human body. One of the gifts of the Five Elements is that it allows you to understand how your body and mind (actually a bodymind) function and interact. It also gives you a clear understanding about how to bring your consciousness into harmony with all life.

Each of the five elements describes a unique phase of the circle of life and how to come into harmony with that phase of the cycle:

1. WOOD: How you assert yourself. The nobility of your ideals, the magnificence of your dreams, and the thoroughness of your plans

give depth and breadth to your character. These are sacred parts of your character that must be developed if you are to be whole. Your **liver** and **gallbladder** are the organs of the element of wood.

2. FIRE: Love. Through this channel you learn that the purpose of life is to cherish everyone and everything. Your heart makes everything you focus on have "reality" in your own unique world, no matter whether it is something you want, or something you would never want. Your **heart** and **small intestine** are the organs of the fire element.

3. EARTH: Resonance: the horizontal aspect of the cross. Its lessons are that you are safe, loved and have clear boundaries. Home and hearth are the basis of security. Earth is the largest element. Its organs are your **stomach, spleen,** and **pancreas**.

4. METAL: The power to grieve. Metal is the vertical aspect of the cross, which predates Christianity, connecting you to the spiritual dimensions. Through your **lungs** and **large intestine**, you take in and let go. Through this element you develop the fire in your belly.

5. WATER: Fear. The water element within your body represents your emotional energy. The **kidneys** are your intuitive brains. Your **bladder** expresses your feelings. Since feelings are most like the energy of your spirit, feeling your feelings gives you access to the energy and wisdom of your spirit.

- CHAPTER 2 -

The Five Elements Through the Seasons

Nothing ever stays the same. Everything is in a constant state of transformation and change. Change follows predictable cycles, much like the seasons of a year:

Springtime (*wood*) is the beginning phase of growth of any cycle or relationship. That is when everything is growing at its fastest rate. It feels like the upward surging growth will never end, or even slow down.

But when the cycle or relationship enters the summertime phase (*fire*), the upward surging growth slows down slightly and softens, blossoming into a blaze of colors, fragrances and tastes that inspire joy and fun within every being. As the days lengthen, the warmth of unconditional love helps everything and everyone achieve their potential.

Indian Summer (*earth*) is the last twenty days of each season. That's always the time of greatest activity in the insect world. The end of summer is the time of ripening the harvest, providing us with the sweetness of life.

In the autumn (*metal*) of any cycle, the energy slows even further. There is a chill, a melancholy in the air, a time of reflection. If we have trouble with transformation and change, this can be a difficult part of any cycle for us. It's like everything is dying.

The winter of any cycle (*water*) is the time when there is the least amount of energy for growth. It is a time for contemplation, for turning inward, for choosing the seeds we will plant in the coming spring.

All our relationships follow similar transformational cycles. Every cycle has its beginning, its time of maturing, its season of loss and times when very little energy is available. There always comes a time of greater darkness. Our relationships are constantly going through these seasonal changes. For relationships to endure, we must embrace them *throughout all their changes*. They must be able to transform and change, or they wither and die.

Transformation and change are the building blocks of your reality. All life goes through these cyclical movements. When a relationship is in the phase of winter, it can seem so bleak because that is when the least amount of energy is available. But the springtime that inevitably follows has the most exuberant energy of all the seasons. When something evolves as far as it can, it immediately begins to change and transform. Everything in the whole universe is made up of the rhythm of going from light to dark and back to light again.

All life is a dance, a spiral nebula, a river flowing to the sea. I invite you to become aware of and embrace the richness of each season in all your relationships.

You may want a situation to stay in the spring or summer, but it may be in the fall or winter of that particular situation. You may be in the summer of your relationship with your best friend, but in the winter of your job. You may be in the springtime with your family. There are such exquisite experiences for those who say "yes" to *all* that comes at them.

If you think a situation "should not be happening to you," that you should not have to deal with *this*, you condemn yourself to experiencing that situation over and over again. If you cannot face the winter of a situation, the spring cannot come forth.

In the fast pace and complexity of modern life, we can easily have thirty or forty situations happening simultaneously. Each will be in some phase of the cycles of transformation and change. The more we live in the moment, without comparing ourselves with others—or what's happening now to the past—the clearer we can see our noble elegance. Living this way is exciting, challenging, and more than a little scary. But the fruit of saying "yes" to all of life's lessons is the opportunity to live wide awake. You spend more time in the higher realms of thankfulness and gratitude where life is rewarding and fulfilling.

By observing all life as existing in cycles of transformation and change, we can experience the magnificence of each moment, no matter which part of a cycle we find ourselves in. Every moment is exquisitely what it is. Magic happens when we say "yes" to what is. When we face life more courageously, with gratitude, we get a feeling for the movement of energy and a greater understanding of its patterns.

Chapter 3

The Element of Wood

The element of wood can be thought of as the phase of growth during springtime. It is symbolized by a delicate shoot pushing upward through the hard earth with an exuberant force that is not seen in any other time of the year. Those shoots can also be compared to new friendships or your plans and dreams.

In the element of wood, your liver is the part of your consciousness that listens in on everything that pertains to your ideals, dreams, and plans. That also includes everything you think, feel, believe, and talk about with your friends. So if you let your unruly mind ramble on and on thinking about problems in the world or all the problems with people around you, your liver must keep busy thinking up and creating more problems in *your* world.

It is important to remember that you do not live in the same world with any other human being. Each person lives in his or her own reality. So if you want a life of fulfillment, focus on the things that make you feel the most alive, and make *that* be the focus of your attention.

Your bodymind relates to everything as if it is here and now. It assumes that *whatever* you focus on—real or imagined—is happening here and now. It makes no difference whether you like what you are focusing on, or you hate it. The polarities of wanting something, or not wanting it, are irrelevant. They are not even considered by your body-mind. No matter what you are thinking about, the part of your consciousness located in your liver system is drawing up plans to have more of *that* in your own unique world. *Whatever you focus your attention on is being drawn toward you.* That's how life works for a creator.

Manifesting is much easier than most people think. The biggest problem is figuring out what you want. Then the hard part of manifesting is training your unruly mind to stay focused on your heart's desires. *Committing* to your plans and dreams is very much like putting your automobile in gear. Nothing happens until you commit. Then you have to keep your eyes on the road. There are so many distractions.

Are you focusing on the things you want to do in this life? Or are you—like most people—letting your mind focus on all the stuff that you don't like, situations that are going wrong?

Most of us dissipate large amounts of our life force on the problems of the world. It's because we believe that we can correct those problems by thinking about them. This does not work. It has not worked. It will *never* work.

Einstein famously stated, "You cannot solve a problem at the same level of thinking that created the problem." Following that up, he also said, "Continuing to do the same thing and expecting a different outcome is the definition of insanity."

If you want to make the world a better place, focus on doing whatever makes *you* feel most alive. The good done by one person—when they focus on doing what they love, and love what they do—is more healing and beneficial to the world than thousands of people staying current with the news and voting in every election. Remember, every moment that you are focusing on the problem, you are part of (the creation of) the problem.

If the world were a perfect place, what would your heart desire to do? If you could do anything you want, be anything you want, what would you do? These are the questions you want to entertain. Focus the force of your attention on dreams that scare you a little, dreams that blow the doors of your heart wide open. Dare to dream. Then act on your dreams. Stop wasting energy thinking about what's wrong in the world.

Once you begin to see the direction your life wants to take, begin it. Bold action has its own genius and power. You do not have to wait until you see clearly what you want. Rarely do you know at the beginning of something how you want all the steps to turn out. You can start by taking baby steps toward your heart's desires.

Commit your precious attention to your own plans and dreams. Make *them* happen. The world needs your contribution. You must be the change you want to see in the world. It doesn't happen any other way.

As you come to understand your spiritual nobility, you ultimately realize that you must train your unruly mind to *stay focused* on your dreams, plans, and ideals. Commit to your dreams and ideals with the same certainty that you believe the sun is coming up tomorrow.

CHAPTER 4

Willpower and Your Sense of Purpose
·*Liver*·

In medical physiology, we learn that the liver is an organ that has from 50,000 to 100,000 filtration lobules. As it filters more than a liter of your blood every minute, it effectively eliminates debris and pathological bacteria in the process. It stores and releases glucose to stabilize the blood glucose levels, stores vitamins A and D, and is absolutely *essential* in protein and fat metabolism.

In the Chinese understanding, your liver is much more than just an organ. Parts of the liver system are the four muscles that make the electrical energy your liver uses. You also have meridians on each side of the body that begin in the middle of your torso and terminate at your great toes. Your liver functions on all seven dimensions. All of this together can be considered your liver. When the liver is in distress, the muscles and meridians also suffer distress.

The part of your consciousness that resides in your liver system governs willpower and your sense of purpose. The way you develop these qualities is to *stay focused* on plans and dreams that make you feel alive, that excite and challenge you, and that cause a twinge in your gut when you first consider them. Dare to dream dreams that stretch the imagination of who you think you are—then *commit* to them.

Commitment engages your whole liver system. The moment you commit to a goal or dream, your liver starts up-taking *all the energy* you will need to accomplish that goal. The energy of your liver is a forceful energy that wants to shout, "I'm doing this!" My father had a saying where he worked as a welding foreman, "The difficult tasks we do immediately. The impossible take a little longer." He really understood this principle.

When you make excuses—or let yourself believe that someone or something outside yourself can prevent you from achieving your dream—you block the exuberant energy of your liver. That causes anger and irritation to immediately start forming up in your bodymind. The longer and more completely you feel blocked, the greater the anger. As you work through the blockages and obstacles that confront you, you develop willpower.

Your liver is continually drawing up plans to have more of what you believe and what you are talking about with others. It combines your values and beliefs—and your fears—into plans that give form and substance to whatever you direct your attention toward. Your bodymind makes no distinction as to whether it is something you want, or something you would never want—something you love, fear or hate.

I hear people say things like, "I can't do that." Or "I'll never be able to get down to the weight I want to be." And it's true! What you believe will happen happens, just as you thought. Your words are powerful commands. Your bodymind takes everything you think and feel literally, and unfailingly gives you what you expect.

Like it or not, what you believe is what you get. Take responsibility for what you believe. So when you hear yourself thinking or saying something that doesn't feel right in your gut, something disempowering, ask yourself this question: "Is *that* how I want to create my unique world?" If it is not, kill that belief. Shoot that sacred cow dead. Then don't forget to replace it with how you *do* want to create your world.

It is so important to understand that you seriously dissipate your precious life force by focusing on all the problems around you. It is so easy to fritter your life away. I see very intelligent people obsessing about what others are doing, and spending large amounts of time gossiping, talking about politics, conspiracy theories and government or corporate shenanigans. Your life can be great when you train your unruly mind to stay focused on *your* heart's desires.

But if you focus on something that you cannot personally change in the next few days, *all you are doing is making yourself impotent.* Focusing your attention on things that are wrong in the world depletes your life force. It makes you feel like you have no future, no growth potential.

You can't change any of the problems of the world by focusing on them. That is the grand illusion. *You can only change the world by focusing on the contributions you want to make.*

What will you leave behind when this life is over? The fabric you weave into the tapestry of life with your positive contributions is more valuable, by a factor of thousands, than all your concern about the world's problems combined.

Doing the Slow Turn

When you find yourself getting frustrated, irritated or angry, it's time to do *the slow turn.* Slowly turn around the circle of your life while looking for "what you don't want to keep putting up with in the same old way anymore."

When you find it, the next step is to ask, "if I don't want to keep putting up with that, what *do* I want?" This can be a subtle process: a quick flash and it's gone, so really pay attention.

Once you know what you want, *commit to it.* The instant you commit, all of the irritation or anger instantly transforms into one of the heartfelt emotions like thankfulness or certainty that it will happen. When the irritation to your consciousness is gone, the heat of inflammation dissipates almost immediately.

Your liver is on your right side, just up under your ribs, just above where your right elbow hangs down. If you are angry, you can feel the heat coming off your liver. That's inflammation. This is interesting to know, because the very next instant after you commit, all of the heat of inflammation in your liver will be gone. Check it out yourself.

All the heat will also dissipate in the lower pectoralis and rhomboid muscles (between your shoulder blades) that make energy for the liver, and both liver meridians. All the heat of inflammation dissipates within a few seconds. Then they are all calm. An important understanding here is that your body is mostly consciousness and energy. According to quantum physics, all matter is actually 99.999% energy (and consciousness).

After you have committed to what you desire and all the inflammation has dissipated, what's left is the positive feeling of your heart, and your liver's calm determination to do what you committed to.

I had a life-changing experience using the slow turn when I was a young man in my twenties. Two weeks into my senior year at Chiropractic school, I was drafted into the Army. Shortly after I returned to college from my stint in the Army my mind refused to study one evening. I couldn't even focus on a single sentence of my studies. I felt incredibly frustrated and angry about missing so much time because of the Army. I was further frustrated because it felt like as hard as I worked—I was a full-time student working a full-time night job and perpetually sleep deprived—there was an arbitrary ceiling to what I could accomplish. At this point I came to full stop, and did a slow turn. I asked myself *what I no longer wanted to put up with in the same old way.*

I realized that I did not like my definition of who I was as a student. I felt like I had an above-average intellect, yet I sweated bullets through all the exams and was always in the last third of the class to finish them. I had no idea what the different professors wanted us to learn. Everything felt difficult. And because I worked full-time it felt like I was stuck at a 3.15 grade point average. At this point I realized that I needed a new definition of who I was as a student.

When I focused on defining myself as a student, a new definition immediately popped into my head: I realized that I was *brilliant.* That was not too much of a stretch because even though I worked full-time, my grades were as good as many of my friends who studied full-time and did not have to work.

The moment I considered myself brilliant—believed in that image and *committed* to it—everything changed. No part of me wanted to study the way I ever had before. Breathing out forcefully from my lower abdomen became an essential part of studying, taking notes and taking tests.

I found myself wanting to speed-read my notes, and my breath glitched at every line where I wouldn't get the answer right. So I put an asterisk on each line where my breath had a glitch.

Anytime you read past a part where you have part or all of it turned around backward, your mind kicks out of gear, and you read on with no comprehension, like a car that kicked out of gear. So I would back up, challenging each word and phrase until I came to one I was unsure of, and circled it. After finishing speed-reading, since I was brilliant, I only needed to study where the asterisks and circles were.

That cut my study time from thirty hours a week down to ten, and I *knew* ahead of time what each professor would ask because of where (and how many) asterisks there were. If there were ten asterisks on a particular line, there would be ten questions on that subject. Tests became fun and exciting. All this occurred because I *committed* to being brilliant.

The next day no part of me wanted to take notes the way I always had. And when it came to exams, no part of me wanted to take tests the way an average, middling, struggling student would. From then on I did everything like a brilliant student. And that changed everything for the better. After that I got "A's" in all my classes. I was the first one out of every exam I ever took.

When you harness the raw power of your anger, it is an unstoppable force. This is how you develop "willpower." Doing the slow turn can absolutely change your life. The steps again are:

1. Look around the circle of your life until you see what you do *not* want to put up with any longer.
2. Ask yourself, if I don't want this anymore, what do I want instead?
3. Commit to what you actually want.

This is how you make the power of anger work for you.

CHAPTER 5

Decision Making and Discernment
· Gallbladder ·

Your gallbladder concentrates the liver's bile about 10-fold and stores it for release into the small intestine after you have eaten a meal. The bile emulsifies fats and allows you to digest proteins.

Your gallbladder system includes the four muscles that make energy for the gallbladder, and the gallbladder meridians on both sides of your body. The meridians begin in the corner of your eyes, go back and forth along the side of your head, and eventually terminate at your fourth toes.

Each acupuncture meridian holds out its portion of your aura, which is an egg-shaped energy field extending out about three feet from your body in all directions. Functioning together, your meridians form up a fairly dense and palpable energy field that insulates you from having to hear other people's thoughts and feel their feelings. The insulating qualities of your aura allow you to experience your own thoughts and feelings without other people's thoughts and feelings merging with yours. This allows you to experience an autonomous life.

Your liver and gallbladder—the two organs of the wood system—are like blood brothers. They work better together than either can separately. The part of your consciousness that resides in your liver is always drawing up plans for *whatever* you focus on, whether you want it or hate it. Your gallbladder is the part of your consciousness that faithfully executes all the plans you develop in your liver.

The qualities of a healthy liver and gallbladder can be likened to an architect (the liver) and the contractor (the gallbladder) in the building of a house. Neither is as powerful individually as they are together. Through your liver you see the vision of your life, why you came to this incarnation. You develop noble ideals, have wonderful dreams, and make mighty plans. But you still need the contractor's skills to make all the decisions that bring your visions to life.

When the liver and gallbladder are healthy, you have elegance in your movements and flexibility with your tendons and sinews. You exhibit good structure to your logic, which leads to enhanced powers of reasoning. Your thinking process has the kind of clarity that allows you to "see" your vision. You get your point across clearly to others. You can visualize a positive future for yourself.

Your musculoskeletal system gives structure to both your body and your plans and dreams. Imbalance in the element of wood can show up as bad posture, like letting your torso slump and break over, which makes your head project way out forward. You might let your feet toe out like a duck. These kinds of postural faults lead to creaking joints, stiffness, and movements that are jerky. Tendons easily sprain. When your posture is poor, the integrity of your thinking process is similarly impaired.

Good posture and flexibility gives your liver and gallbladder the clarity, strength, and flexibility that lead to clear thinking and emotional stability. This gives staying power to your attitudes, and provides power and flexibility to your beliefs. *A strong, flexible body helps build a strong, flexible mind.*

Your liver cannot make sound decisions and create plans that have integrity without good discernment. Each and every plan you make depends upon the discernment and good judgments of your gallbladder system. Do not let fear of being judgmental cloud your thinking. *You need to make good judgments and discernments about everyone and everything you encounter.* For most of us, this is the part of our consciousness that has been most heavily socialized—and compromised.

Good judgment might come into play when you are deciding whether to be friends with someone. Do their values align with yours? They may be exciting to be with, but do their actions and beliefs enhance or detract from your values and principles? Besides you, what kind of people do they associate with? Are they kind? Is this person someone who can be stubborn and choose not to do something just because he or she gets an attitude about it?

Being judgmental would be to put someone down or name call, like saying "he's a jerk." But good discernment from your gallbladder allows your liver to make sound, integrous plans relative to that person. Then you can wisely decide how much—or how little—energy you want to commit to that person.

Each moment you stand at the nexus of eternity. Will you choose this or that? Will you go here or there? Your gallbladder is the part of your consciousness where you discern the merits of each decision. This decision-making process shapes your world for better or ill.

CHAPTER 6

Creating a Heroic Character and Stepping Into It

The power of the slow turn is that it lifts us beyond the limitations of what we are conditioned to believe is reality. In the slow-turn example from my school days, one of the powerful ways I lifted myself into the top tier of graduates in my chiropractic school is that I created a new self-image, a brilliant character, and stepped into it.

The moment I assumed the identity of that character, all the brilliance of that character was mine: not only the ability to study and take tests with ease, but more importantly, to assimilate and master the material presented.

I have repeatedly seen the power of this technique over the years. A character that we just "make up" proves to be more real—and infinitely more powerful—than who we have been conditioned to believe we are.

I highly encourage you to create a character who represents all the positive qualities you would embody "if the world were a perfect place." Ask yourself,

What would I do, or who would I be if the world were a perfect place?

Dare to invent a character in a role that is a little bit scary, that stretches the limits of what you thought you could *ever* be. Use your imagination to create that role in a perfect world where you could do or be whatever you want to be.

Then step boldly into your creation. You have to know that the moment you commit, all the fears that have previously kept you from assuming that role are going to come rushing up to the surface of your awareness with a monster-like fury. They always come as soon as you step out of your comfort zone.

Feel whatever fears, frustrations, worries or anxieties as they come up. Feeling them through dissolves them into nothingness, letting your new character take root. It's important for you to realize that you have every talent and skill you will ever need to handle every challenge that comes at you—if you don't chicken out. And the world is, indeed, a perfect place.

Just after I started in practice, I decided to employ this technique once again to define myself as a practitioner. I created a Super Healer character who could help patients get through every imaginable disease or problem. He was a brilliant doctor who could figure out and resolve any health problem that came up. He demystified medical jargon so he could explain everything to his patients in simple words. He did not resist criticism. He saw every patient anew, like a child seeing something for the very first time. He wore polo shirts instead of a tie and lab coat.

Then over the next thirty years I woke up a thousand nights around 3 A.M., sweating, frustrated because I was stuck with the progress of a particular patient. I would wake up two or three nights in a row, frustrated at not knowing how to resolve a specific health challenge. Then by the second or third night, I would wake up with "the answer." Remarkably, my insights were always right on target.

If I had not created such a bold character—and stepped into it—I would not have had all those 3 A.M. wake-ups, nor would I have achieved those delightful insights. The revelations gave me in-depth insights that also helped me understand a host of similar problems with other patients. With each success my expertise grew.

One step at a time you ultimately become your heroes. Imagine you are watching a movie of your life: in every scene you have the option of being the leading lady or man. Dare to dream. Start paying attention to the background dreams you secretly long for. Often they are dreams you think you can't do, or that someone *else* should do them, but they keep coming up in *your* consciousness. As you allow the dream to form up, you begin to see that you are "the one" to do this.

Slay Your Dragons

There is a sense of magic when you first aspire to a dream. But as soon as you start taking your courageous first steps, fears start floating up to the surface of your mind. The dragons of our old myths represent those fears. Feeling the fears dissolves them, slays the dragons. We all need your dreams, the threads that are your contribution to the tapestry of life.

Your life and your contribution are precious. Most people are waiting around for a dozen doves to fly by in the sign of a cross or some other divine sign before they commit to their life. Here's the deal: *Everyone's* contribution in this life is essential. Everyone.

Everyone has genius in one or more areas of their life. Everyone! As you live into one of your genius qualities it starts fleshing out, then the next genius quality begins to bubble up into your awareness. If you never step out of your comfort zone—if you hold back because of your fears—if you don't risk going for it, you will have many regrets at the end of this lifetime.

If you boldly "go for it" in the areas your heart opens to—the dreams your mind will not quit thinking about—you *will* experience your genius qualities. Most people let fear and complacency stop them from doing what their heart profoundly desires. As a result, they never discover their genius. My prayer is that you find *your* genius.

Lean into Life's Difficulties

I love downhill skiing. It is such a great metaphor for life. When you ski, your skis only work for you if you lean forward into your ski boots. In other words, you must lean *into* the difficulty.

When the slope is steep—or life is hard—saying "yes" to the difficulties, feeling your feelings, and committing to your path is like having the hottest new ski equipment. They make it easier for you to get through difficult terrain gracefully.

If you focus on holding back, like trying to skid to a slower speed, everything gets harder. Your skis are not designed for holding back. Like life, your skis only work well when you lean into the difficulties of the terrain ahead.

We all suffer from socialization. There are thousands of subtle ways that society has conditioned us to hold back from our greatness, to not stand out, to be safe, to give our power away. For example, researchers studying family dynamics observe that the typical parent says "no" to their children in about three hundred different ways each day. But they only say "yes" about five times. School and church reinforce this pattern. Since your friends are similarly socialized, they also reinforce this pattern. By the time the child is seven years old, they have completely internalized the negative reinforcement. "No" automatically comes up anytime their mind thinks of positive directions.

We peel away layers of societal conditioning by training our minds to say "*yes*" to all the difficulties that come up. Saying "YES" to your difficulties is like leaning into your ski boots. It's the only way to take the hill.

CHAPTER 7

Reframing

When you know what you want but think you can't have it, your gall-bladder will immediately become inflamed, and stay inflamed until you can see your way through the situation. *Resentment* is the normal healthy feeling that will naturally come up. If you do not feel the resentment, more dishonest feelings like stubbornness come up. You might stubbornly assert "nothing ever works out for me."

Other, less honest emotions that come up when you fail to *feel* and work with your resentment are feeling galled or repressed. The trouble with these less honest emotions is they become entrenched and hang around for years, sometimes for life. You see it in the person at work who always complains about their job, or the partner in a marriage who constantly complains about their spouse. These less honest feelings distort and define what you consider reality.

First feel the resentment. Do that immediately. Then reframe the picture as if what you want is happening right now. After all, this is *your life*. Live it wide awake. Create your life in a way that your eight-year-old self would be proud of.

One of my patients presented with an inflamed gallbladder. When I asked her what she wanted but thought she couldn't have, she said, "I have been in two failed marriages and several other relationships that went nowhere. I don't think I will ever find the right guy." I had her get in touch with her feelings of resentment so they would dissolve.

Knowing the power of reframing I said, "Why don't you make a list of the qualities you desire in a man, and the qualities in yourself that you would embody in a perfect relationship." She went home and wrote down all the qualities of her own perfect character, and the qualities of her perfect partner. Three weeks later they serendipitously met. Letting go of the resentment freed up her energy to let the goodness in. They have been happily married now for fifteen wonderful years.

Almost everyone in high-pressure situations burns out periodically. The pressures outweigh the pleasures. That is when reframing helps. If you are feeling burned out on some part of your life or relationships, you need to go back to when you originally fell in love with what you are currently doing, or when you fell in love with whom you are with. That's the time to remember all the ways your loved one has been there for you and refocus your awareness on what is important. Reframing can also be used to resolve short-term issues.

Not too long ago my wife and I were quarreling, and I was so angry that my eyes were trying to cross. She was holding onto her position like it was a sacred cow. I said one more word and she huffed into the other room. Then I realized, "Oh my gosh, she is my best friend in the world, and she is always there for me." Just as I thought that she walked back and said, "Can we hug and start over?" When you reframe a difficult situation by focusing on how much you love the other person, *that* can change everything. That simple realization ended the confrontation more than words ever could. It blew away the stuck energy. Everyone is telepathic, whether they know it or not. Reframing—even though it might just be in your mind—can change everything.

Start noticing when you feel resentment building up. At that point, ask yourself "what is it that I want, but think I can't have?" Thinking about lack generates more lack. Wanting something guarantees that you will always *want* it. A far better strategy is to reframe it to where you see yourself *having* the object of your desires now. You own it now, even if it is to arrive sometime in the future of linear time.

Your dreams come from within you and manifest outward. Honestly, there is nothing *outside* of you that can block you from doing what you desire. And no one outside yourself can tell you what you are supposed to do. There is no scroll on the other side of the veil that has what you are supposed to do written on it. You do it. Only then is it written.

"Reframing" is a habit successful people practice. It is an easy skill to learn and develop. Simply reframe the picture—the situation—until you can imagine yourself having or doing what you truly love *in the present moment*. While you are imagining this outcome, don't forget to breathe.

Imagine walking around in your reframed reality, feel it, smell it, play with different aspects of it as if it currently exists. That's called "five sensing it." Imagine yourself experiencing as many aspects of what you want as if it exists here and now. If you want to be a pilot, imagine your hands on the steering yoke of the plane. See it sitting on the tarmac. Imagine the lift-off, banking off around big old fluffy clouds, setting it down in a perfect three-point landing. Use your imagination to play in your visualization. Imagination is one of the creative faculties of your higher mind and one of your most powerful tools.

There are nine driving energies of the wood element: *hope, vision, future, vitality, exuberance, birth, growth, activity, and regeneration.* These qualities exist both outside of you—like a spring rain or the dynamic growth of springtime—or the vitality you feel at your celebratory dinner after completing a challenging goal. When your wood element is healthy, you can feel the noisy exuberance of your plans and dreams wanting to burst out from within your being. You have vision. You have a bold future to manifest into being. You want to shout it out. Nothing can stop you.

You want a life of action, not one of holding back. Do not hold back for fear of making mistakes. *Give yourself permission to make mistakes—even big ones.* They are your greatest teachers. The greatest among us will readily admit that they failed their way to success. When you do something stupidly or in a way that you do not like—and learn from it—you learn far more than you can from doing a thousand things right.

When you first start to do something, rarely do you know how it will actually turn out. You may need to think or move in the direction of your dreams for a while before they flesh out into something you can share with others. Take action. Don't hold back.

The more engaged you are with your hopes and dreams, the healthier your liver and gallbladder are, the better your flexibility and stability, and the clearer you can see the visions of what you want. Your noble ideals and magnificent dreams give purpose to your life. They expand the depth and breadth of your character. *All this* is the function of your liver/gallbladder system (wood) within your bodymind.

CHAPTER 8

Anger Is Your Friend

Anger is like a wild horse running across the prairie, racing the wind, making you feel like you are *all that*. It is the raw energy of your liver, divinely inspired, vigorous, and forceful. It needs to burst out. It is intimate, and does not need to be unkind. After all, love is its driving force.

Most people misuse their anger by projecting it onto others. They may protest the lessons that come at them, which comes from a deep-seated fear that someone or something *outside* ourselves is holding us back, that somehow "they" are controlling our fate. The truth is that after you commit to something (either consciously or by defaulting to your fears), your own spirit and soul create *most* of your lessons. Say "yes" to your lessons. Life is so much more exciting that way.

Anger that is misused takes on a tainted appearance. When most of us think about "anger," horror stories come up about when it got out of control or when it turned violent. The news media capitalizes on sensationalism, providing horror stories every morning and evening about anger gone wrong. As a result, society has demonized this childlike force and made it into something "mean."

You need not fear your anger. It is a wonderful tool in your consciousness. It is the catalyst that breaks you out of deep old ruts, helping you overcome stifling inertia. It literally shoves you out of old patterns of grief, confusion and depression or other emotions that hold you back.

Often you cannot get out of your funk until you get righteously angry. Then you need to do "the slow turn," and perform the three steps mentioned earlier to use your anger properly. Again they are: Figure out what you do not want to keep putting up with. Determine what you want. Commit to it.

We need to liberate our anger, see it for what it is. It is a vital ingredient of any intimate relationship. When we start to lose the profound truth and love in our relationships, anger is right there to push us back on track. When we get stuck in a rut of indecisiveness, it's anger that lights a fire under our rear-end to get us moving on the right track.

In a healthy state, anger's mantra would be something like "either lead, follow, or get out of the way." The more you ignore anger, the more its pressure builds up, which can be distressing. Anger continues to mount until you figure out what you want. It is a kind of divine discontent. *Anger is the honest emotion of your liver.* Anger is your friend.

LEARNING TO CHERISH

- CHAPTER 9 -

The Element of Fire

Every minute of your life, about 5 liters (1.3 gallons) of blood pass-es through the heart, traveling through almost 62,000 miles of blood vessels. But the heart is much more than just a pump. Your heart has enough neurons to be a brain, and 60 percent of them go to direct your brain's functions. Every moment you are spiritually aware, your heart functions as the emperor of your consciousness.

All through history, humanity has let the brain do the thinking. Your brain is an operating system that divides all life into polarities like the past versus the future, right versus wrong, etc. Without your heart direct-ing it, your mind continually reverts to divisiveness. This way of think-ing has consistently divided mankind into "us versus them." When your heart is not controlling your brain, life is hellish.

Unlike your brain, your heart lives in the present moment. It consid-ers everything you focus on as if it is happening *here and now*. It wants to love and include everyone, and let them love you back. When your heart is in charge of your consciousness, all your organs become like a benevolent ruler's wise and highly esteemed cabinet members. Your heart invites all of them to contribute their areas of expertise and wis-dom into the *singularity* of your consciousness.

Your heart wants to focus its attention on loving what you have, and focusing on what you love. The present moment—if you thoughtfully consider it—is the answer to all your prayers and dreams. The trouble is, if you have not felt your fears, and are only thinking and talking about them—your heart is taken offline. Your mind's default is to focus on all the problems, which creates more of what you fear.

Everyone lives in his or her own unique world. You manifest into being that which you focus your attention on. When you "think from your heart," your whole life finally starts making sense. With your heart making your decisions, all your organs come on-line. All their wisdom is included in making the best possible decisions. *Your heart*—not your mind—*is the true emperor of your world.*

The ancient Chinese called the heart the "supreme controller." They did not use words like "supreme" or "great" lightly. Your heart is the closest thing to God you will know on this side of the veil.

Your heart can be thought of as the root of life itself. Like our great central sun, your heart bathes everyone and everything in its warmth. Your heart's warmth and unconditional love—and the insights derived from unconditionally loving—nurtures you, and everyone and everything that matters to you, toward their highest potential.

Your heart naturally loves. It never relinquishes its childlike quality of loving, no matter how badly you may have been hurt by life. It wants to love everyone and everything and allow them to love you back. Always. You do not have to teach your heart to love any more than you need to teach a child to play.

The power of cherishing allows whatever and whomever you focus on to blossom and develop into fruition.

That is the most important sentence I will ever write.

Every cell and organ functions best when it is receiving the warmth of love that comes from your heart. Without that love, no part of your body can grow or mature to its full potential. The same is true with your splendid plans, dreams, and relationships. They only come to fruition when your heart focuses its love upon them.

We literally love our friends, family and loved ones (even our pets) into being the best version of themselves. For example, if we expect our children to be loving, kind, and brilliant, they will consistently exceed our expectations. If we expect them to be screw-ups, they will consistently exceed our expectations. When your heart governs your thoughts, its love improves every aspect of your world. And you experience your best, illuminated self.

- Chapter 10 -

Forgiveness Rewrites your History

When any negative feelings about others come up, and you don't actually feel them, your heart is immediately taken offline. Your brain takes over and translates the negativity into stories that are familiar. The stories are based on fears of the future or negative experiences of the past. The unfelt feelings generate thoughts and actions that form walls between you and others; they block your hopes and dreams; and they stand between you and everything you cherish.

Each negative feeling builds up pressure that generates thousands of negative thoughts. Your bodymind takes everything personally. It assumes that any negative thoughts you are aiming at others are actually aimed at you personally. The impact of negative thinking impairs all of your own cells' functions, forcing them to operate at much lower levels of efficiency, often self-destructively.

Most people think they are feeling their feelings when they are actually only *thinking* about their feelings. Usually they are thinking or talking about *how and why* those feelings impact them.

To be sure you are actually *feeling* your feelings:

- Come to a full stop.
- Only let your mind have the one sentence that brings up the negative feeling, like "That makes me angry." That's enough words. Now experience the anger.
- You can become aware of where that emotion is in your body. It may be a tightness in your chest. It may be a knot in your gut. It may be a feeling of tiredness. You may feel it in any part of your body, or over your entire body.

- Stay with this feeling—without dialogue, or trying to change the feeling in any way—until it dissolves.
- Keep going back to the incident and feeling the next feeling, until you go back and the feeling is at least up to the level of joy (the lowest love-based emotion).

Forgiveness is simply *feeling* any negative feelings that stand between you and others until they resolve. If you do not actually feel the feelings, all the pain and suffering associated with them gets triggered dozens of times a day by similar people, events or circumstances. Feeling the feelings dissolves any walls that were created between you and others. When the negative feelings are gone, your mind stops generating negative thoughts.

Ultimately you want to forgive everything and everyone. When you feel all the feelings that come up as you go through your day, you are living the spirit of forgiveness. You are literally forgiving the world. No matter what you must physically do when dealing with others who are toxic, feel the toxic feelings. This is a powerful transformative tool, and you are an agent for change, a spiritual warrior.

Forgiveness brings your heart back online. The way your heart considers the situation rewrites the memory of it through the lens of unconditional love. Every event you forgive changes everyone involved in wonderful ways. Your past becomes transformed by the profound goodness of your spirit. You change everything. Your forgiveness rewrites history.

You are always overwriting your DNA. But by simply feeling your feelings, you change the past, present, and future. You rewrite your DNA strands in a more loving and empowering way. And your forgiveness helps others to rewrite theirs.

In some relationships there are a lot of painful memories. Sometimes it takes many years of faithfully forgiving one painful incident after another before the walls come down. There may be a lot of karma to undo, yours or theirs. Nothing ever stays the same. Your relationships are always getting better—or worse. All during the time you are forgiving the other person, they are changing. *You* are also changing. Forgiveness changes both of you in wonderful ways.

After the long process of forgiving, you will look back at your history with that person, and everything will be different. Both of you will be more empowered and more loving. Issues that used to divide you will seem irrelevant. Strengths that were latent will come forward and be part of both your characters. That changes your DNA, and the people you forgive. It changes your world in wonderful and powerful ways.

Stay Focused on What You Love

Your bodymind—also known as your innate intelligence—assumes complete responsibility for whatever you are thinking about. It is *completely* literal. Anytime you focus on what is wrong "out there," your mind is forced to develop insights about the problems you just focused on. The dark side of that is your mind must develop insights into having more problems like that in your life.

All during the time your mind is focusing on problems, your heart is taken off-line from providing the warmth, unconditional love and insights that all your organs and every part of your world needs. And that also draws your heart's love away from all your plans, dreams, and relationships. They all suffer.

This can be likened to an apple tree that should be producing hundreds of big juicy red apples. But without the unconditional love, warmth, and guidance your heart provides, your tree can only produce fifteen or twenty paltry apples in the whole season. Your plans and dreams, as well as your health suffer immensely when your negative thinking forces your heart to focus on all that is wrong around you.

Your heart radiates unconditional love that personifies the finest qualities of your spirit. Every moment that your heart is focusing its precious attention onto what it loves, it is developing insights into how you can have more to love. That's how it works. The more you love, the more loving your world becomes until you are completely surrounded by love. Year after year every part of your life keeps getting better. This is how to live.

Based on the insights your heart develops from unconditionally loving, it issues the operating instructions that all your cells and organ officials need so they can bring your desires to fruition. Then, the fruit of your tree is abundant and fulfilling.

In your busy life, you can find yourself in dozens of different environments in a single day. In each and every situation, the insights from your heart allow you to manifest a more loving world and create healthy limits and boundaries. Your deepest desires flourish under the nourishing warmth and insights your heart continually provides.

Begin focusing your awareness on what you love. Love what you have. Cherish others. Forgive. Say a resounding "yes" to all your lessons and difficulties. After all, your spirit and soul brought you those lessons and difficulties as vehicles that will most directly deliver your heart's desires to you. Now that's something to ponder. Feel how happy your body feels when you say "yes. Yes. YES!" Then every part of your life makes sense.

CHAPTER 11

Sorting Things Out

·*Small Intestine*·

In medical physiology we learn that our small intestine is about 30 feet long. Its inner lining looks like velvet due to millions of villi—finger-like projections about one millimeter long—resplendent with veins, arteries and lymphatic vessels that effectively digest about 95% of the food you eat. Non-nutritive substances are allowed to simply pass on into the large intestine.

On all the higher levels of your consciousness, your small intestine is the heart's first imperial bodyguard. Its job it to protect your heart (the emperor)—and your kingdom—by taking in everything that is nutritive while letting non-nutritive substances pass on by. *Pass on by* is the operative concept.

Your small intestine's job is to accept everything that is nourishing and send it to your heart. In the ancient texts, this quality is described as "sorting the pure from the impure." Its job on the higher levels of your consciousness is to sort out thoughts, feelings and observations that are not nourishing and let *them* pass on by. Letting things that you might consider evil or bad to "pass on by" is infinitely more powerful than resisting or fighting against them in some way. The good you do is much more healing to the world than fighting evil.

Your heart cannot provide warmth and unconditional love to its subjects while simultaneously defending itself. Those are mutually exclusive actions. The genius of your bodymind is that your heart has three imperial bodyguards. Their *primary duty* is to keep your heart focused on what you love and what is beneficial to your world.

If you allow your rational mind to focus on all that is wrong or stupid, that action forces your heart off-line. Days, months, or even years can slip by while your heart is too distracted by problems "out there" to provide the unconditional love that your friends, your family *and* your plans require. That time could be spent providing the love and insights your kingdom needs.

When you allow your rational mind to continually draw your attention toward all that is wrong in the world, all that negativity invades your small intestine until it can hardly digest your food. "Food" includes thoughts, feelings, attitudes, values and beliefs. Your small intestine also digests all your relationships, work, religion, politics and everything else you focus your attention on.

When you let your unruly mind focus on all the problems and how bad things are happening around you, negativity floods into your heart creating tremendous dis-ease to every part of your health and well being.

I notice that patients with small intestine ailments are *always* obsessing on problems. A mother may be obsessing about her family's troubles so intensely that every part of her own health suffers. A father may be focusing all his attention on struggles at work, problems with his friends and family, or politics. In every case, digestion is impaired.

To restore normal function to your small intestine, come to full stop. Really appreciate each wonderful thing as it is happening. Re-visit it several times. It may be a beautiful scene, an act of kindness or anything that brings you joy. You only have to do this a couple times before your small intestine returns to normal function. Your small intestine starts functioning correctly the instant you *get* this concept and commit to it. Applied kinesiology confirms this.

Here is a test for you: When your small intestine is healthy, you remember all the good things that happened in the last three days. In ill health, you can't remember the good things that have happened in the last few days, but you remember *all* the slights that happened to you in the last fifteen years. Which camp are you in?

Your heart must be protected from having to dwell on foolish or negative things. Your small intestine's job is to stay focused on everything in your life that is nutritional, good, kind and whole. Focus on that which you would want more of in your life. The whole time your heart is focused on what you love and on your own plans and dreams, it is providing wonderful insights that direct all your other organ officials to manifest more of what you love. Then your heart becomes the loving Emperor who rules over a happy, thriving kingdom.

– CHAPTER 12 –

Keeping Your Focus on Love
· Pericardium System ·

The pericardium system is the sac around your heart. It is the second bodyguard in charge of protecting your heart. It is known as "your heart protector." It does just that. It absorbs the physical blows, as well as the mental and emotional traumas and shocks that would otherwise traumatize your heart.

Ancient texts called this system "circulation sex" because muscles that make energy for it—the piriformis, all three buttocks muscles and the adductor muscles that draw your legs together—are essential for making love. These are powerful muscles that make the energy your pericardium uses. That should give you an idea of how much energy your pericardium utilizes, and how important it is.

Your heart is not a pump. The top of it isn't thick enough. The heartbeats generate 10,000 times more electromotive force than your brain, producing a energy field that appears much like the north and south poles of Earth's energy field (which stabilize our atmosphere). Your heart's energy field projects outward approximately 10 feet in all directions, affecting everyone and everything in its loving energy field.

The heart protector official—not the heart—controls your arteries and veins. It directs the peristaltic action of your arteries that sends your heart's warmth and love all the way out to every cell in your body and brings it back thousands of times each day. It distributes your heart's unconditional love, warmth and insights to all your cells and organs— and also to everyone and everything you think about.

The Ambassador to All Your Relationships

It is important to realize that relationships hold the universe together—everything from atoms to friendships—and y*our heart protector is the ambassador to all your relationships*. Its job, as your heart's ambassador, is to keep all your relationships healthy by extending the heart's unconditional love to everyone and everything, while maintaining clear boundaries. That is its job as Imperial bodyguard.

Authors and speakers Gay and Katie Hendricks talk a lot about the difference between *relationships and entanglements*. They explain a relationship very simply:

- A relationship exists when two *whole* people come together to share their essence.
- A relationship allows the entire gamut between intimacy and aloneness.

These two definitions are deceptively simple, and yet they take years to master. In a relationship, both parties walk away with more energy than they had when they met. In order to consider a person to be "whole," you must assume that he or she has every skill they will ever need to handle *every* problem they will encounter. For a person to be whole, you also must consider that their essential nature is Christ consciousness or a Buddha in training, no matter what their level of spiritual development is at this time.

If, on the other hand, you worry about someone or make excuses for their behavior, in your world they are no longer whole. Your assumption handicaps and invalidates that person from being a powerful spiritual being to being a second-class citizen. Demoting that person into being less than whole in your world causes them to react to you in ways you will not like.

Everyone reacts to your thoughts, regardless of whether they are psychic enough to consciously *hear* your thoughts. You come into a better sense of relationship and harmony with others when you think about them as if they could hear your thoughts.

In the balance between intimacy and aloneness, when a person needs space and you give it, magic happens. You are giving them what they need—what they want. When you give people the space they need, they can more quickly resolve whatever problem has arisen. In that scene, you allowed them to feel safe.

You can also observe this concept with shy children or pets. When they react to you with shyness *and you completely withdraw your attention from them*, invariably they become more interested in you. Their innate response is, "Who is this person that's ignoring me?" Within minutes the shy child is bringing a book for you to read to them while the parent looks on incredulously.

When a person wants intimacy with you, it usually doesn't require that much. It usually only requires briefly listening or a touch or hug to fulfill their need. But when a person wants intimacy and—for whatever reason—you push them away, you create a dysfunction that invariably takes *much* more energy to handle. You have created an entanglement.

Any encounter that does not fulfill the two definitions of a relationship is an entanglement. If someone wants space and you cling to them, that is an entanglement. If you make excuses for them or feel sorry for them, that is also an entanglement. The emotional undercurrents that follow suck the life out of an encounter. Both parties go away with less energy than they had. Currently, most people's encounters with others are not relationships. They are entanglements.

Entanglements take hundreds, sometimes thousands of times more energy than the little amount of intimacy or space the person needed from you in the first place. And, unlike relationships, they are *never* fun.

If you simply wonder how much intimacy or aloneness a person wants, you innately know the answer. A person may want 10 percent intimacy and 90 percent aloneness. Give them space. A short time later that same person may want a completely different ratio. When you ask yourself the right question, your spirit answers. Sometimes you just *know*. Everyone is psychic to some degree. Some people *hear*, others *see*, while others simply *know*.

As you observe the two simple rules of relationships, most of your encounters turn into relationships. They give back much more energy than either of you expended. Relationships provide increasingly more protection and health to your heart. Cherishing others is the greatest protection you can give your heart. As a result, your heart—the emperor—is able to keep your kingdom safe, peaceful, productive and healthy.

CHAPTER 13

Controlling Your Curiosity

·Three-Heater System: Your Body's Heating Engineer·

Standard medical physiology leaves a giant hole when it comes to understanding how our heart works. By adding in "five elements" physiology, we come to understand our heart's functions in a more fundamental way. The most wonderful understandings come as we bring our lives into harmony with the heart's three imperial bodyguards:

- three-heater regulating system
- heart protector system
- small intestine system

The third Imperial Bodyguard of your heart is named the "three-heater" official or "triple warmer." Its job is to keep your curiosity focused on cherishing yourself, others, and everything you have. Every moment your curiosity focuses on what you love transforms your unique world into a more loving and lovely place.

Triple warmer is the part of your consciousness that is responsible for keeping the temperature at an even balance in the three warming spaces into which your trunk is divided, regardless of the outer temperature or circumstances:

- The upper warming space of your chest contains your heart and lungs.
- The middle warming space is the part of your torso that includes your liver, gall bladder, pancreas, stomach, and spleen.

- The lower warming space includes your small and large intestines, kidneys, bladder, and sexual system.

The organs within your trunk are the officials that govern every aspect of your consciousness, and your body's health. It is important that the temperature is regulated just the way all your organs like it.

When one or more of your three warming spaces becomes over-heated all those organs get agitated and function with less efficiency. What overheats this system is spending a lot of time focusing on things or events that irritate you. The anger, frustration, worry, or other nega-tivity that results pushes out into your energy field from one or more of your three warming spaces, affecting you and everyone around you. If your attention is focused on all that is wrong, the negativity stifles your energy. It also has a stifling effect on everyone around you.

On the other hand, when you become indifferent, there is not enough warmth. You can have cold hands and feet. You can feel depressed or just uninspired. When there is insufficient heat to nurture your plans or dreams to fruition, your mind can feel lackluster and weary. You lack the enthusiasm and drive to actually accomplish goals you were previously excited about. You do not have enough energy to commit to life or your loved ones. When your fire element lacks warmth and joy, it feels like your spirit cannot match energy with the other party revelers.

When your triple-warmer official gets out of balance, you lose the ability to keep your emotional and social thermostat in balance. You can blow hot and cold. These kinds of mood swings and difficulties drive friends and loved ones to desperation. When you oscillate between overenthusiasm and indifference, it is difficult for others to maintain anything like an appropriate balance with you. This particular imbalance has sent a lot of people to counseling.

For this reason the triple-warmer official has been referred to as the "heating engineer." When the temperature is heated or cooled just the way you like it, you can more easily achieve your maximum creativity and productivity.

You maintain the healthy temperature of your three warming spaces by focusing your attention toward everything you love, and withdrawing it from things you don't love. When you let your mind focus on unpleasantness, the problems of the world or dysfunctional acts of others, *that* always knocks your three heater system out of balance. Always. The unintended consequences of focusing on all that's bad affects you most of all.

Why Did He Do That?

One sure fire way to knock the triple warmer system out of balance is wondering *why* someone does something in a dysfunctional manner. Just wondering, "Why did he do that?" runs all of that person's unconscious logic—like how they rationalize that it's all right acting out in such an inconsiderate, cruel, thoughtless, bullying or helpless way—through the matrix of *your* heart. Ouch!

That question takes your heart off-line for as long as it takes to develop insights into why he or she did it. Figuring this out can take hours, or days, just to figure out that one silly question. Curiosity about why anyone does anything dysfunctional always throws your three warming spaces out of balance. It is "the curiosity that killed the cat."

Make it a habit to define those kinds of acts by saying, "That was inconsiderate," or whatever defines that particular dysfunctional act. I learned this lesson profoundly a few years ago while riding my mountain bike. I had been riding for an hour at moderate intensity when I got my second wind. Then I started riding over slight hills without gearing down, going for it. I was in the zone.

I rode up a mile-long "second-gear hill" in third gear with energy to spare. I stopped at the top to gather my forces. There is a steep hill to get to my house, and I wanted to take it without having to do switchbacks. Although the road was very wide, a car went by me so close that he knocked gravel on my shoe. I shook my fist at him, and that would have been fine, but then I started thinking about *jerks like him*. That single thought caused me to run all the unconscious motives of that guy—and others around here who show no respect to bicycle riders—through my body.

Suddenly my left knee felt unstable, my neck was tense, my stomach was queasy, and I had a slight headache. Then it dawned on me, just a few seconds before I was pumped, experiencing the high of endorphins and growth hormones. To recover, I projected my consciousness half-way down the hill I had just climbed—back to before I took in all that negativity, which in turn took my heart offline.

Re-experiencing my joy and physical prowess slowly pushed all the negative energy out. I felt all those nasty feelings release out through my hands and feet. When the negativity cleared out of my bodymind, I felt really happy again.

I was back. Down by my left foot I saw a shiny new penny, heads up. I picked it up. It was heavily nicked from being run over. I put that penny in my pocket and kept it for a year and a half. It was like a talisman that kept reminding me to not *ever* wonder why anyone does anything dysfunctional—and to keep bringing my focus back to all that I cherish. One day I accidentally spent the penny, but not before learning this valu-able lesson.

When you become aware that you are focusing on something you do not like, your three heater's wise counsel is to quit gawking at the ugliness of unconscious activities, and re-focus on the beauty that is all around you. There has always been unconsciousness in the world. The great news is that every day more people are waking up. The goodness and beauty all around you is what deserves your attention.

Putting your attention on bad things that are happening takes your heart off-line. Your heart goes offline when you are focusing on prob-lems you have little influence to change. As a result, *your* bodymind, and *your* kingdom are left without an emperor—and that's never good.

"Fight, Fright, Flight"

Your bodymind takes everything you focus on personally, as if it were happening to you. It reacts to alarming events by going into sympathetic dominance, which is called the "fight, fright, flight" response. This is a great response pattern when you are in danger. You can react with speed, strength, and clarity that far surpass any of your normal capabilities. But it's really unhealthy to *live* this way.

Watching the news is actually quite harmful to your health. Their emphasis on graphically showing us violence and sensationalism as many times a day as possible throws everyone's nervous system into hyper-vigilance, or sympathetic dominance. You may be watching the news about people at war on another continent, but your bodymind reacts as if opening your front door you will see tanks and soldiers running by. Sensing danger, your sympathetic nervous system immediately shuts down your digestive, immune, and sexual systems. And you know that *can't* be good for you.

All those systems are superfluous when you are facing imminent danger. The energy from those beneficial functions gets diverted to your muscles and your sense organs so you can perceive and react instantly. Your bodymind shuts down those non-essential functions for the whole time it feels threatened—so it can *instantly* respond to the (implied) threat.

Where the news is mostly sensationalism—like in America—people live their entire lives in this hyper vigilant mode of sympathetic dominance—and they have the digestive, immune, and sexual problems to prove it. Well over a hundred billion dollar's worth of drugs are sold in America each year, just for these problems. The irony of the situation would be hilarious if it were not so calamitous.

When you focus your attention on the problems around you—as most people do—your bodymind firmly believes the world is a hostile place. For most of my life, my focus was on the problems of the world. I was fascinated by the news, politics, conspiracy theories and stories of corporate malfeasance. Many parts of my body suffered as a consequence. As soon as I started training my mind to focus on loving what I have and focusing on what I love, those problems ceased to exist.

When the triple warmer does its job, your whole body feels safe and loved. Your digestive, immune, and sexual systems get turned back on. They get all the energy they need.

When your heart controls your mind, you feel safe and loved. Your parasympathetic nervous system comes back into balance. It generates thoughts that come from *knowing* you have plenty of time, people love what you do, the universe supports you and approves of you. Life is good. These kinds of thoughts make your digestion work well. Your immune system keeps everything healthy. Your sexual system gets all the energy it needs to function well. As a result, life *is* good.

Keeping Your Three-Heater System in Balance

You further stabilize your three-heater system by not letting yourself get so overly excited and worked up when things are good that your thermostat gets stuck overheating. And you don't want to get so overly depressed when things go bad that your thermostat gets stuck in not generating enough heat. In manic depression, you can get so overly excited about something you performed well, that you plunge into the deepest of depressions afterward.

Your three-heater's job is to keep redirecting your focus back to your plans and dreams, and to everything you love. Revel in beautiful sunsets and all the wonders of this blue-green paradise world. Devote time and energy to reflecting on loved ones. Those are the things you want your heart to focus attention on, which creates more of *that* in your unique world.

In the circle of life, the love your heart feels is the agent that heals your heart. Keep focusing on aspects of loved ones that you admire. That allows your heart to develop insights into loving the best aspects of that person into being. It is incredible how powerfully your love affects everything, and everyone it focuses on. Focusing on what you love creates a more loving world. The love in your heart makes everything you focus on sacred.

BEING HELD

- CHAPTER 14 -

The Element of Earth

To understand the qualities of the Earth element, imagine *being held,* not only when you were a baby, but in this moment in the arms of a loving universe, getting all the *nourishment* you need every day of your life. The fruit of your activities are continually providing you with the *sweetness of life*. You feel safe enough to develop *firm boundaries*. You have *good distribution* in all areas of your life, and you always have *enough*. You train yourself to *resonate* with the positive traits of others—rather than feeling sorry for, or having concern for people's problems. You want to resonate with the higher qualities of people you love and admire, instead of resonating with their problems.

A healthy element of earth within you feels like you have *an abundant harvest* on every level of your life—body, mind, and spirit. All these qualities—italicized above—are the contributions a healthy earth element bestows on your unique world.

Within your bodymind, the element of earth is similar to the love a mother gives her child. That love provides the foundation for feeling secure. *Your greatest security comes from feeling safe and loved*. Every dysfunctional thing any of us does comes from that lack.

Most of us did not get all the love and nurturing we needed as children to feel safe and loved in this world. If children do not get the support or attention they need growing up, they can act out in all kinds of desperate ways, fixated at an early stage of childhood development. As adults they may still be crying out for love, support, attention or sympathy—acting out unconsciously in attempts to get the attention they are missing.

Lack of nurturing can manifest outward in a number of ways in adults. They may:

- Unconsciously crave the missing nurturing or nourishment, often projected onto food or some other addictive/compulsive avenue
- Not recognize the bounty of their own harvest
- Develop eating disorders or other destructive behaviors that try to fulfill their longing for sympathy
- Excessively fish for compliments, or sympathy, but never seem to get enough
- Be so focused on getting their own needs met they are unable to nurture others
- Feel *entitled* to the love and attention they desire, acting out when they do not get it
- Give away their harvests (even though they really need them) until they fade away into martyrdom
- Obsessively nurture others, whether they need it or not, to make up for their own lack of nurturing

On the opposite extreme, they may:

- Refuse sympathy of any kind
- Avoid asking for help, and will reject it if it is offered
- Lack sympathy for others

A big part of waking up to your full potential is developing the positive qualities of the element of earth within your own inner nature. If you didn't get the nurturing that you needed growing up, it's time to develop these qualities within yourself now. Stop blaming your family for "why they are the way they are." You chose them. Live your life as if you had a nurturing mother, father, and siblings, whether you did or not. Blame is not a good strategy. It doesn't fix anything.

Here is a powerful visualization to connect you to the nurturing and nourishment that strengthens your earth element: Imagine you are a child, lovingly being held in your mother's arms as she feeds, loves, and cares for you. Feel the sweetness of her as she cuddles you. Hear the loving sound of her voice as she sings to you. Hear her teaching you your first words. Think about her softness, the sweet smell of her, her presence as she holds you.

Now switch your perspective and become the loving mother or father, sending love and care to yourself when you were a baby or young child. Let your younger self know that he or she is safe in your loving protection for their whole life. Help them to feel all the fears and frustrations in the difficult parts of their childhood. Show them how safe and easy it is to release any awful feelings they might have encountered. Tell them how wonderful life is when they stay focused on what they love.

The sense of *lovingly being held* is a quality you can cultivate or nurture at any point in your life. Choose to associate with people who make you feel that way. Feeling safe and loved is the basis of your security.

CHAPTER 15

Ripening Your Thoughts, Plans and Dreams
· Stomach ·

On the physical level your stomach churns your food while secreting hydrochloric acids into the mixture to ripen it, then releases it into the small intestine at a controlled rate so your intestines can digest all the nutrients. If your stomach does not acidify (ripen) your food adequately, the bile from your liver is unable to break down the fats and proteins you ate. The enzymes from your pancreas are similarly ineffective. Not ripening your food causes most of your digestive problems.

On the higher levels of your consciousness, your stomach ripens your thoughts, feelings, attitudes, principles, values, and beliefs by thinking them through—which is equivalent to chewing your food well. Your stomach's job on the higher dimensions of your bodymind is to ripen your plans, dreams, hopes and ideals until they can nourish and provide a healthy satisfaction for your body, mind, and spirit.

Most of us are a little weak in this area. Often our instincts are so effective at just reacting to what is happening around us that we don't make the effort to fully ripen issues or relationships that matter the most to us. We hurry through life without thinking things through to completion. On the physical level, the digestive issues from this way of thinking—even though temporary—may have gone on since childhood. They may seem permanent.

A healthy stomach requires you to think your thoughts through, similar to chewing your food well. When you become aware that you have been thinking about something, that's your cue to spend some quality time thinking about how it affects your values and principles, and how that shapes your life. Until we think things through, most of us don't even know what our values or principles are.

You ripen your plans and dreams by imagining them as if they currently exist. Within your imagination, spend quality time enjoying your plans and dreams as if they were here and now. This brings back the joy you experienced as a child playing, creating and imagining. When you do, every part of your incredible bodymind gets to participate in the process of manifestation. The power of your imagination makes manifesting your desires fun, effortless and a lot more exciting.

Play with your plans and dreams in the finished product like a child playing make-believe. If you are a writer, it is seeing your finished book sitting on the bestseller shelf at the bookstore; if you are a medical student, it is seeing your diploma hanging on the wall of your consulting room.

Ripening your dreams takes them out of the "wish" category by fleshing out all the aspects that make these dreams come true. This process keeps filling in more of your attention until what you desire becomes tangible. Your imagination keeps filling in more of the picture until your goal becomes crystal clear. Your imagination, one of your seven senses, is developed and honed in your stomach.

Bring all your senses to your visualization: Smell what your brand new book smells like. Feel the texture of the cover. See the crowds lined up with your book in hand, eagerly waiting for your autograph. Hear their accolades about how much your book means to them. Taste the victory champagne. *Hey, that's what I'm doing!*

This one step—imagining your dream as if it exists—is huge. Your bodymind is completely literal. Visualizing the end result clearly in your imagination makes it *real* to your bodymind. This shifts the paradigm from, "oh my gosh, how am I going to get there?" to "I've already seen it, so I *know* I can do this," or "this is doable."

Think through how your values and principles influence and shape the picture. If, switching examples, one of your highest ideals is freedom, and your dream is to find a lifetime partner, part of ripening that dream is to really think through how freedom might be expressed within this relationship.

One way might be to imagine someone who honors your need for a lot of alone time, someone who values their own freedom as much as you value yours. When you include your values and principles into your dreams, it brings clarity and integrity to them, ripening them in delightful ways. Ripening your plans and dreams helps you to become single-minded, and that makes you unstoppable.

When you do not think your thoughts through, they have not ripened, and are all but impossible to digest. When you do not feel the fears that invariably come up, it allows your mind to dwell on worst-case scenarios, or limited thinking like "how can I *possibly* do that?" That sours your food. This chaotic way of thinking sabotages your dreams and plans by forming a competing picture to muddy everything up.

Fears *inevitably* come up when you make a plan. They push your desires further and further away from you. If you experience the fears—without dialogue, or taking actions intended to distract you from your fears (like watching TV or having a snack)—they simply dissolve.

After you have experienced the fears, what are left are the positive feelings. As they float up, bringing up the sweetness of life, and you savor that, the positive feelings attract your desires to you. You experience the great fullness of life.

Food as Fuel

With minor exceptions, *fruit and vegetables are alkaline* and everything else, like meat, grains and dairy is acidic. We need alkaline food for physical endurance, mental stamina and to keep our emotions stable. Alkaline food creates an internal environment that provides enough fuel and stamina to give constancy to our values and beliefs.

When our diet is mainly alkaline, our energy remains rock solid from one meal to the next. Eating five to seven servings of vegetables or fruit per day is your greatest insurance against *all* diseases. A serving is the size of your closed fist. Seventy percent of your food needs to be vegetables and fruit, the more organic the better. Food is fuel.

All the by-products of your physical activities are acids. If your diet does not have enough vegetables and fruit, your whole body becomes acidic. Your joints swell up, which is your body's attempt to reduce the acidity. You can tell if you are too acidic because the swelling makes your first steps in the morning painful.

When your diet is too acidic, it chemically shoves your body into "fight, fright, flight" responses, which is called "sympathetic dominance." This is similar to how your body responds to bad news on TV. Having a diet that is too acidic causes your body to shut your sexual, digestive, and immune systems down. Sensing danger, your body diverts energy from those systems to your muscles and sense organs, making you hyper vigilant so you can respond instantly to the supposed threat.

Your bodymind reacts to every thought, feeling, and belief as if they are also food. In essence they are. Positive thoughts are alkaline. Negative thoughts are acidic. Just as with our food, we need a certain amount of both.

A small amount of fear is healthy. If you have no fear, you might step in front of a bus, give your Social Security number to a scammer or do some other foolish thing.

Examples of nurturing and supportive alkaline thoughts are:

- I am safe and loved
- I have enough time and resources to accomplish what I need to do
- I love what I'm doing in this life
- I am appreciated
- I am respected
- My family, friends and life are supportive

Resonance

Sympathy is an action of your stomach. "Sympathy," as developed by the Chinese in the five elements probably translates more accurately to the word Resonance.

If you take two guitars, tune both of them, and pluck the "C" string on one of them, you will hear the "C" string from the second guitar vibrate (as if it had been strummed), even if it's across the room. They are resonating together.

In daily life we resonate with everything around us, just like those two guitars. Another way to say that is: we are constantly, and somewhat unconsciously influencing each other. When we associate with someone who always makes excuses, we unconsciously start offering up excuses ourselves. When we spend our time hanging around with people who are loving and kind, loving ourselves and others just seems like the normal thing to do. Who we associate with directly influences all our thoughts, actions, values and beliefs.

Sympathizing, or resonating with the pain of others means *you* ripen *their* pain within your own body. Sympathy means: I suffer with. Likewise, surrounding yourself with negative and toxic people draws out your own latent negativity and toxicity, which directly influences all your own thoughts and actions. In effect, you are souring your food.

Who you associate with is vitally important. Choose well who you associate with. Evolve your life toward spending more of your time with people you admire. When you associate with people whose ideas and ideals you admire, the positive resonance strengthens and fortifies your own values and principles. Those profound moments become deep reservoirs of wisdom and friendship that resonate through time, moments that you can draw from many times throughout your life.

CHAPTER 16

How "Unfelt" Feelings Affect Your Stomach

Ultimately, you want to feel *all* your feelings—both good and bad. When you feel the good feelings, they expand into every part of your body-mind, giving you great fullness of joy and happiness. As good feelings expand they can fill your life to overflowing. You can allow the feeling of peace and contentment to fill up your bodymind and radiate out into your energy field until it overflows into your world.

When you feel unpleasant feelings, they dissolve into nothingness. You liberate yourself from negative attachments to those people or situations. If you have long-term digestive problems, then most likely you have been hit with painful feelings that, for whatever reason, you considered too difficult to feel. So you stuffed them.

From early childhood, you may have stuffed anger, frustration, fear, anxiety, sadness, and any number of difficult feelings into your stomach. The build-up of negative feelings causes myriad symptoms including:

- Thinking you have too much to do
- Feeling unappreciated
- Thinking you don't have enough time
- Dizziness and nausea
- Wanting to withdraw from life
- Long-term depression
- Recurring bouts of anxiety
- Migraine headaches

During stressful or exciting times your unfelt feelings—combined with all the feelings happening in the moment—can overwhelm you. *Thinking* about your problems just stuffs them further down into your bodymind, where they continue to build up in intensity. The buildup of unfelt feelings causes—by far—the majority of your pain. You develop a chronic "pain body" of built-up emotional pressure.

Any time your pain builds beyond a five on a one-to-ten pain scale, you can bet that at least half the pain is emotional pressures that build up because you are not feeling your feelings. If you hit your thumb with a hammer, it often hurts at ten on a one-to-ten pain scale. But thirty minutes later it only hurts at a one or two, unless you bump it again. When your pain continues to build until it exceeds an eight or nine, it is probably 80 to 90 percent emotional. Emotional pain is *much more painful* than pain that is only physical. You can tell it's emotional when it continues to build.

One of my patients complained of a feeling of impending blackness so thick it felt overwhelming. She had terrible anxiety and apprehension. She kept running around, scattered, convinced she did not have enough time. She experienced profound dizziness and nausea when she turned her head too fast.

She was terrified of the overwhelming anxiety attacks. I talked her through how to muster the courage to confront the anxieties by simply feeling them. I encouraged her to avoid making up stories about how the anxieties were "too much to face." By simply feeling the anxieties and the *feeling* of impending blackness, she found that they went from fire-breathing dragons to just another feeling she could easily dissolve.

Feeling all the anxieties allowed her to start making sense of her situation and figure out what was happening, what was causing her distress. It turned out that during the entire time she was experiencing the emotional distress, her husband was in love with another woman. He admitted that he was having an affair.

She, like all of us, is telepathic. Her bodymind was aware of, and responding to knowledge her rational mind was not yet conscious of—but it showed up as digestive distress and anxiety. After she split up with him, her dizziness, anxieties and stomach issues cleared up. Since then she has had no further stomach issues.

Healing Emotional Issues of the Stomach

Because you are a creator, when you focus your attention on something, anything, any negative feelings you have regarding that issue immediately surface, whether they are terrible things that have happened in the past, or fears regarding the future. Here are some things you can do:

- Feel all negative feelings or body sensations that come up.
- Breathe out strong from your lower abdomen and sit up straight so you are not compressing the area around your stomach and contributing to its distress.
- Question whether what you are thinking about is an accurate reflection of how you want to create your life. If it is not—it's not *your* truth—focus instead on plans and dreams you want to create in your own unique world.
- Use your seven senses, including imagination to ripen your dreams and desires until you can fully enjoy them as if they exist here and now.
- Let your values and principles shape your dreams so you create *your* world exactly the way you want.

Realize that you are always creating your reality by what you are focusing on. You can do it *consciously* by focusing on the grace and love that's all around you, which creates a more graceful and loving life. Your life is *your* precious picture to paint. Moment by moment you can heal your stomach and bring it into harmony by ripening the life your heart desires. It's all so simple.

CHAPTER 17

Having Good Distribution in Your Life
· *Spleen* ·

From medical physiology we learn that the spleen tucks under your rib cage just forward of your left elbow as it hangs down. As blood passes through the spleen and liver, they cleanse it of bacteria and foreign bodies. Blood cells live about 120 days, and—as they get old and brittle—many of them rupture and are recycled as they pass through your spleen with its enormous maze of blood vessels.

From five elements physiology, we learn that your spleen's job is *distribution*. Your spleen is in charge of transporting all the nutrients to every cell, and transporting all the waste products away. It faithfully distributes all your bodymind's needs twenty-four hours a day to every cell and organ. That is a huge and vitally-important job.

The part of your consciousness located in your spleen can be likened to the head of a trucking company. It is the official that transports and distributes all food, energy, and commodities to every cell and organ in your entire bodymind. If it flows or moves, your spleen moves it. On the mental, emotional, spiritual levels of your consciousness, your spleen represents the distribution of all the aspects of your life.

Does your life feel like you lack the time or resources to do what you want? Are you languishing in one or more dead-end situations? Do you dislike the balance of your life? If you are having these kinds of thoughts, your spleen official (who takes everything personally) firmly believes *it has let you down*—that it has failed you. You know how bad you feel when you let a loved one down. That's how your spleen feels.

Thinking this way causes your spleen to suffer immensely, and in its distress it malfunctions. When you notice that you are feeling this way, it is time for you to reflect on all the goodness that exists in your life, to basically give your spleen a pat on the back. Like you, *it needs to be appreciated.*

When a steady diet of unappreciative thinking distresses your spleen, you get overly stiff from working or playing hard because you are not getting rid of waste products as efficiently as you can. Your digestion becomes sluggish. Sleep is affected. In times when you hate your life, cancer, leukemia, autoimmune disorders, tumors and blood disorders are the kind of disorders your spleen can develop when it believes it has completely failed you. What kind of thoughts and feelings are you sending to your spleen official?

It is not difficult to imagine the resulting health problems if this official becomes weak and can only transport *some* of the commodities to *some* of the population. When the spleen official is weak, you cannot get enough supplies transported into your muscles. You cannot get all the waste products carried away quickly enough. Movement, and the motivation toward movement, becomes progressively difficult.

When transportation to and from your nervous system is inadequate, your mental stamina and agility is diminished. It's a lot harder to concentrate and think things through. You can feel stuck.

On any given day you literally have millions of things to be thankful for, and maybe a few hundred things you can get upset about. And yet, your brain's tendency is to focus on problems, on what you don't have or don't like. Every moment you are complaining causes your spleen to malfunction, similarly to how *you* tend to malfunction in situations where you give your all, but are not appreciated. Ouch!

When you allow your mind to focus on negativity—like how messed up the government is, things you dislike about your job or problems with people around you—it uses up the energy your heart would commit to loving your world into being. This can cause your spleen official to become so challenged that you:

- Become entrenched in your ways
- Feel too stuck to start anything new, including things you really *want* to do
- Become lazy or overwhelmed
- Get stuck in behaviors that are destructive or addictive
- Solve everyone else's problems, while achieving nothing for yourself

Each of us experiences these problems at one time or another. You can always extricate yourself by taking the following actions:

- Make the time to really play
- Create time for contemplation
- Spend quality time with loved ones
- Have an artistic outlet
- Get enough sleep
- Commit to doing the things that make *you* feel most alive
- Add more movement into your life
- Appreciate the goodness that you contribute
- Be grateful for the goodness that is all around you, goodness you may be taking for granted
- Breathe in the wonderful moments of your life

You don't have to make big changes to feel happy. Sometimes little changes make all the difference in the world. Take your loved one for an evening walk. Make time to go dancing, put in quality time figuring out how to pull off a fantasy vacation. Little changes spice up everything. It doesn't take much to spice up your life.

When considering the health of your spleen, I cannot overstate the importance of movement. Make it a habit to get movement into your life. Everyone feels better if they take a walk every day. If you have difficulty figuring out how to have healthy movement in your life, consider joining a health club, or put on some fun music and dance at home. Unplug your TV for a while and see what else excites you.

When you were a child, you naturally had lots of activity in your life. Lack of movement was *never* an issue. As you get older, it takes planning and commitment to get enough movement into your life. You have to make it a priority, and commit to it. In societies where people are long lived, working up a sweat every day is the norm.

When you don't set aside time for movement and action, all the essential qualities of your life suffer. Your spleen's ability to transport and distribute food and waste begins to clog up. Old age usually takes the rap, but that's just ignorance.

Check in with yourself regularly. Ask yourself: Am I moving as much as my body needs? Life is so much better when you make time for what *you* feel is important. You are the one that creates your life. So create positive changes that make your life feel like you have good distribution. You deserve it.

I once had a patient come in with a spleen that was hot and inflamed. As she talked about her frustrations at home, I saw that she had a "distribution" problem. Her three children were really involved in sports and activities at school. She loved living out in the country, but felt frustrated about being "mom's taxi," having to drive into town and back several times a day to accommodate her children's many activities.

I told her about a lovely community near the high school that has magnificent views of the South Yuba River Canyon. If she lived there, her children could walk to school. They could wake up ten minutes before class and still make it to school on time. More importantly, they could get to all their extracurricular activities on their own. The moment she decided to move closer to the high school, her spleen calmed down. Years later, even after her children have all graduated from college, they still enjoy living there.

Your thoughts are healing you—or killing you. Time just adds it up. Because your bodymind responds to every thought—and takes everything you think literally and personally—what you think matters. So when you think your life has good distribution, your spleen displays good internal distribution of nutrients in and waste products out.

The instant you come into harmony with how any of your organs operate, *that organ instantly calms* down leaving you free to enjoy health and well being.

- CHAPTER 18 -

Having Enough

When is enough? "Enough" is not something most of us consider. We don't notice when we have eaten enough, when we have shopped enough, when we have played enough, or worked enough. When it comes to the topic of *enough*, most people fall into extremes between wanting more and feeling like they don't have enough.

When we compare ourselves to others and believe we are being deprived, especially when we're young, we can become polarized into a lifetime of wanting more: more money, more food, more clothes, more cars, more of *whatever* we have addictive compulsive behaviors toward. We can be insatiable. We never feel the satisfaction of having enough. There's always the sense that we need more just to "get by" in the world, even though we may have way more than enough on every level.

The other extreme is a profound sense of lack that creates a driving obsession to save and scrimp and hoard. We tell ourselves we don't have enough time, money, resources, education or opportunity to have or do *that*. There is never enough, no matter how much we have. This fear-based thinking keeps us deprived. We can't do the things that bring us enjoyment. We can't afford to do any of the fun things, "because there's not enough."

As you make it a habit of focusing on all the ways you have enough, your life begins to naturally unfold in ways that let you experience the great fullness of life. Say "yes" to the things your heart desires. Everything has a gestation period. When you "see yourself having it," actually having it becomes a foregone conclusion. Own it now in your consciousness, and let it manifest in God's time. You just make your life up. Why not make it up with you having enough?

There is a moment while eating, playing, or working when we experience the exquisite quality of "enough"—but only if we are looking for it. If we are not paying attention, we go past all these exquisite moments in a blur without recognizing them. We become aware later, after we have eaten too much and wished we had stopped earlier. Many of us don't notice that we have worked enough until we have used up all our stamina and are totally exhausted.

In your own life there is a delicious moment in dining when you have eaten just enough. When you observe this phenomenon, the enchantment of the dining experience takes you to whole new levels of appreciation. Similarly there is a moment when you are working, a moment when you know you have done enough for today. When you become aware that you have done enough, you can look for the cutting off place where you can put everything away and bring the job to completion. By not working yourself to exhaustion, you leave room in your consciousness for inspiration from your own spirit.

When you pay attention to that "moment of enough," you also notice when you have *not* done enough. You might need to do just a few more things to bring the project to a truly satisfying conclusion. When you pay attention to these little things, it makes all the difference in the world.

Boundaries

Boundaries are all the ways you respect your own principles and values without allowing others to override or negate them—or you to override theirs. It is how you stand up for, and say "yes" to what you want. It is how you guard your precious time and energy by saying "no" to what does not work for you. The more decisive you are with your "yeses" and "noes," the clearer and stronger your boundaries become.

Your boundaries are not meant to be rigid. They are not weapons designed to control others. You can be flexible in the ways you negotiate with others. But, in a healthy state, there is a line that you will not go beyond in compromising your values, principles and beliefs.

One of the ways people attempt to crash through our boundaries is through manipulating our feelings. Another way is to create a perceived threat that makes us voluntarily give up our boundaries. One example is after 9/11 we gave up our right to privacy because of the perceived threat to our safety. Benjamin Franklin said, "Those who would give up their freedom for security deserve neither." You can also see emotional pain and manipulation in families with guilt trips concerning lifestyle choices, controlling shared space and controlling each other's time and energy.

We crash our own boundaries by needing to "fit in," giving up our choice, not wanting to seem pushy or selfish, believing our choices are not valid, feeling like we are not "good enough" or that our needs don't matter.

We can never be whole if we don't have firm boundaries. When creating our boundaries, we need to include the right to create the world we want to live in. We need to make our "yes" be "yes," and our "no" be "no." Then we can manifest the world we want to live in, consciously, with firm boundaries.

DEVELOPING CHARACTER

- CHAPTER 19 -

The Element of Metal

The qualities of metal are your *drive, strength, determination, persistence and power*. Metal represents the strength of your character and your drive to succeed. It is the fire in your belly.

When your metal official is strong and healthy, you are someone others trust and respect, someone who is wise, someone others look up to. You do what you say you will do. You are true to your word. You know you are an integral and necessary part of your community, your world. One positive step at a time, then another, leads you to becoming this person.

When your metal official is weak, you may feel cut off from Creator or from your own divine spark, or you may experience a void within you that feels like a canyon that cannot be filled. You can experience a feeling of emptiness and coldness that is far beyond a mere lack of warmth.

You can go from one guru or quest to another, always searching externally for what is missing inside you, never satisfied for long by what you find. Without your divine spark, it is difficult to find any value within yourself or anywhere else. You can become quite negative about yourself, life and about everything you do.

Weakness in any official usually manifests as behavioral extremes. A person whose metal is weak can be the most scruffy and unwashed person you know, or they can be compulsively tidy and fastidious. They might live in squalor or compensate for inner emptiness by putting up an immaculate façade. They may eat only the purest food, or wear ostentatious displays of gold, silver, or precious stones to cover up the void inside.

If you want to understand the metal official within your bodymind, it helps to understand metal's reaction to heat: metal is flexible and can maintain incredible strength of form. The talents you forge into the makeup of your "character" can display the strength and malleability of the finest metals. With the right amount of heat—the right balance of love and boundaries from your parents—your metal becomes malleable. Your talents, and your particular genius can be shaped into tools that are useful to yourself and society.

If too much heat is applied to metal, it can lose its form. This can be likened to a child who is adored with no limits—regardless of what he or she does—with little or no consequences for poor behavior. No matter what the child does, the parent says, "That's OK." They cover up and make excuses for the child.

This kind of love burns up the child's metal, leaving it unable to hold heat or form. Under pressure, their metal no longer holds up. Under stress, their character shatters and fragments. Their inner fire does not glow.

The result is a person who does not stand true to their values, who folds and gives up easily. They start out with noble intentions but give up at the slightest test of their mettle. At the opposite polarity, there are parts of their life where they can be very rigid in their perspectives, with little consideration of others due to the gravity of their own perceived needs. Often people with weak metal display the behavior patterns of both extremes.

When someone's metal element is out of balance, they do not seem to reach their potential. The word "lackluster" captures this quality best. It is as though they perform all their functions without ever being fully engaged.

If you display the imbalances described above, there are two things you can do to heal and purify the metal element within yourself. *The first is to forgive,* especially your father and other father figures in your life. Any time a painful memory comes to your awareness, go back to that moment in time. Get in touch with the emotional pain of that moment. Then without dialogue, keep going back to that incident and feeling the next negative feeling that comes up. When all the negative feelings clear, you have forgiven that incident. Staying with this process, until you release all the feelings, including the subtle ones, lets the mystery of that situation reveal itself to you.

As you let go of old painful traumas, a weight lifts off you. Old aches fade away. Your inner light increases its radiance and shines more brightly. Your metal starts holding its form better, and you start standing tall when trials and difficulties occur.

Some of what you forgive may be your father's actions or behaviors that were abusive or dysfunctional. Some emotional pain might involve abandonment issues. Even though you can rationalize the "reasons" why your father was not around when you were growing up, or not supportive because he was so busy, your bodymind still experiences abandonment, which needs to be forgiven in the same way an unkind act is forgiven. That releases the emotional pain out of your bodymind.

The archetypes of Father (metal) and Mother (earth) form about 60 percent of your internal makeup. The biggest portion of your worldview is occupied with these two archetypes. Holding onto painful memories about your parents and siblings cause the majority of your pain.

Ultimately, you must forgive everyone and everything that causes you emotional pain. Once you clear out the old pain, there is plenty of room for inspiration. The more you forgive, the easier it is for your spirit to inspire your higher ideals and guide you to create and live the life of your dreams.

The most primal action that strengthens your metal element *is breathing out strong,* which progressively enhances your self-esteem, strengthens and stabilizes the element of metal in your character, and creates a stable foundation for living powerfully. You breathe in all that is good, and breathe out what no longer serves you.

While most people experience decline in their vitality every year after age thirty, *you* can experience ever-higher levels of vitality as you age. You can live every aspect of your life powerfully, even into old age.

CHAPTER 20

The Ability to Grieve
· *The Season of Autumn* ·

The element of metal is associated with the season of autumn in which the energy of growth slows dramatically. The air becomes heavy with mist and rain. Leaves die and fall to the ground. Death and dying—a natural part of the cycle of life—returns essential nutrients and metals to the soil to nourish vigorous growth the following spring. So it is in all aspects of your life: death and dying of what no longer serves you creates the space for new dreams and aspirations to grow.

It is normal to grieve when someone or something is lost to you. *Your lung official grants you the power of grief.* But if you cannot move beyond your grief, any new loss hits you like a punch in the gut, leaving you defeated. Instead of living life head-on, you spend your time focusing on your rear-view mirror thinking "if only." You give up your power to regret, wishing things were like they used to be. If you cannot let go of the past there is no room for inspiration, no space to create a future, or even contemplate one.

Everything has seasons of change. Everything. Let's take relationships as an example:

- Spring is when the relationship is growing vigorously. You are spending a lot of time together, growing, learning and sharing a wealth of experiences.
- The summertime of a relationship is when the energy slows down slightly, becoming softer. This is a loving time when your shared experiences form buds that grow into flowers and eventually bear fruit.

- The time of Earth, Indian summer, is the time of harvest. You are usually so busy, there is less time together, unless you are harvesting something together. Even then, the focus is on the harvest, not on each other.

- As relationships or situations enter the season of Fall, even less energy is available. Your focus is more inward and less on the relationship. It is a time of personal contemplation.

- Winter is a time when the least amount of energy is available to the relationship. Each person tends to focus on being cozy and comfortable. If there are no demands or expectations, this is a time to enjoy each other's company. But often this is a time when others do not have time for you.

It is important to say "yes" to each phase of life as it is happening. When a relationship enters the autumn phase in your life you may contemplate its value to you: "What inspired me about this relationship? Did we both share in the bounty of this relationship, or did one benefit more than the other? Is this relationship something I really want to invest the time and energy in to make it survive the test of time? Did it bear fruit and bring fulfillment? Is there anything that we need to let go of or invest more energy into for this relationship to continue and flourish in the years to come?"

The Autumn of any cycle is a time for contemplating any feelings that you may have projected onto a relationship or partner, like disappointment or frustration. This is a good time to look at any expectations that you or the other person must *be* a certain way. There are things that may need to die so the cycle of renewal can bring new life to the relationship, and nourish vigorous growth the following spring.

- CHAPTER 21 -

Living Your Truth
· Lungs ·

Your diaphragm—the wall-to-wall floor of your lungs—is a very effective bellows. As you breathe out strong, your diaphragm pushes up like a dome, forcing carbon dioxide out, purifying your blood. Then when you involuntarily breathe back in, your diaphragm pulls down like a bowl, allowing your lungs to infuse your blood with a big mixing bowl's amount of life-giving oxygen.

In the higher dimensions of your bodymind, your lungs are the officials who receive the pure energy from the heavens. Your lungs don't just breathe in air. They breathe in the visions of your life; they breathe in truth; and they expel beliefs and assumptions that no longer represent how you want to create your own unique world. Your lungs and large intestine are the organs associated with the element of metal. They both symbolize the steady rhythm of taking in and letting go.

The ancient Chinese medical treatise *Nei Jing Su Wen* describes the lungs as the "lid" of all your organs. The lungs receive "pure energy" from the heavens, and send it downward. The pure energy can include higher truths, your life's visions, or noble thoughts. The lung's downward-dispersing action disseminates the essence of inspiration that every cell and organ needs in order to live a fulfilling life. When you breathe out strong, and thus breathe in strong, your lungs give the other officials all the energy they need to accomplish the dreams you commit to. You live large.

Various forms of lung congestion are due to the lungs' inability to send energy and fluids downward. Asthma, bronchitis, emphysema, pleurisy, and upper respiratory infections can all be traced back to fluids not getting dispersed downward. Lung congestion, in the higher levels of your consciousness, comes from not downward dispersing the higher truths and visions of your life, or refusing to believe that you could *possibly* step into your vision. Your bodymind is mostly energy and consciousness. Letting your unruly mind talk you out of your vision or higher truths is the main cause of lung and bronchial problems.

When I ask people what they want, most tell me all the things they do *not* want. When pressed about what they want, many of them only have vague ideas, like "better health" or "less stress." Your bodymind is image oriented. It needs clear, fixed images to work toward: can you imagine hiking mountains and swimming rivers into your late eighties or beyond? How about running a marathon? Can you imagine your mind sharp as a tack until the day you die? Can you see yourself at your ideal weight? Can you see yourself doing the exact things you would want to do if the world were a perfect place? These are the kind of images your bodymind can grab hold of. Then they are so much easier to implement.

Choose image-oriented goals—goals that scare you a little—that stretch the imagination of who you think you are. If your bodymind does not have *specific* images and goals to emulate, it can perceive no way to get there.

Instead, most of us tend to cling tightly to mean, discouraging or dismissive things others have said about us, which form the basis our own limiting thoughts, feelings and beliefs. As we *feel* our feelings about disparaging statements, they dissolve into nothingness. If we cannot let go of old conditioning, we have no room to take in new concepts. This can manifest as not even *trying* to make sense of what we are hearing. When we are in that state, talking to us can be like talking to a blank wall.

Fear of death, in the element of metal, shows up in thousands of subtle and not-so-subtle ways like: not wanting to be pushy, worrying about what others think of you, thinking that you are inadequate or that you do not belong, needing to be understood, or wishing things were different than they are. The negative thoughts, which are generated by your fears, cut you off from your spiritual connection.

When you do not *feel* a fear that comes up, your body's immediate reaction to your fears is to slump and start breathing shallowly. For as long as you breathe shallowly, you feel separated from your own divine nature. You see your God as something outside of you.

Breathing out Strong changes your life. As strong as you breathe out is as strong as you breathe in. You breathe in the inspiration from the heavens. When you are breathing out strong, you simply *know* that you have always been connected to the guidance and authority you desire. You realize that the source of creation has never, ever been separate from you. Every moment that you are breathing out strong, the power of love, the nobility of truth, and your right to be here—just as you are—are self-evident.

- CHAPTER 22 -

Letting Go of What No Longer Serves You
· Large Intestine ·

Your large intestine, or colon digests the last five percent of food, mainly metals like calcium, phosphorus, magnesium etc. It also extracts the last of the water so your stool can firm up. It purifies your blood by eliminating the dregs.

Your large intestine is responsible for *transformation and change* in your life. It is responsible for getting rid of the garbage. One of the ways it accomplishes this is by letting go of the toxic thoughts, feelings, and beliefs you are exposed to each day. When you hang onto garbage, your mind and spirit become toxic.

If you keep dredging up the past and what went wrong, you don't have room for all the blessings life *wants* to bestow on you. You have trouble moving on. You become locked into rigid beliefs and ideas.

This rigidity shows up in your character as viewpoints of life that leave no space for new possibilities or inspiration, for transformation and change. If rigidity has shown up in your character, it can manifest as frozen joint problems. Mainly affected are the wrist, elbow, or shoulder. That's where the large intestine meridians run through. But you can also have ankles or knees that freeze up due to rigidly holding onto old pain or limiting beliefs.

Inability to let go of toxic memories can also coincide with inability to let go of possessions that no longer serve any useful purpose. It may be time to clean a closet and take clothes you no longer wear to Goodwill. Or it may be time to clean the garage. Clearing out debris in your home coincides with getting your inner house in order. What do *you* need to let go of?

If the colon fails to get rid of the garbage, all the officials in your body suffer. The toxicity makes it difficult for your organs to perform their duties.

Diarrhea, the opposite problem, can be just as bad. The food passes through your intestines so quickly you cannot get nutrition from it. Everything seems to slip away too quickly, like sand slipping through your fingers. Without adequate breath, the nourishment from your food, including thoughts, feelings, and beliefs go right through you and come out only partially digested. Breathing deeply oxidizes and activates your food, helping you get all the nutrition out of it.

The meridians of the large intestine run full out from 5 AM to 7 AM. For most of our long history—when we did not have electricity—that's when we would wake up and have our morning bowel movement. This is also the time when we feel inspired to do all of the things we want to get accomplished for the day.

There is a symbiotic relationship between your lungs' function of taking in inspiration and courage, and your large intestine's function of letting go of wastes to keep your blood pure and sacred. Keeping both functions in balance is essential to a healthy body, mind and spirit. Breathing out strong helps maintain that balance.

Letting go of the pain and limitations of your past, and breathing in the courage to face each moment with strength and conviction, empowers you to stand at the very center of eternity. Within each moment is the power to transform you, changing you into the best version of who you can be. This is the gift of the lungs and large intestine within your bodymind.

- CHAPTER 23 -

The Element of Water

In the higher consciousness of your bodymind, water represents your feelings. Water gives your plans, dreams—and all life—the ability to endure. When your water element is healthy, your mind has fluidity. Thoughts and ideas flow effortlessly. It is easy to think things through.

On the other hand, when the water element gets into trouble, it can manifest the extremes of drought and flood. You start experiencing drought in your life when all your thoughts *and feelings* are fixated on what you don't have, how life is slipping away from you, or on all the things that have gone wrong. Thinking this way for a prolonged period of time begins to dry out your hope, dreams and possibilities. When you steadily focus is on the things you can't do—that there is not enough money, resources or time, that you are "stuck—hope evaporates.

In drought:

• You believe that no matter what you do, you cannot get ahead

• You fear you will never have enough

• The ground does not feel secure under your feet

• Your focus is on how hard your life is

• Every day you seem to have less

- Life is uncertain
- You believe the abundance you do have is slipping away from you
- Your toxic feelings and limiting beliefs manifest problems which confirm that, "yes, you are losing ground"
- Your life feels like there is little or no harvest
- You have fear and anxieties about the future
- You have doubts about whether you can survive
- You feel hopeless
- You can feel this way about your loved ones, worrying about them, wondering how they can possibly make it

Other people in the same situation may have a totally different perspective, and not experience a drought at all. Most of the pain and suffering we experience comes from our mind putting a negative spin on situations. When we do not feel our negative feelings, our mind can create quite morbid stories.

Overpowering Feelings Feel like Being in a Flood

Flood is when you let unfelt feelings—which you may have deemed too painful or toxic to feel—build up to such a great level that they flood over you, swamping you, inundating you with fears, anxieties and other difficult feelings until there is no safe place for you.

In flood:

- There are many things in your life, or your loved one's lives, to fear or worry about
- You push feelings deemed "too toxic to feel" deeper into your body-mind by thinking about them instead of feeling them
- Your unfelt emotions build up until life feels overwhelming
- You are inundated with feelings like grief and sorrow

- Life seems hard, and even small things feel like they are too much to deal with
- You are so busy trying not to drown, you lose sight of your own plans and dreams
- You dislike how your life, or your loved one's life, has turned out
- Your overwhelming feelings trigger thousands of fearful thoughts that leave you stunned and immobile
- Your own self-preservation, or that of a loved one, dominates your mind

Moaning or groaning is an unconscious sign of difficulties in the water element. A person who moans or groans, even though their life may not be worse than anyone else's, indicates that they are either drowning in unfelt feelings, or that the drought they feel is so severe they see no future for themselves.

The pressure of unfelt feelings can build up until life becomes overwhelming. Worry and unfelt feelings are the two principle causes of high blood pressure. So when you catch yourself moaning or groaning, it's time to start feeling all the overwhelming feelings your rational mind might *deem* too toxic or scary to feel.

Ears are the end organs of the water element (just as eyes are the end organs of the element of wood). Kidney stress can sometimes feel like you have water in your ears. You can also experience low back or knee pain, teeth problems, hearing loss and excessive fear and insecurity. A water imbalance often shows up as dark circles, a bluish-black hue and puffiness around the eyes. Puffiness around your eyes is a sure sign you are letting feelings build up to toxic levels.

Feel, Rather than Think, Your Feelings

The first key to working with the element of water is to not intensify negative feelings by *thinking* about them, or talking about them with others.

If a painful memory comes up, the correct way of dealing with it is to go inside and *feel all the feelings*. If your mind keeps going back to the same painful event, that means there are more negative feelings or body sensations from that event that still need to be felt. Feeling your negative feelings dissolves them. *Then* talk about them if the issues are still important.

All your unfelt feelings create thoughts that are like grappling hooks that keep you attached to unhealthy relationships, memories and situations, binding you to painful memories and toxic people. The more you feel all your feelings—including body sensations that come up, like tension in your gut or tightness in your chest—the more completely you release the negative attachments. Feeling those feelings releases the grappling hooks. Then your spirit is free to connect you to the beauty that is all around you.

Water has great power. It can move mountains to achieve what you desire. But when you are not feeling the negative feelings that come up, the powerful force of your feelings (water) pushes your desires further away from you, while pulling what you fear toward you. What you feel is hundreds of times more important than anything you think. Once you feel the negative feelings, your heart naturally focuses on what you love.

Water has no boundaries of its own. It is an inexorable force that cannot be stopped. It will always find a path through anything in its way. It never "gives up." It can bring down mountains. When your emotions align with your plans and dreams, the force of your feelings empower your flexibility, endurance, ambition, and determination. *You* never give up. *You* can move mountains.

The Season of Winter

In winter, the time of night far exceeds the time of light. Water replenishes the earth, dissolving leaves to return life-giving nutrients back to the soil.

Winter is the time to reflect on the true values of your life, the time when you ask yourself the deeper questions regarding your life, like:

Who am I? What did I incarnate into this life to do or be? Am I doing what I really want to do in this life? What are my deep, abiding values? What principles and values do I hold dear? Am I living a life that is aligned with them? Would my eight-year-old self be proud of who I am today? If the answer is no, what needs to be different?

When you ask these profound questions, your spirit answers. New avenues open to you where none existed before. You access profound information about the pathways and destiny of your life.

In this mysterious time when darkness far exceeds the time of light—when the energy of the seasons is at its lowest ebb—you have time to reflect on the directions available to you. It is the time for going inside and curling up by the fire with a good book. There is plenty of time to ponder the specifics of your life, what you have accomplished, where you are heading. This is the time when you carefully select the seeds you will plant in the coming spring. If the world were a perfect place, which seeds would you want to grow, blossom and bear fruit in the coming year?

- CHAPTER 24 -

Developing Intuition
· *Kidneys* ·

You are graced with two brains. The brain most people are aware of is the rational mind up there between your ears. It is actually your lower mind.

You really should love your brain, and cherish all the wonderful things it is capable of doing. But as incredible as your brain is—compared to your kidneys—it is slow to figure things out and overly prone to rationalizations. It is constantly projecting what may happen to you in the future, based on what has happened in the past. Your brain is more than a little afraid of *the infinity* of the present moment. So it retreats to the familiarity of using your five senses to predict the future based on the past. When in control, its past/future way of thinking severely limits the infinite possibilities of the present moment.

The kidneys, on the other hand, are your higher brain, filtering twenty percent of your blood per hour for your whole life. Each kidney has between fifteen thousand and twenty-five thousand filtration units, called "glomeruli," *which are completely lined with gray matter.* In your brain, gray matter just happens to be the *thinking* portion. That means your kidneys are some kind of brain.

The fact that your kidneys are some kind of a brain has been common knowledge in the study of anatomy for over 200 years, but anatomists had no place to put that knowledge. Thinking your brain was not the absolute controller of your consciousness was considered heresy. Now, within the holistic community, it is becoming common knowledge that your heart is the true emperor of your consciousness. Your kidneys, with their intimate connection to your spirit, report directly to your heart. In five elements physiology, your brain is considered part of your kidney system.

Your kidneys receive, and translate feelings and insights from your spirit. Spiritual energies and emotional energies are the most similar. They are both all-encompassing and fill up all the space wherever you are. When you let yourself experience and ponder your "first feelings," your insights from pondering those feelings develop your sense of intuition.

Accessing Spiritual Wisdom in the Everyday World

Your kidneys, through your feelings, translate the information your spirit is communicating to you. The moment you think about doing something—even though it may not occur until later—your spirit is experiencing it as if it were occurring here and now. Your spirit is not limited by time and space. To your spirit, everything is happening here and now. The first feeling that comes up is your spirit's exact preview of how you will feel if you actually do it.

You can use this quality of your feelings not just for discerning larger issues like whether to go to an event, change jobs or move to a new location. The real alchemy of your life happens when you begin to notice your feelings about the dozens of little things that come up all through a typical day.

The wisdom of your kidneys shows up as an immediate knowing of what is going to happen, before it happens. Over the course of your life, whenever something did not turn out well, you always had a bad feeling about it first, but you often did it anyway. When it went wrong, the realization was, you *knew* it would. It's like déjà vu because your spirit already experienced it going wrong and had sent you a bad feeling to warn you.

You want to become progressively more aware of your feelings, not just about things you get a bad feeling about, but things that you get a good feeling about. You have a lot more magic in your life when you engage with what you have a good feeling about. And you get a lot less hard knocks when you avoid doing the things you *know* will go bad.

Imagine you start to park in a parking space at the mall and get a bad feeling. If you were to back out of that space and look around to where else you could park, your eyes would naturally focus on your spirit's better choice. When you return to your car later, after the sun has gone down, the place where you were first going to park just happens to be plunged into darkness because the light in that part of the parking lot is out. Where you were guided to park just happens to be the brightest part of the lot. I have had so many experiences like this where my spirit led me away from what had the potential to be harmful.

Part of waking up is paying attention to your feelings, especially your first feelings when you think about doing something. If you honestly think about it, you got a bad feeling before every bad thing that *ever* happened to you. And you had a good feeling before every good thing that ever happened.

When you think about something that's coming up, and you get that warm fuzzy feeling in your heart, that is your intuition telling you that you are *really* going to enjoy whatever that is. Your first feeling is subtle and only lasts for a moment, yet it contains the wisdom of your spirit. Space out and you miss it.

A friend of mine, Penny came in one day and said, "I have fifty tickets for my fifty best friends to see Les Miserables." I immediately got a warm fuzzy feeling in my heart. I *knew* that I wanted to go, so I immediately said, "Count me *in*."

However, she felt that she hadn't convinced me yet, so she had to tell me that it was the original cast who had finished their *long* run on Broadway and were now coming to Sacramento on their world tour.

After the musical, a bunch of us were standing on the steps of the convention center and I noticed that I had the same warm happy feeling I had the moment Penny first said she had fifty tickets. But now the feeling was because the *experience* of the musical with dear friends had been so exquisite. My spirit knew and communicated exactly what kind of experience I would have weeks before my brain ever could.

If you pay attention to your feelings—especially your first feelings about what you are thinking about doing—you innately avoid all the minefields of life.

Years ago I was turning onto the freeway from Nevada City, heading toward Sacramento, when I saw a hitchhiker thumbing a ride. He looked like a nice, friendly young man. But as he opened my passenger door, he whistled for some friends across the street, and everything inside me went black. My insides instantly felt like ice when I turned around and saw his hard-looking friends start to get up. I *knew* something really bad was going to happen if those guys got in my truck.

My innate intelligence took over and I observed myself peeling out, leaving the hitchhiker standing in the road. It took thirty minutes for the icy feeling in my heart to thaw out enough to feel normal. I *know* my intuition saved me from a terrible fate.

Many years ago one of my friends came home and backed his work truck into its usual place, got a bad feeling and moved it further back. When he got up the next morning to go to work, a huge pine tree had uprooted in the night and fallen. It smashed his truck flat, like something out of a cartoon, stopping the tree about three feet above the roof of his house. If the truck had not been there, the tree would have gone right through his baby daughter's bed. His intuition saved her life.

These are a few examples of how your feelings connect you to the wisdom of your spirit. When you feel your feelings, and reflect on what those feelings mean in the context of the moment, you get in touch with the wisdom of your spirit.

In addition to your feelings, your kidneys transmit your spirit's messages to your consciousness in several intuitive ways:

- Auditory: You *hear* messages warning, advising or chiding you as you move through life.
- Visual: You *see* the direction that you need to go. You see what you need to do or not do. My wife sees something happening before it occurs.
- Kinesthetic: You have gut feelings and body sensations, or an inner knowing about how it's going to turn out. Don't ignore them.

I am more kinesthetic, so my spirit communicates with me mostly through my *feelings* and body sensations. Often I just *know* what I need to do or not do.

Remember, you are a spirit having a human experience. Paying attention to all the messages from your spirit during a typical day gives your innate intelligence the clarity to handle all life's difficulties more easily. As you get better at these skills, you move with infinitely more grace in your life.

Worrying and Wondering What Will Happen

Because you are a creator, wondering what is going to happen in your life totally freaks your kidneys out. The Emperor has abdicated the throne. You are literally *asking* outside circumstances to create your destiny for you. Instead of focusing your attention on what you want and committing to it, you are giving outer circumstances—or other people—control of your life. Anytime you are not creating your own reality, someone else is doing it for you. And *that* never turns out the way you want it.

To turn this around, start by breathing out strong a couple times to interrupt old disempowering patterns. Then ask yourself, "What would I do if the world were a perfect place, and anything were possible?" Sometimes small steps toward fulfilling your own plan or dream make all the difference in the world.

Sometimes you have to take a number of steps in the direction your intuition points out before the larger picture of your vision can reveal itself to you. When you move in the directions that make your heart happy, your entire bodymind and the whole spiritual kingdom has the opportunity to lend their assistance. As a result, it magically turns out that the world *is* a perfect place.

Worry is just as bad as wondering what will happen to you. Worry projects your fears onto the destiny of your loved ones. Those kinds of thoughts hinder, rather than help your loved ones. This is a gross misuse of your kidneys.

Worry is an unconscious reaction, one of those kneejerk spells we all get caught up in. Our entire society is conditioned to worry. The implied belief is: if you don't worry, you have no compassion.

Worrying about others is like throwing a blanket of *your own gloom and doom* over the top of their already difficult situation. It does absolutely nothing to make their situation better or help them in any way. Worse, the great power of your attention directly influences their outcome in the negative direction you were worrying about. Everyone responds to your thoughts. Worry's effect on others is so destructive that it's like you're doing voodoo on them. The sick joke is: it turns out the way you worried, justifying your worry; enabling you to worry more.

Worry causes the muscles over your kidneys to spasm. The instant you start worrying about others—worrying about how things are going to turn out, or wondering what is going to happen—the spinal muscles over your kidneys go into spasm, radiating pain into your low back. For people who constantly worry or wonder what is going to happen to them, those muscles are always moderately spasmed. This is one of the principle causes of low back pain.

There is a much better way. When you catch yourself worrying about a loved one, take a couple cleansing breaths (fast deep breaths) to break the spell. Then go over a checklist of that person's strengths and assets. As you think about their positive attributes, they light up in that person's consciousness, helping them to see their own better qualities. *That* actually helps them to see a way out of their difficulties.

Every time you catch yourself worrying about a loved one, go over another checklist of their assets. If you catch yourself worrying about them twenty times a day, go over a checklist of that person's strengths and assets twenty times a day. During all the times you are going over the checklists of their strengths, your thoughts influence their awareness toward positive things they can do. *That* is real help. My patients and I have done this for a great number of people during difficult times. The results are impressive. You really help people this way.

Your Wellspring of Superhuman Strength

Classic Chinese philosophy considers the kidneys your storehouse of ancestral energy, an exquisite energy that is passed down from your parents. They call ancestral energy one of the "three treasures." Your spirit and qi (the life force that animates all life) are the other two treasures.

Ancestral energy is very much different from the energy you make and use every day. It is your finest energy. You tap into the wellspring of ancestral energy during your most difficult moments.

During adrenaline rushes, times when you mightily exceed the limits of your everyday abilities, you draw directly from this energy. During these moments, time can slow *way* down. You can muster clarity and power beyond anything you normally possess. You can, and most likely have performed superhuman feats.

When I was nineteen years old I was driving forty miles per hour in my Ford pickup when a boy on a bicycle crossed the road through oncoming traffic and skidded to a stop right in front of me, forty feet away. My mind instantly did the math. At forty miles per hour it takes one hundred and twenty feet to stop. *He's dead!* In my head I screamed *NO!* and time slowed *way* down. I jammed on the brakes as hard as I could, but realized that I was still going to hit him.

I tried to turn the steering wheel but with the brakes locked up, I could not turn it and was still going to hit the boy. I heard myself scream *"NO!"* again. With the second surge of adrenaline I broke the hard outer covering of all three spokes of the steering wheel, and broke the metal frame of the seat I was sitting on. But I got the front tires to turn just enough so my left front tire swerved to the right of him.

It felt like I energetically pushed my feet all the way through the floorboard, deep into the ground. I severely bent the brake pedal on my truck (completely impossible), but I stopped my truck about two inches before my left rear tire would have run over him.

My rational mind's version of reality (fate) had me running over the boy, but my spirit's version of reality was me doing *everything it took* to keep from hitting him. If I had not screamed *"NO!"* to my rational mind's version of reality, I would not have accessed the reservoir of ancestral energy that gave me superhuman power that day.

You access this reservoir when you say *"NO!"* to fate. Who you are—including what you are capable of doing—is leagues beyond the limitations your brain considers to be reality.

In times of danger, your rational mind's version of reality is not the ultimate reality. When you say an emphatic *"NO!"* to the dire fate your brain presents, you access this powerful reservoir of superhuman capacity that is not normally available to you. In a moment of clarity, you see or know what must be done. When *that* becomes your reality, you have entered an altered state. The normal laws of gravity and physics are reduced to suggestions. They can be transcended.

Within the normal laws of gravity and physics it was impossible to stop my pickup within forty feet—but that's what I did to save that boy's life.

A second example happened to me when I was twenty-one years old. Four of us were hiking down into the Feather River to go fishing. It was so steep that one of our friends and I waited until my cousin and brother-in-law were at the bottom so we didn't landslide each other. As I walked around a boulder, I saw that it was about nine-feet in diameter. My friend behind me jumped on it, dislodging it by mistake. He yelled, "Look out!"

I looked back to see that boulder bouncing toward me. I realized I couldn't get enough traction to move laterally without the boulder stamping me flat. When I rejected that possible "reality," I saw that my only choice was to jump straight up. I waited until the last second, and did a flatfooted jump that was high enough for the boulder to pass under me—impossible under normal consciousness. Due to the steepness of the hill, I landed a good sixty feet down the hill. I came down on my feet, but due to the rockslide immediately landed on my back sliding feet first, really fast. Three hundred yards down the hill my cousin Brian ran over to where I was headed and started *fiercely* kicking footholds into the bank. Rocks were bouncing all around him. As I got to him, I spread my legs, and he tackled me. I wrapped my legs around his waist, and for a microsecond we stopped.

Then we both started sliding toward the edge and my cousin Brian—who was the most fearless person I ever knew—looked terrified! I *knew* I had to do something fast. I pulled three small trees out by the roots without stopping us. I reached behind me and pushed the fingers of both hands about three inches deep into hard red clay, stopping us, with Brian's feet dangling precipitously over the edge of a sheer cliff.

Instantly the pain in my forearms maxed out to a solid ten on a one-to-ten pain scale. It was the worst pain I had ever experienced, but I couldn't let go. My brother-in-law quickly laid down with his feet splayed wide, grasped my forearms, and I his. Brian climbed up over us like a spider, and we all got up.

When we looked over the edge, we would have fallen sixty feet onto wet, slippery granite rock. Brian and I saved each other's lives that day by tapping into ancestral energy. Both of these examples point up how we only gain access to the reservoir of ancestral energy when we completely renounce fate, and then fiercely commit to the reality our spirit points up.

- CHAPTER 25 -

Expressing Your Feelings
· Bladder ·

In the higher consciousness of your bodymind your bladder is the official who expresses all your feelings. When you have a healthy relationship with your bladder, you experience all the feelings that come up without unnecessary dialogue or being judgmental about what we are feeling.

Most people think that expressing their feelings means acting them out, talking about them or thinking about them. *Expressing your feelings is simply feeling the feelings that come up, experiencing them without the mind doing anything to change them.* Feeling a feeling does not require logical thinking or physical action.

All feelings you do not feel, whether positive or negative, build up pressure in your body. The cumulative pressure from unfelt feelings builds up until it causes pain. And that pain causes your brain to generate thousands of toxic thoughts. All that toxic thinking makes life seem so difficult, even when it is not. One of my friends calls it "stinking thinking."

Since your bodymind takes everything you think personally, the unintended consequences of negative thinking depress all your body's functions. The constant stress creates inflammatory processes that impair physiology and shortens your life span significantly.

Check in on your feelings as often as you can. There are two categories of feelings—love and fear—each with about a hundred separate feelings. The lowest feeling on the love side is joy. When you check in on your feelings, if you are not at least feeling joy, then you are definitely in one of the fear feelings. Some of the feelings are so subtle that you cannot even define them. You just don't feel happy.

Experiencing the subtle feelings opens you up to the mysteries of your own life. A habit I recommend, and have done first thing every morning for years, is to check in on your feelings when you go into the kitchen to put the water on for tea or coffee. By the time you finish your tea you have usually dissolved the negative feelings you woke up with. As the more subtle feelings release, you find yourself fully immersed in the mystery of your own life. This really sets the day up right.

When you do not feel your feelings, they build up over months and years, creating stagnant or polluted water. The build up of negative feelings causes the bladder and kidney officials to suffer distress. Blood pressure goes up. Negative feelings you do not feel create progressively more pain until you actually develop a "pain body," with your etheric body stuffed so full of the pain of unfelt toxic feelings that you hurt all over. Emotional pain builds into pain that is much more painful than pain that is only physical.

One of the ways you develop a pain body is by listening to, absorbing and taking in other people's problems. Often you are feeling sorry for them, empathically resonating with the emotional pain of "their story," concerned about them, suffering with them. This causes you to take the negative feelings into your bodymind, as if they were your problems.

Worrying about, or feeling sorry for anyone is *never* a good spiritual strategy. It diminishes them to a second-class citizen in your world by assuming their difficulties are greater than they are. Remember, everyone is exactly where they need to be to learn the precise lesson they are here on Earth to learn, and everyone has *every* talent they will ever need to handle every problem they will ever face.

Instead, ask yourself *what does this powerful spiritual being need to learn from this lesson?* Take a deep breath as you go over a checklist of their strengths and assets. As soon as the conversation opens, ask your friend what kind of lessons they think they need to learn from this? Resonate with their strengths, not their weaknesses.

If you are one of those people who listens and takes in everyone's problems, this is incredibly damaging to you. *This is a huge boundary issue for you*. Taking their burdens onto your own shoulders does nothing to help them spiritually. It is just another way of giving your own power away.

When people try to keep dumping all their problems on you, you need to keep asking them, "What are the good things that are going on in your life?" It's important for them to focus on the good that is happening in their life—their triumphs, the sweetness—not just their tales of woe. Tragedies are always bittersweet. To achieve balance, inquire about the sweetness in this situation.

Friends listen to each other's stories so they can help each other work things out. That's what friends do. But many people habitually dump their problems on others. Those kinds of people are too toxic to be around. After they dump their trash they feel good. They dumped their trash. You feel bad. Whoa!

You may need to separate yourself from people who do not respect this boundary. In the end, *you* are the one who suffers from *their* problems. When you keep taking in everyone's problems, this weakens your own bladder.

Not Feeling Your Feelings Distresses Your Bladder

When you keep stuffing your feelings, the pressures of life can build up until your worldview is completely bleak. Your bladder can become quite distressed when you feel so mired in desperate views that it's hard to see any future for yourself, when you think your hardships are beyond the pale of human help. Your bladder official can become terribly distressed. These desperate states come from trying to escape from hopeless feelings instead of just feeling them.

There are many people who think they have no resources, drowning in despair. Being overwhelmed by their own negative view of life, they often sigh or moan and groan. They usually have sagging postures, their voice is flat and monotone. There can be an overriding urge for self-preservation, or the extreme opposite: the person can seek escape from it all by denying there is any danger at all. At this extreme are the ultimate thrill seekers.

Your Need for Water

Most people don't drink enough water. They are chronically dehydrated, which causes 128 low-grade symptoms such as constipation, headache, fatigue, and swollen joints. None of these symptoms will kill you outright. They just dim your life force down until your whole life feels difficult. All your body's functions suffer when you do not drink enough water. When you're dehydrated, your brain shrinks. I'll bet that gets you drinking more water.

I recommend putting a full glass of water by your bedside at night, and drinking all of it *before* you leave your bedside in the morning. Although it might seem counterintuitive, drinking a big glass of water first thing in the morning makes you thirsty all day. When you're thirsty it's easy to drink enough water.

But if you do not drink water until later in the day, you've trained yourself to be a camel. Then it's all but impossible to force yourself to drink adequate amounts of water. You are slowly killing yourself if you do not drink enough water. Coffee, sodas and alcohol actually dehydrate you—including your brain. You can drink them if you want, but you can't count them.

Stagnant, unfelt feelings show up as bags under your eyes and edema in the lower abdomen and legs. The situation escalates when you don't drink enough water. The unfelt feelings create stagnant water in your body which negatively affects both your kidneys and your bladder system, including the meridians and all the muscles that make energy for them.

Because impurities and unwanted minerals are not being flushed out, your system is gradually poisoned. The resulting toxicity stresses your kidneys out, especially when you add an overload of unfelt feelings. The intuitive feelings that help you avoid the problems of life get so obscured that your intuition is diminished.

On the other hand, if conditions like diarrhea or prolonged grief cause your bladder to eliminate wastes too quickly, water reserves fall low and you can have dry skin and hair, headaches, general discomfort, loss of appetite, tiredness and irritability. Your eyes and mouth get dry. In times like this, you may need to take supplements that bring up your electrolytes.

Your bladder system runs its energy most intensely from 3 to 5 P.M. The way you feel at this particular time is a direct reflection of the health of the entire bladder system, including all of its muscles. The erector spinae muscles that run up both sides of your spine, and most of your lower leg muscles make the electrical energy your bladder needs. That's why your ankles swell when your bladder is distressed.

If you want your water/emotional system to work well, *drink a minimum of eight large glasses of water every day.* You need more if you are sweating in the heat or exposed to the drying effect of the north wind. You also need more water when you are dealing with intense feelings. Just drinking a glass of water clears up a lot of pesky symptoms, like headaches, weak digestion, dry skin, and feeling listless. Water is an incredible solvent to hundreds of problems.

CHAPTER 26

Becoming Decisive
· Ileo-cecal Valve ·

Even though ilium and cecum are words used long ago to describe your small and large intestines, the valve between them is still called the ileo-cecal valve. For your digestion to remain healthy, this valve must stay tightly closed all of the time. It only opens for a moment when the small intestine makes its peristaltic (snakelike) movement that pushes the waste products into the large intestine.

After the evacuation, the valve shuts tight, triggering a neurological reflex for your appendix to inject two squirts of mucous. The mucous lubricates the stool, which is especially important at times when your stool gets too dry. Then your large intestine extracts the last of the metals like calcium, phosphorus and iron, and extracts enough water to firm up the stool.

Your intestines not only digest food. In the higher dimensions of your multidimensional bodymind your intestines also digest all your thoughts, feelings, beliefs, judgments, values, politics, spirituality, relationships, your work, and literally *everything* you take in. When you are decisive, this one-way check valve only lets digestion, and life move in one direction. As you become more decisive about all the little things in your life, you become crystal clear about the big picture of your life. *You become single minded.*

If you fail to make a decision—especially with little things—your indecision divides your consciousness by making contingency plans for all the possible ways you might go. It *must* make contingency plans for all those possibilities. Your bodymind is forced to run all the scenarios as if you were going to do all of them. Do you *get* how badly that screws up your life? You lose the awesome power of single-minded focus that directs your attention into an unstoppable force.

You are a creator. The foundation of your character is a triangle. The three points of your triangle are cherishing, being truthful, and being decisive. When all three points of your triangle are functioning together, supporting each other, they empower you to create your life simply and effectively.

Now the bad news. All the little indecisions weaken your love, devalues it. They diminish your truth. You wind up not standing for anything. The values and principles in your life lose their meaning. You give others control of your choices, which hardly ever works out the way you would choose.

For example, if a couple were making a new garden and one of them says, "I'm going to get flowers for the garden. Want to come?" If the other says, "No. Whatever you get will be fine." Then after the garden is planted they say, "Why didn't you get petunias? You know I love petunias." The other person feels resentful. Bad feelings build up, and soon they are fighting about something entirely different. It's all the little things adding up that make or break relationships.

Families and friends that are honest with each other in answering all their little questions are developing the tools that let them understand and appreciate the breadth and depth of each other's character. Each person is truly magnificent, but most hide their light from others because of one fear or another. Indecision is one of the main ways we hide from each other.

When you are asked what you want, and you go inside and think "what would I want if I could have anything I want?" the answer flashes through your consciousness instantly. It is usually subtle, and if you are spacing out, you miss it. The clearer your answers are to all the little questions in your relationships, the clearer each person's understanding of the other becomes. Then we all start getting what we desire.

Decisiveness—making the decision, instead of deflecting in some way—is every bit as important as being loving and truthful. It's a triangle.

Each point supports—or detracts—from the other two. The irony is, being decisive about the little things focuses the big picture of your life until it becomes crystal clear.

My friend James tells his daughter when she is indecisive: "Mary, you're not exercising your ileo-cecal valve." That always makes me laugh.

Indecision literally throws a monkey wrench into the gears of your life. Here's how it works: when you decide to pursue a goal or plan, all manner of situations are set into motion because of your decision. The spiritual kingdom starts setting up all the things that need to happen at each intersection of your life as you proceed on with your plan. Remember, you are a *spiritual* being having a human experience.

Then—if you become indecisive—your own forward progress stalls out. Since the gears have been set in motion, the opportunity goes on ahead and presents itself. But because of your indecision or procrastination you were not there at those particular intersections to receive it, and unbeknownst to you, you missed yet another golden opportunity.

Now the good news! As you become more decisive, you end up getting your heart's desires. Manifesting your desires is the easy part; figuring out what you want and staying committed to it until it is manifested is, by far, the most difficult part of the equation.

Start taking the necessary action steps toward your desires as soon as possible. The universe loves immediate action. Then, as you arrive at each of the intersections of your life, the spiritual kingdom has things lined up. The teacher is there. The gift is there, and so is the mystery. They are always there at all the main intersections of your life. Start looking for them and you will see. By being decisive, you are there to receive them. Your life has more grace. People think that you are just plain lucky. And you are.

How Indecision Causes Physical Pain

Your small intestine is extremely effective at digesting *everything* you take in. The food you eat takes about eighteen hours in transit, going back and forth through your small intestine until it finally arrives at your ilio-cecal valve. Your small intestine efficiently extracts 95 percent of the nutrition out of it. What is left over is highly toxic, but still has the consistency of a fruit smoothie.

Any indecision, no matter how small, causes your ileo-cecal valve to become flaccid. Then, every activity that tightens your abdominal muscles—which you do hundreds of times a day—forces toxic wastes back up into your small intestine. Your small intestine does its job, which causes it to absorb the toxic wastes into the bloodstream. This is called auto-toxicity, self-poisoning.

Ninety percent of your lymph glands—your sewer system for eliminating toxic wastes from your blood stream—are located in your armpit and groin. The toxins quickly overwhelm the lymph nodes in your groin area, causing your pelvis to go out of alignment.

The result is that one side of your pelvis twists forward, and one hip pushes up higher than the other. The high-side hip usually pushes the shoulder up on the same side. This causes the whole spine to twist up and rotate. It causes a number of vertebrae to subluxate (go out of alignment with pathological consequences).

Indecision causes your pelvis to misalign so badly it appears that you have a short leg, which can seem permanent if you are chronically indecisive. The pelvic misalignments also cause your knees and ankles to misalign. *The main cause of scoliosis* (curvature of the spine) *is indecision*, not committing to what you know. At least 90 percent of short-leg situations are simply the inevitable results of indecision. I bet you didn't know that.

All fourteen of your powerful circulatory systems are greatly compromised by scoliosis and the misalignments caused by indecision. Being indecisive—even though it seems like such a small issue—creates an enormous amount of dis-ease. Your whole body suffers. Over time the dis-ease morphs into disease. When you comprehend how devastating indecision is to your overall health—to your whole life—you realize that no one, especially you, can afford its terrible costs.

Decisions are Emotional

Your ileo-cecal valve—even though it is between your small and large intestine—is part of your kidney system.

How you *feel* about something you desire is the most significant part of your decisiveness. Your feelings are like amperage in electricity, the pressure of electrical flow. How you feel about a plan or dream is much more important than anything you think.

While you are focusing on a desire, any negative feelings create *pressure* that keeps pushing your desires and dreams further away from you. Positive feelings attract your desires to you.

The problem with positive feelings is, you cannot sustain positive feelings about anything when negative feelings are lurking about and have not been experienced. It's just not possible. Unfelt negative feelings almost always win out. But once you feel the negative feelings, they dissolve. Then they are gone. Once the negativity is out of the way, it's easy to revel in the positive glow of your magnificent plans and dreams.

Joy is the lowest emotion on the positive scale. Gratitude is higher. Happiness and the knowingness that everything is exactly as it should be are above that. The higher up on the emotional scale your positive feelings are, the greater their attraction is to your plans and dreams. So whenever you are thinking about a dream or something you want to do, always check in on your feelings.

Thinking positively about a goal or plan while *feeling* negative feelings is a classic example of indecision. This particular inconsistency between thinking and feeling will always make your ilio-cecal valve go flaccid, with disastrous results.

Experience all the fears that come up until they dissolve. This is how you slay the dragons and monsters that would otherwise block your heroic journey. Then you are free to experience all the positive feelings that draw your desires toward you and enhance your journey.

Oceans

I have a feeling that my boat has struck,
down in the depths, against a great thing.
And nothing happens!
Nothing . . . Silence . . . Waves . . .
Nothing happens? Or has everything happened,
and are we standing now, quietly
in the new life?

—Juan Ramon Jimenez

SECTION II – SPIRIT LIVING IN MATTER

- CHAPTER 27 -

A Spiritual Being Living in the World of Matter

This section explores the ways your spirit and bodymind work in harmony, how neither can achieve what they desire without the other, and how you—as part of Creator—co-create the world you live in.

We are all angelic beings who volunteered for this assignment: to come down to this dense planet and clothe ourselves in biological raiment in this grand experiment, learning the lessons and experiencing the trials of an earthly existence. We come here to learn and grow and evolve—and to achieve our deepest desires, the desires of our heart. Our lesson plan includes bringing our bodymind up to the level of our spiritual awareness.

The body you are living in for this lifetime is like a lens that distorts the information you receive into particular perspectives: like whether your body is athletic or artistic, male or female, skinny or large, the level of health you experience or the part of the world you grow up in. As you plumb the depths of your capabilities, this world provides trials to your physical body, your thoughts, feelings, values, principles and beliefs. The body you inhabit for this lifetime is the unique lens through which you observe the world, and your own inner nature.

Your spirit's lesson plan is to teach you how to cherish, be truthful and decisive—and to keep these three qualities in an exquisite state of balance throughout all the difficulties and experiences you encounter. The lessons you learn as you navigate these incredible dimensions become the crucible of fire that transforms you from mere potential into a fully-actualized being. This is the essence of alchemy.

Navigating Your Seven Dimensional Body

Your spirit lives in the eternal moment, the gap between time and space. When you chose to live in the physical universe—and you did make that choice—you incarnated into a physical body that gave your spirit access to seven wonderful dimensions. Each of the dimensions has such profound wonders for your spirit to experience:

- *Physical:* Your physical body gives your spirit access to all manner of movement and adventures: all of the different sports, dancing, hiking, swimming, making love, eating sensuous foods and enjoying the world through the five senses.
- *Etheric:* This is the energy double to your physical body and is the most direct reflection of your overall health. When you hold a blouse or shirt up to the mirror and look at how the color of the garment either enlivens your face or diminishes it, what you are looking at is your etheric body. This body directly responds to the quality of your food and drink, exercise and rest. When you look at the "color" in a person's face you are glimpsing their etheric body. The color reflects their vitality.
- *Mental:* The third dimension gives your spirit access to all the physical sciences, philosophies, religions, mythologies, cultural mores and all the ways you communicate with others. The mental realm operates through your brain and nervous system. Until quantum physics, all our sciences were restricted to only considering the physical and mental realms, as if the other dimensions didn't count. Scientists are awakening to the wonders of a multi-dimensional universe.
- *Emotional:* Every moment that you feel the feelings that come up, and reflect on them, you gain instantaneous access to the eternal wisdom of your spirit. Becoming aware of, and feeling all your feelings,

expands all the horizons of your awareness and helps you spiritually evolve at a much faster rate. Your kidney/bladder system rules this dimension.

- *Causal:* The fifth dimension is ruled by your acupuncture meridians, which exert enough stable pressure to maintain your auric field, a discernable energy field that extends out from your body about three feet in all directions, including above your head and below your feet. Your aura, or auric field has the shape of a big energy egg surrounding your physical body. It insulates you from having to experience everyone's pain and thoughts when they are in close proximity to you, giving you autonomy to live your *own* life without undue influence from everyone around you.

- *Attitudinal:* The sixth dimension—ruled by your endocrine system—produces hormones that stabilize your emotions and allow you to discern sensory and extra-sensory perceptions, and translate them into a language your heart-ruled mind can assimilate. This is where you develop your attitudes about what you want to do, what you like or dislike, what you accept or reject. When your awareness expands into this system, your values and principles define your attitudes, thoughts and actions.

- *Enlightened:* The seventh dimension is ruled by your chakras. You have seven principle chakras, representing the seven levels of your enlightenment. Your chakras are the most subtle organs of your body, with very subtle, flower-like petals that spin faster and develop pure rainbow-like colors as you become more loving, truthful and decisive. When you have unresolved emotions like jealousy, anger, malice, or worry, the colors of your chakras become murky and dark, making them less able to access the spiritual wisdom that is all around you.

Why Life Seems Difficult

The denseness of gravity here on Earth makes desires for food, shelter and material wealth seem so all-consuming that they can easily take control of your life. For most of history, so much of our consciousness was channeled toward meeting our physical needs and desires that we severely sublimated our spiritual growth.

As we start to wake up, we realize that at any given moment we have millions of things to be thankful for, and only a few hundred that cause us consternation. But our unconscious default is to focus on the problems and complain instead of saying "yes" to the lessons our spirit and soul bring us. We can become so preoccupied with the problems of the world that we forget how much we have to be thankful for.

As your spirit evolves—and your inner world becomes more important than the outer world—you learn to rise above the dense gravity that draws you down into your needs, desires and your mind's "stories" about all the problems around you. You learn to align yourself with the finest qualities of your heart. In this crucible of time and space, you get to refine and flesh out all the finer qualities of your spirit.

This *is* a difficult world to incarnate into. Life can be hard. But actually, we humans crave difficulty. We need it! And we all volunteered to be here. More importantly, we chose our parents—partly for their strengths, and partly for their qualities that we rail against. We chose *this* life.

There are so many obstacles to overcome just in a normal day, not to mention the really hard days. But we are here because Earth is where we have the most opportunity for transformation and change, for real spiritual growth.

- CHAPTER 28 -

Your Spirit's Job:
Making Your Body Feel Safe and Loved

Your spirit and your bodymind have similar goals. But neither can get what they deeply desire without being in a loving relationship with the other. Your spirit wants to fulfill the deepest desires of your heart—not necessarily of your mind. In order to get what you desire, your brain must learn to take all its direction from your heart, not the other way around.

Your body intelligence, under your heart's guidance, is infinitely greater than the limitations of your brain operating system. When your brain is in charge, it reduces your awareness to only the physical and mental realms. Rumi, the thirteenth-century Persian mystic poet hinted at this by saying, "Out beyond the doing of good, or the doing of bad, there is a field. I'll meet you there." In that field—the eternity of the present moment—your heart invites all the talents and powers of all your incredible organs into a unified bodymind that is as capable of greatness as any of your great heroes.

In order to get outside the limitations of your mind, start listening to your feelings. Notice the longing you feel when one of your heart's unfulfilled desires is mentioned or thought of. Start noticing persistent desires that keep recurring in your thoughts, desires you might *think* are beyond your capabilities—or dreams you think someone else should accomplish.

Let your principles and values inform your beliefs, and let *that* motivate your thoughts and actions. When your mind serves your heart, then you are using the full capacity of your body intelligence. Only when you use all seven dimensions of your bodymind are you capable of making wise decisions.

The body you currently inhabit is the lens that dramatically affects all of your spirit's perceptions during this incarnation. It is similar to the way an equestrian's awareness of a ride is influenced by the qualities and unique personality of the horse he or she rides. An artistic body can compare to the thoughtfulness of a Morgan; an athletic body to an Arabian that can run a hundred miles in a day, but can be more hard-headed and arrogant. Your body may be athletic or artistic, high strung or mellow, sickly or healthy. But whatever your body is, it is the finest gift you will ever receive.

The horse's eagerness and the committing of its intelligence to having a great ride profoundly affect the rider's assessment of the ride. The horse must desire direction from the rider if the adventure is to be fun and fulfilling for both of them. If the horse is eager and the rider appreciative, magic happens.

Your bodymind is like the horse. Your spirit is the rider. Neither is as powerful by itself as both are when operating cooperatively. Your heart, the Emperor of your bodymind, innately desires what your spirit wants.

When you are in harmony with the simple functioning of your organs, your personal power nearly doubles every year. Life becomes so much more exciting and new. You are living in beginners' mind, beginner's heart, seeing everything with the same awe and wonder of a child seeing or doing something for the very first time.

Does eagerly giving up control to your spirit scare you? I have feared giving up control to my spirit ever since I first considered it as a young kid in church. I think everyone struggles with control issues to some degree.

My worst fears were that I would have to give up all of the fun stuff and be a "goody-goody." I feared that "being spiritual" meant I would have to get rid of my wildness, ambitions, and desires and become religiously correct. As it turned out, none of those fears had even a shred of substance.

Your spirit actually likes all your quirks. Each of your so-called faults is connected to one of your genius qualities. For example, your impatience is connected to "the passion you have for life." The quality of being reticent and holding back more than you would like is connected to your deep contemplation about everything in life. Your anger may occasionally rear its ugly head, but channeled into commitment, the driving force of that anger is one of the qualities that make your will so powerful. If you got rid of your impatience and your anger you would have no motivation to do anything. It would be hard to just get out of bed in the morning.

Look at your quirks. Then imagine what genius qualities link up to them. Squash the fault, and you squash the genius quality. Your spirit does not want to get rid of your troublesome qualities. Neither should you. You just want to keep gaining better control of them like an accomplished equestrian controls the reins of a spirited horse, calming him, complimenting his great qualities, making him or her feel safe and loved. All your quirks and idiosyncrasies are reflections of your DNA.

Your DNA reflects your character. It represents all the strengths and weaknesses from the lineage of both your parent's lines, honed by the millennia of time. Every moment, every decision, you overwrite your DNA. You can overwrite it with the same old tired stories you have been telling yourself. Or, you can rein in and have compassion for your lower qualities, while steadily transforming your character. As you spend more time in mindfulness, focusing on what you love, you start becoming the promise of yourself. You rewrite your DNA in whole new exciting ways.

Each ego personality has its own dysfunctional needs and attitudes, what it fears and frets over, the stuff *it has to do* because, "That's who I am." Your spirit accepts all that. Your personality also has its genius qualities, qualities that set you apart from all the others and contribute so much to the world. You are unique. You are one of a kind. Your spirit celebrates that.

Your dimensions as a spirit are probably impossible to fully imagine. As a spiritual being, you need to take control of your bodymind with patience and a firm loving hand. In this world of duality it is difficult to know who you are, or who anyone is just by looking at them. You only see yourself, or others, by observing the fruit of their tree. When you think with your heart, and keep your bodymind attuned to the simple operating systems of your organs, the fruit of your endeavors gives the best reflection of who you truly are.

Your day job, as a spirit, is to continually teach your physical body that it is safe and loved. Every stupid thing any of us have ever done is because we didn't think we were safe, loved or both.

Experiencing The Tide of Your Spirit

Cranial work, which was developed by osteopathic physicians, has allowed me a glimpse into how powerful we are as spirits. There are three subtle "tides" that cranial work taps into. The first tide subtly moves all the parts of your body to allow adequate circulation to each and every part of your body. Like tides, the different parts of your body move one way for about three and a half seconds, then the other way for three and a half seconds, even if you sit or lie perfectly still for hours. The tide of your energy field expands upward and outward around your head for ten seconds, then contracts and moved downward for ten seconds, which pumps cerebro-spinal fluids through your brain and spinal column. By stopping the first two tides, the physician can get in touch with the subtle tide of the patient's spirit. The insights and efficacy of this work are incredible.

For fifty seconds, your spirit's tide contracts into the dense body you live in. You connect to the unconditional love and gravity of Mother Earth. After fifty seconds of contracting, the tide turns, and for the next fifty seconds your spirit expands as far as you can imagine, easily out into the entire solar system. This back and forth rhythm of your spirit's tide continues for your entire lifetime.

Cranial work has opened me to glimpses of the greatness and generosity of our spirit. Cooperation with my spirit does not feel like an obligation any longer. Instead, it feels like partnering with a highly-evolved being that *always* has my very best interest at heart. Now I feel safe giving up control of my mind to my heart and spirit. It has taken me a while. Previously, all I could see was what was wrong with the world. Now I spend most of my time focusing on what I love and loving what I have. I never imagined life would get this good.

- CHAPTER 29 -

What it's Like to Have a Body

As spiritual beings having a human experience, the amount of time we have been in this incarnation is but a blink of an eye compared to the time we have existed as spiritual beings. We, as spirits, exist in a magnitude that is difficult to grasp. We are both the created, and the co-creator of all that is created.

From the beginning of our scientific explorations, our scientists have limited their observations to *only* how we are living here as an integral part of creation. In the early part of the twentieth century, physics began transforming into a meta-physics called "quantum physics." Now quantum physicists are discovering just how difficult it is to comprehend how we—as part of Creator—are "the observers" who are always co-creating all that we observe. And we inextricably exist in both realms.

With each new discovery, scientists and science teachers—who used to be defiant atheists—are sounding more like mystic poets. There is an ever-increasing percentage of the population whose background reality includes the underlying principles of quantum physics. We are becoming more aware of how we affect all that we observe.

One of the most fundamental truths is: You do not live in the same world with anyone else. Each person lives in his or her own unique world. What you focus your precious attention on all day long, every day, is your unique world. Focusing your attention on something—anything—makes it real in *your world*. The Great Mystery is how all our unique worlds coexist in the greater dream of Creator.

My world is seeing patients four days a week, working out three mornings a week, writing this book, skiing and riding my mountain bike when I can; while my wife's world is running my office, checking in with her loved ones, walking by the river, making fine pottery and fused glass jewelry. Last night we were sitting on the back deck. She was drinking a glass of wine and enjoying the sunset while I was feeling the nearness of her and thinking about how wonderful our life is together. Even though we share so much of our life together, our experiences are so very different. We lovingly share our worlds, but at the end of the day, Judy lives in Judy's world, while I live in John's world.

Within your world, if you just look at something, all its possibilities and probabilities are affected. Objects and situations are affected in predictable ways: since your values and beliefs have so much control over thoughts, actions and feelings, the more profoundly you believe something, the more it will influence the outcome.

One of my friends was talking about how everything that can possibly go wrong around his son seems to go wrong. He went on and on about all the misfortunes that keep happening to his son. When I asked about the son's finer qualities, he revealed that in most circumstances the things his son did were outstanding. I asked him why he didn't talk about those qualities. We always have the free will to choose.

I asked him to consider how every time he talked about his son's misfortunes, even though his son was usually not present, he was spotlighting his son's worst qualities, queuing *them* up in both his and his son's lives. I suggested he shift his focus to his son's outstanding qualities instead of his misfortunes.

My friend had to chew on that concept for a couple of weeks before he could accept it. Gradually, after he and his wife quit talking—and thinking—about his son's calamities, and started thinking about all the wonderful things his son was doing and involved in, his son quit having things go wrong.

Everything and every situation have potential possibilities and probabilities of up to 360 degrees of a circle of movement. It could go all these different ways. The power of your attention is such that it effectively collapses most of the possibility and probability waves that do not align with how *you believe* it could turn out. In the end, situations end up pretty much the way you thought they would.

You can say, "It would have turned out that way anyway." No! Not necessarily. Not if you hadn't *looked* at it. This question, "How does the observer affect all that he or she observes?" is the question that ushered quantum physics into being.

The basis of quantum physics is: You are both the created and the creator of your own unique world. In this brave new world, your attention is *the* most important tool you have for manifestation.

You have so much power in your attention, which is the focus, the lens of your awareness. Your attention is encoded with all your beliefs, values, principles, attitudes, feelings and thoughts. Just you "looking at something" brings all that encoded power into play. Do not dissipate your precious attention by focusing on all the problems and negativity in the world. So many people are not yet awake that, until a critical mass of people awaken, bad things will continue to happen. You have the opportunity to create a brave new world, *your* world. Start training yourself to keep your focus on what you love, and to love what you have. Use your attention wisely.

Focusing Your Power of Attention

Most people walk through life with minimal awareness regarding what they observe, much less how their attention influences the outcomes of what they observe. You love others into being the best version of themselves by focusing your love onto their positive traits.

Your loving attention spotlights their better traits, makes them more noticeable, even if you say nothing. Then if you verbally praise the positive traits that your attention pointed up, you more consciously reinforce those traits, influencing people to want to live into those traits. There are times when the right thing said can change a person's life forever.

We have all had a loving aunt or uncle, a schoolteacher or coach, who saw the better qualities we had and pointed them up to us. They might have been the person who turned us around. They helped us believe that we could be the best version of ourselves. They were our inspiration. Often they were the ones that nudged us into believing we could do what we ultimately have done.

There are always "unintended consequences" that result from the power of your attention. You can be the catalyst that nudges people into dysfunctional behaviors by projecting negative feelings toward them— while expecting them to screw up. You may love that person completely, but make excuses for them, while inwardly expecting them to fail. Your attention may be the tipping point. You have that kind of power. Have you given much thought to the power you have just by *observing* something or someone?

You can observe the effect of your power of attention on your children and pets. If you expect them to be wonderful, mindful and brilliant, they will exceed your expectations. If you expect them to be screw-ups, they will exceed your expectations.

Part of waking up to the present moment is becoming more aware of the positive (and negative) effects your attention has on others. You also need to notice how other people's attention affects you. You become aware of their negative attention toward you by the negative feelings that come up when you are around them. What they are projecting toward you becomes apparent as *the feeling you experience while in their presence.*

Most people are not psychic enough to "hear" your thoughts or "feel" your feelings, but *their bodymind reacts as if they do.* Any thought or feeling you have about another person impacts them directly, either positively or negatively. Ultimately, you are responsible for the unintended consequences.

When you find yourself focusing on another person's negative traits or weaknesses, you can shift your attention onto their positive traits, even if you have to really work at it to find them. You can make a positive impact on that person and love them into being the best version of themselves.

Your physical body takes *all* its direction from your spirit—you. It is important to realize that what you think about your own body—or any of its functions—directly affects *its* ability to function well. Loving your body influences it to function at its best. Focusing on your body's negative qualities influences your body to malfunction. It is important to remember that you are a spirit, and your body responds to your every thought and word.

When you focus on admirable traits—whether yours or someone else's—you put the spotlight on that. If you love your body, it will gladly take you anywhere and everywhere you want to go.

Who You Associate With Matters

People tend to gather into groupings based upon their intentions. People who want to contribute to making the world a better place tend to associate with other people who are working toward making the world a better place.

People who are more fear based tend to gather together with other fear-based individuals. When fear-based people come together, their conversations tend towards things that have gone wrong and problems in the world.

Whom you associate with is crucial. It directly influences everything you do and everything you think. Whom you associate with has greater effects on your thoughts and actions than your disciplines.

CHAPTER 30

Changing Your Beliefs Changes Your World

You see your world *the way you believe it is*. What you expect mysteriously turns out to be what happens. If you believe in lack and limitation, everywhere you turn limitations bar your way. It is hard to get what you need, much less what you *want*. You can have a whole lifetime, even endless lifetimes of lack. As long as you expect to get less than you need, you get less. If you believe in injustice, everywhere you look you will see injustice.

A great metaphor for life is "the holodeck" on the old television series *Star Trek: The Next Generation*. In the holodeck, a crewmember can create a personal fantasy program. He or she sets up the exact situation they want to experience. Then they get to experience that program as "reality." The program they set up can be mountain climbing, equestrian riding, combat against multiple foes, or whatever the crewmember can imagine. The holodeck is a great metaphor for your life. If you do not like what appears to be coming at you, change what you believe (the programming).

Much of our culture has unwritten customs and values, hidden programming that most people don't question. They just accept it as "the way things are." For example, in most Western societies we are taught that worrying about loved ones is a loving, compassionate thing to do. The assumption is: if we don't worry about someone who is in the throes of catastrophe, we are not very loving or kind.

In truth, *worry is praying for what you do not want*. That is what most people do. They read the paper, listen to the news and talk with their friends about all of the things that are going wrong, or might go wrong. In the unconscious state, people spend their days and nights focusing on issues and events they would never want to create. Then, how they feel about that folds over to create how they are going to feel in the next block of time. What they focus on is exactly what they are creating in their own unique world. Naturally, what comes at them next will *feel* the same way. That is how humanity, as a whole, creates dissatisfaction.

The universe is a lot like a clerk at Burger King. If you drove up to the window and said, "I want a hamburger with no lettuce, no tomatoes, no sauce, and no bun," there would probably be a short pause. Then the clerk might say, "OK, You mean you just want a slab of hamburger meat?" If you say yes, they will probably say, "That will be three dollars and ninety-nine cents," (or whatever a hamburger costs).

The clerk wouldn't say, "Are you nuts?" They would just deliver it to you as you requested. In that same unquestioning way, the universe delivers what you expect.

The universe can also be compared to a genie in *The Arabian Nights*. No matter what you focus on, the genie assumes *that* is what you want and says, "Your wish is my command." He delivers what you are focusing your attention on. Your Genie focuses on *the image* your mind creates, without regard to whether you want it or not.

There have been a lot of jokes about a genie's wishes that were literally interpreted. The wish comes out in a way the person had not intended—like the guy who wished for a million bucks, and came home to find his yard and neighborhood filled with a million male deer. Consider that your Genie is attracting *whatever* your mind is focusing on. The polarities of like or hate are totally irrelevant.

As a creator, become aware of what you are feeling, thinking and talking about during your day. Your feelings, what you believe, and the principles and values you maintain precisely determine the nature of what you will manifest into the world. You may have difficulty with this law, but it is the law.

My wish for you is for the difficulties in your life to be mainly in the planning and execution of *your* elaborate plans and dreams: once you have overcome all the difficulties, you get to experience such magnificent feelings of accomplishment.

You can immerse yourself in hobbies or sports or professions that have such steep learning curves that you will never be bored. Joseph Campbell calls this "following your bliss." *The big idea* is to do it consciously, rather than by default, which comes from thinking about your fears, worries, or anxieties.

Do not hold back from stepping into your dreams or ideals because of the difficulties. You are going to live a long time anyway. You may as well have something to show for it. There is such pleasure in working toward mastery of something you love.

Your greatest joys come from having something to do that you can throw all your passion into. Imagine the great joy of having accomplished your splendid plans and dreams against all adversities. *That* is fulfillment.

CHAPTER 31

The Universe Wants to Communicate With You

The entire elemental kingdom—plants, animals, rocks, rivers, and wind—desires to communicate with you, and functions as an extension of your subconscious mind. All of nature is in fact intelligent, and desires to be in relationship with you.

When you accept the fact that there are no random events, life's mysteries open themselves to you. Native Americans have long believed that birds and animals act as messengers of the spirit world. Their presence in your life always has meaning. For example, if a skunk or a deer in the road forces you to slow down or stop, the deer may be your subconscious mind telling you that you need to be sweeter and gentler, that there is great power in the innocence of love.

The skunk may be telling you to be more aware of how your reputation affects the world around you, or of not releasing your sexual energy so casually. Your sexual energy may need to be elevated to the level of passion for what you are doing. Sexual energy is just one octave of the energy that flows from the energy center below your navel (second chakra). The octave above sexuality is your passion for life. The octave above that is charisma. The highest octave of sexual energy is compassion.

When a red-tail hawk flies past me, I immediate ask myself "what was I thinking just now?" Invariably my thoughts were of something I was considering doing. The hawk's message in that situation is, "Yes! Do it." There are two books that outline what the animal and bird kingdom wants to tell us: *Medicine Cards* by Jamie Sans and David Carson, and *Animal Speak* by Ted Andrews. A lot of our friends use these two books as reference books for their encounters with these messengers.

Your spirit's voyage of discovery is to explore not only the universe outside yourself, but also the dimensions within: you have vast dimensions within your consciousness that await discovery. You have so much richness to discover in the higher, subtle kingdoms of your bodymind. You have even more to access in the spiritual kingdoms.

As you open up to the glories of your inner life, your current vistas become the starting point of a journey in which the world of your heart, mind, and spirit keeps on doubling in size and glory. To embark on this voyage of discovery, your rational mind, your brain, must relinquish its role as master of your consciousness, and allow the real master, your heart, to take control.

- CHAPTER 32 -

Getting Back in Phase With Life

When I was eight years old, I had six intense spiritual experiences spread over a month-and-a-half period. By the end of that time, I was left with a lot of clarity about the nature of the conscious and unconscious states, especially for someone my age.

I observed then that of the approximately four hundred people I personally knew, there was only one person, my Uncle Ted, who was actually awake. Unlike the other people I knew, he continually chose to cherish others. He never created dramas. His focus was on the goodness within each person. He lived his values. Everything about him seemed right as rain.

At that time, my observations were that only the teeniest trickle of people's energies went *inward* to the goodness within themselves. Almost all of their energy, as far as I could tell, went outward toward objects or concepts they unconsciously considered "outside themselves." Inner values faded into the background any time money or their way of life was challenged. Most people spoke of higher values, but when it came down to what they did, *outer* circumstances usually took precedence over inner values.

The way people related to each other seemed backward. It went the opposite direction that consciousness should flow. People's value systems seemed to be turned 180 degrees opposite of what was real.

I firmly believed there had been a terrible error. Somehow a mistake had placed me on the wrong planet. These were not my people. The meanness and intolerance everywhere was depressing to observe. From today's perspective, 1951 was an intolerant period. We have evolved a long way since then.

124

During that time, my father asked me to help him when he was tuning a car in his shop. He asked me to start the car, put my foot firmly on the brake, put the car in drive, and slowly let off on the brake so the car would creep forward. I did that, and the car crept backward. He yelled, "Put it in drive!" I told him it was.

He came around and stuck his head in the side window and saw that the car was indeed in drive. He told me to put the car in reverse and slowly let off on the brake. I did, and the car crept forward.

He had me put the car in park and set the emergency brake. Then he said, "Turn the radio on." When I did, all we heard was loud static. He revved the engine from under the hood. Static and the sound of pistons firing was all that could be heard through the radio's speakers.

He had me shut the engine off. He said he had put the distributor in *180 degrees out of phase* to how it should be. That caused the pistons to fire in reverse order. It made the crankshaft rotate opposite to the normal direction. That was why the car went backward in drive and forward in reverse.

When I asked about the radio, he said, "With the pistons firing in reverse order, the electrical current to the condenser was on the wrong side of the coil. The sound of the pistons firing had already occurred before the current into the radio could be suppressed."

After he got the engine running and timed, the car crept forward when I put the transmission into drive. This time, when he asked me to turn the radio on, sweet music, beautiful and clear, came through the speakers.

I realized that when a person's focus is 180 degrees out of phase, positions are more important than cherishing people. There are "reasons" for not loving others. Huge blocks of their time are taken up with protesting what is, thinking this problem should not be happening to *them*, or wondering *why* it was happening to them. That way of thinking always creates pain and suffering.

I saw that when we are spiritually awake, most of our awareness goes inward toward our heart's values. Inner values and principles drive our thoughts and actions. A person who is focused on doing something positive and focusing on the good in others is like clear sweet music. They are so much more interesting than people who are focused on any concept that has rules imposed from *outside* themselves, like politics or religion. A person who really "hears" what others are saying is so much more refreshing. Most people listen with their mouth open, only waiting for the other person to stop talking so they can say what *they think*.

When I thought about my Uncle Ted, I could see clearly that in the presence of a conscious, loving person, it is easy to see that cherishing others, and yourself, is the path to walk. His awareness went toward cherishing people and accepting "what is." He seemed to spend more of his time in the here and now. His presence had a liberating effect on everyone around him.

Everything "out there" simply reflects our inner values and principles. When we focus our precious attention on what we cherish and what we want to do or be, we are creating our own destiny. Our actions tend to be inclusive; they invite others to participate. Our lives move in positive directions. Our choices show others better ways of being in the world. When cherishing others is our motive, we tend to blaze new paths, which leave trails for others to follow.

- CHAPTER 33 -

When We Achieve Critical Mass, Everything Changes

Willis Harmon headed up a study program at Stanford Research Institute during the 1970s and 1980s called "Energy Futures, Human Values and Life Styles." In this research project, his team searched through opinion polls and other research data for a time period that showed the greatest amount of tangible social transformative growth.

The three-and-one-half years between 1964 and 1967 stood out dramatically in the study. It was a time of tremendous transformation. During this time, more than 51 million people in America alone changed their core values and became what Harmon's team defined as "inner-directed" people. Later researchers renamed this same population grouping "cultural creatives." Most of the awakening people at that time were from the baby boomer generation, born right after World War II. This awakening is still happening. It is gaining momentum all over the world.

Any of us can change our attitude in an instant, especially when we realize that it is based on inaccurate or incomplete information. Values—like making our decisions based on well-thought-out and deeply-held principles—are completely different. They are deeply ingrained and usually take generations to change.

The "inner-directeds" in the study went from having outer circumstances guide their choices to making choices based on their own principles and values. There was never a time when so many people were waking up. This marked a radical change in how a large segment of society conducted its affairs. In all of history, *so many people waking up* should have been the banner news story in every media.

During this period people became focused on performing random acts of kindness, volunteering in organizations like the Peace Corps and other humanitarian organizations. Children sang in old folks homes. People got involved in other inclusionary activities. The United States focused on sending a man to the moon and bringing him back. African Americans gained their civil rights. Women achieved greater equality in the workplace.

Becoming directed toward inner values instead of reacting to circumstances based on the values laid down by previous generations is one of the first signs of spiritual awakening. Instead of letting the priest, rabbi, minister, doctor or politician tell us how to live, we trust our gut. We put more trust in how our heart feels about situations than on some outside authority. When a doctor gives us a diagnosis, we do our own research. We ask for second opinions. We discern for ourselves the relevancy of the diagnosis. We take back our power to choose.

The awakening that first mushroomed during the 1960s has continued to grow. Up to that time, most of the monies spent on technology went toward fighting war or fighting disease, instead of technologies that transform all the ways we live our daily lives. Now every day in every town and city in the world, more people are waking up. You can see the signs everywhere you look—if you look.

Socially-conscious technology (that makes people's lives better and more fulfilling) is still in its infancy. It increases in direct relationship with the number of people awakening. Now we can see these types of technologies starting to build momentum and get a serious foothold. The closer we come to a critical mass of people waking up, the faster technology that makes people's lives better will develop.

I believe the laws of human dynamics and the laws of thermal dynamics operate by very similar principles. If you want to blow up a stick of dynamite, have a thermonuclear detonation, or awaken enough people to ignite a social movement, you must initially get 9.1816 percent of the mass (or people), which is called "critical mass," to participate.

That is less than 10 percent of the population. The good news is that we don't have to wake up 70 percent of society to awaken and transform the larger body of society. We only need to help one or two of our friends to wake up for all this to work. I find that exciting!

You can see this transformative process in all kinds of organizations. To transform any group to a higher level of organization and effectiveness, you only need to get a little more than 9 percent of the members behind the plan. Looking back ten years after a transformative change happened, the 70 percent who thought it was a good idea but dragged their heels at the time will honestly say, "I was for it all along."

There will *always* be 10 percent of any population that will vehemently oppose any new plan. In physics, that group represents inertia. Inertia means that an object at rest wants to stay at rest, while an object in motion wants to stay in motion. Inertia can be observed as the members who want things to fundamentally stay the same.

An example in the Episcopal Church demonstrates the concept of igniting a critical mass of people. Sometime in the 1980s, the church decided to ordain women. When they achieved a critical mass of people pushing for the ordination of women, it hit the tipping point. At that point the 70 percent, who were dragging their feet but thought it was a good idea, were swept along in the rush. Women were ordained.

Then the Episcopal Church decided to accept openly gay parishioners. You can imagine that 10 percent opposed that change too. When a critical mass of parishioners arrived at the belief that gay parishioners deserve a place in their church—just like anyone else—it happened. In society there are now many examples of movements achieving critical mass, and everything changing as a result. You can observe this in every field of endeavor.

At this point I need to emphasize that critical mass is not some huge number like 50 or 70 percent. It is only slightly more than 9 percent of the people involved. When an organization or something you are involved in is striving to evolve, you might want to ask yourself, "Do I want to be part of the critical mass of people who are making it better, the mediocre middle, or the inertia that resists the transformation?"

Right now, it feels to me like there is about 5 percent of the population that is becoming focused on inner values. There seems to be another 10 percent that is trying to remain awake, but are lulled back asleep by the siren song of the world of time. Even though 10 percent are only conscious for short amounts of time, the combined 15 percent are the movers and shakers of the spiritual revolution. There is a steadily-building momentum.

Civilization is waking up from its slumber. We are rapidly approaching a moment of quantum awakening that has been foretold by all the indigenous tribes and all the religions of the world. We are now firmly in that transitional time.

Who Are Your Heroes?

As we wake up we all need heroes in all the fields of endeavor we engage in. I remember in school studying about heroic people like Copernicus and Einstein, and later pioneering women like Amelia Earhart and civil rights leaders as diverse as Jackie Robinson, Mohammed Ali, Malcolm X, and Martin Luther King, Jr.

When I was in school, most of the heroes I studied about seemed totally outside of me. When the teachers were talking about them, I remember thinking, so what? I did not realize at the time how important it is to have role models we admire. It is so clear to me now that we all need heroes in all our fields of endeavors, role models we can emulate when our struggles seem so overwhelming.

When you find yourself struggling so hard, wondering if you will fail, think: "how would my hero handle this?" Then step up. Take steps your hero would appreciate. I have a lot of heroes. I hope you do too. Who your heroes are says a lot about who you are. We all just make our life up. Then we live it.

Because the vast majority of people living right now are not awake to focusing on their own dreams, the inertia can be so entrenched and powerful that it seems impossible to overcome. If we don't have habits that keep waking us up to creating our own unique world, we hardly notice that we are just drifting along in the River of Time. It is so seductive.

I firmly believe that each of us has a heroic purpose. We each have dreams that grab us by the throat and say, "*This* needs to happen!" Usually we agree that it needs to happen, but we think *someone else needs to do it*. For as long as we remain extras in our own movie, the dream never gets off the ground. What are the dreams inside of you that want to come forward? Dare to dream. Then do it!

- CHAPTER 34 -

How Creation Happens
· *The Law of Above Down—Inside Out* ·

In the very first week that I started at Palmer College of Chiropractic in the1960s, we learned a holistic model that explained wellness, healing, and creation. The model was called "Above Down—Inside Out." Here is how it works:

A brilliant insight, truth, dream or plan comes into your consciousness from (above). When you take a dream or the truth (down) into your body, you own it. When you commit to the dream or truth, you move it from (inside) yourself to manifest it (out) into the world no matter the difficulty. This model requires courage.

Above Down—Inside Out also explains how healing works. When you are badly injured, or have a terrible illness, it is often difficult for you to see yourself as vibrantly healthy and whole. It takes courage to even imagine yourself as a powerfully healthy person, but *that* is exactly what you must do.

In the darkest part of your darkest night—times when your health feels like you will never be whole again—that is precisely when you need to come up with, and own a positive image of yourself as a whole and healthy individual. Remember, your bodymind is image orientated. It must see an image before it can manifest it.

See the image of yourself doing fun things, like running a marathon, hiking all over the mountains. Imagine friends telling you how great you look, your color vibrant, and your face beaming. Create an image of yourself in the vision you want to emulate. Seeing the vision is the "Above" part of the equation.

Take that image "Down" into your body. Own it. Be it. Then, against all difficulties, commit to *making it happen*. That is the "Inside Out" portion of the equation. Nothing happens until you have a vision and then commit to it. Nothing.

Coincidently, this model also shows how creation works. Spiritual reality and physical reality both operate essentially the same way. "As above, so below." If you want to heal yourself or manifest something, this is the model. If you want to awaken from the slumber humankind has endured for so long, use this same model.

In the *unconscious* state, the flow of your energies is reversed. For example, something out there happens. Now, because of that circumstance or action "out there," you have to do things differently (outside in). And since that situation now exists, your unconscious mind "thinks" that it must give up its power to that story, that you need to believe differently (below upward). This is 180 degrees backward.

And yet most people unconsciously believe this model in their gut. At this time in history, it remains the dominant paradigm. The medical allopathic model works in this direction. The doctor gives your symptom pattern a diagnosis, then fights against the diagnosis. Once you have been given a diagnosis (outside in), that diagnosis defines the rest of your life (Below Upward). In this model you are defined as your disease: "I am a diabetic, I have a bad back, I am a cancer survivor."

Creative, vibrant, high-energy children are often diagnosed as ADD. Once they are thusly defined, they go from vibrant alive geniuses to problem children that need to be drugged and controlled. The diagnosis often makes these children believe that they are somehow damaged goods, and often defines the rest of their lives.

In our highly-socialized society, we are led to believe that what naturally follows after about age thirty is: every year you give up more of your physical prowess until some yucky disease drags you down—and then you die. When you hear yourself thinking or saying something like "my health is shot," or "I am a diabetic", ask yourself: "Is that how I want to create my world?" If not, change the programing.

There is a huge disconnect between what most people *think they believe*, and what they actually believe in their gut. Most say, "I am in charge of my destiny." Yet when you ask them why they are not doing what they want, they say, "Because of (some circumstance) out there." Because they give their power up to their story, they are not actually in control. They are only reacting. Bacteria can do that.

When the flow of energy is backward, excuses replace goals and dreams. The mind focuses on unending drama, dysfunctions and problems. The entire realm of pain and suffering is created by acquiescence to "fate." Fate is the stories the brain thinks are reality when we leave it in charge.

In the unconscious model, "seeing is believing." How many times have you heard that? That model (known as linear thinking) is totally based on living in the past/future world of time. Everyone has stories about how their past limits their future. They give their power up to the story. When you think this way, your elevator stops just short of the top floor. It goes all the way up to critical thinking and stops just short of the next more conscious step, which is "creational thinking."

It takes courage to think creatively. When you accept a truth or have an idea that needs to happen (above), and own it (down), you must breathe up the courage to be able to *see yourself* making it happen (inside out). As you might imagine, this model deserves large amounts of thought and consideration on your part.

CHAPTER 35

Dreaming Your World Into Being

Every moment that you are awake, you are living within the eternity of the present moment. Within the eternity of each moment, you have the opportunity to create a unique world that resonates with the love you are feeling. In the present moment you are an eternal being, a creator inside the greater dream of Creator. You are the dreamer who dreams your world into being.

Your magnificent dreams are also eternal. Like you, your dreams stand outside the world of time. They simply are. You have the unique opportunity see them as already existing, and play in the finished product, the end game. Then your whole bodymind gets to participate in the manifestation of your plans and dreams.

When you use your imagination to play—as a child would—in a desire or goal as if it exists here and now, your heart uses that time to develop *insights* into how to make it happen in a more loving manner. More importantly, your entire bodymind gets to participate in the process.

While you are imagining playing in the end result, your liver is busy drawing up the plans that *make it happen*. Your gallbladder provides good judgments so the liver's plans have integrity, then it makes all the necessary decisions. Your lungs breathe in inspiration and all the courage needed to pull it off. Your large intestine gets rid of stuff you no longer need to make room for the transformation and change that solidifies your vision. Your stomach ripens your thoughts and plans until they are complete. Your spleen helps you develop clear boundaries and to know when is enough. Feeling all the feelings that come up directly connects you with the awesome power of your spirit and soul. That's the way you do it.

In this more conscious dream, your job is to determine *what* and *why*. What do you want and why do you want it. Ask yourself questions like:

What exactly do I want? Will it make me happy? How will this affect my family, my loved ones? Will this be good for me in the long run?

Then ask yourself why this is important to you with questions like: Why do I want it? Why is it important that this happens? What are my motives? Why does it even need to be? Why is it me that needs to do it?

Your job is what and why. God's job is *how and when.* Give God's job up to God. Then be present. You create the world you live in when you commit to what you want, and why you want it, or why *you* are the one to do it.

After you have committed, it is vitally important to face every situation "that appears to come at you" with courage and gratefulness. After all, you are writing the script. You are directing the movie of your life, complete with where the sets are going to be each moment. And hopefully, in every scene you are the star, or at least one of the principal actors.

It's all just a movie, and we all play parts in each other's projections. There's no scroll on the other side of the veil where what is supposed to happen is written. We all just make it up. Only then is it written.

You have the opportunity to stand—moment by moment—at the nexus of eternity, where all potential and all possibility are readily available to you. I do not know anyone who just suddenly woke up fully conscious. You progressively wake up from the unconscious dream, one step at a time. It is a *process* that takes your whole life. I've never heard of an easy way to just pop awake, not in all the books I have read, or from any enlightened teachers I have studied. No matter what you do for a living, waking up to the present moment is the only game in town.

There is no moment but now. As you relax into the goodness all around you in the present moment, peace of mind naturally wants to bubble up into your awareness. That's your spirit's natural state of being. The turmoil of your mind gives way to the experience of peace and contentment. Happiness can be best defined as complete relaxation. In this state, your best course of action becomes apparent.

In these peaceful moments, the great truths coalesce. When you take these noble truths down into your consciousness *and commit to them*, you are living the spirit of "Above Down—Inside Out."

- CHAPTER 36 -

The Power of a Shared Vision

When a critical mass of people (9.1816 percent) come into agreement, like believing that something is happening—it happens. It becomes the dominant paradigm, the background of shared "reality." It makes no difference to the outcome whether people like it—what they believe is happening—or hate it. It doesn't matter whether they are condoning it or wishing it would never exist.

Remember, your bodymind does not consider the polarity of "like it or hate it." Your mind rules out polarities like loving it or hating it as if they do not exist. To your bodymind, polarities are totally irrelevant. To understand this, try to "not" focus on a dog chasing a cat. Before you had time to censure your mind it probably focused on the image of a dog chasing a cat. Your mind is image orientated, it orients its thinking around images and stories. "Not" is simply ignored by your bodymind.

Take for example a town where a critical mass of people living there believes, in their gut, that the criminal element has taken over their once-peaceful neighborhood. *The people who believe their town is lost to criminals are actually making it happen*, even though that's probably the last thing they would ever desire.

You are directly contributing to the reality of anything you believe is happening. Take responsibility for the fact that you co-create whatever you focus on. What you believe is the *creative* portion of the equation. It creates the outcome.

When you are thinking about a problem as if it exists, you are actually co-creating the problems you believe are happening. Start challenging all the things you believe are happening with the question, *"Is that how I want to create my world?"* If not, shoot that sacred cow dead. Replace it with how you want to create your world.

This formula can just as well go positive. When a critical mass agrees on anything, *that* magically morphs into becoming the background of our shared reality. We all float along in a river of shared intention. Everything we observe came about when a critical mass came into a shared agreement that "it exists."

There are times when we need to believe something, whether or not there is evidence to support our beliefs. These are power moments. Our choice, no matter which way it goes, causes a whole stream of events to occur. It changes everything.

For example, in the late 1970s and early 1980s, there was a movement to build the Auburn Dam in the Northern California foothills. More people hated the idea of what that dam would do than loved it. But that didn't matter. What mattered was that most of the people, including myself, were focusing on the dam *as if it existed,* even though most of us were very much against it.

Our shared assumption that it was going to happen was the perfect formula to "make it happen." Major efforts were already underway to build that dam. They were about two hundred million dollars into construction. It would have been the most expensive dam in US history, costing over a billion dollars.

So many of us love that area around the North Fork of the American River. If the dam were completed, up to fifty miles of richly forested valleys would have been flooded up to the base of some of the best skiing in the world, like Squaw Valley. The lake's modulating affect would mean less snow. The wildness of that area would have gone extinct. When that happens the wildness goes out of us. The rivers are our veins. Our spirit flourishes when we are kayaking, hiking, playing, and meditating there, or even thinking about that sacred river.

I started talking with thirty people in the Auburn area. We all agreed to *see the river running wild and free.* That image became our shared visualization. We agreed to take a few cleansing breaths anytime we heard about the dam, read about it in the news, or even thought about it. The object was to keep our focus on the image of our beautiful river "running wild and free," no matter what we heard or read about the dam. Those people recruited others until there were more than a hundred people focusing on the image of the American River's North Fork running wild and free.

Fear-based intentions only increase arithmetically (one plus one plus one is three). The power of shared intention increases logarithmically, especially when powered by loving feelings. Their numbers multiply times the third power. That meant one hundred people, multiplied by one hundred, and that total multiplied by one hundred. That adds up to the power of 1 million people. That's a lot of power of shared intention.

Early that spring of 1984, we had a major storm the newscasters called the "pineapple express." Our area got eleven inches of rain per day for two days. That was followed by nine inches a day for the next nine days. That's a lot of water. By the fifth day the low parts of the roads in our county had become creeks. A large section of the road going down to the American River slid down into the river. Trees washed down and clogged up the dam's secondary bypass system. The floodwaters rose up over the edge of the earth-filled dam they had built so far. And the awesome power of all that water washed the dam away. Yes!

Two months later, the Army Corps of Engineers issued a scathing report, outlining significant reasons why that ill-fated dam was a *bad* idea. Their main issue was that both sides of the earthen dam were anchored into cancellous rock that could fail under sufficient pressure.

The unstable rock, on both sides of the river where the dam was anchored, went back as far as they could measure. The report said that if the dam failed—which was a distinct possibility—the downriver flood would devastate most of Sacramento. A wave up to forty feet high would have hit the state capital, causing an epic flood.

South Yuba River Citizen's League and Friends of the River formed up later that same year to protect the Yuba and American Rivers. Now questionable EIRs (environmental impact reports) are completely scrutinized. The river is safer now because of the power of shared loving intention. This is an example of the power we have when we focus it positively. We must be the change we want to see in the world.

When a critical mass awakens to cherishing the goodness around them, they create whole new background realities. All throughout history there has never been as many people waking up as there are now. Not ever. That should be the banner headline in every newspaper and newsroom in the world, not the sensationalism the media serves up. Sadly, the government and the media are the last bastions of unconsciousness.

When enough of us change, and that number achieves critical mass, government and the media will always be at the trailing edge of that change.

SECTION III

TAPPING THE POWER OF THE BODYMIND

The next section explores "the seven habits," powerful tools that let you control the incredible power of your bodymind and wake you to the power of the present moment. *These habits are taproots that connect you deep into the strata of all life.* They are the keys to living the life you have always desired.

These seven habits cover the entire spectrum from helping you when you are in the worst possible health, to making your body healthier and more efficient when you are competing at the highest levels of performance. They are habits you will enjoy for the rest of your life as you move into progressively higher realms of health and well being. They make every moment more exciting and fulfilling.

Everyone falls asleep. Everyone. The familiarity of letting your mind dwell on the past or future is so insidious. The issue is waking up. Each habit wakes you up from the spells you so insidiously get drawn into. Once you wake up to the present moment, all these tools and understandings help you to easily manifest your heart's desires. Living in the present moment, peace of mind is easily attainable.

FIRST HABIT

- CHAPTER 37 -

Breathe Out Strong

I was a medic in the Army when I began my adventure into powerful breathing. Our small medical detachment got challenged to a baseball game against a team chosen from the best of a 5,000-man artillery battalion. We only had thirty guys to draw from. I didn't expect much from our team, but I was pleasantly surprised. Unexpectedly, as the game played out, I got a great lesson in the power of breathing.

Our first guy up to bat had a stooped-over posture. He was tall and skinny with Coke-bottle glasses held together in several places with white tape. He had a pocket protector in his shirt pocket full of pencils and pens. When he moved, his joints articulated as if they didn't know each other all that well. He was a nice guy, but definitely not a jock. We all knew he would strike out.

The pitcher for the artillery had an inordinately long windup before his pitch. As the pitcher began his *long* windup, our batter completely stopped breathing—the whole time! When the pitcher finally threw the ball, our batter's swing was uncertain. He was out of breath! He missed the ball by a mile. Then he had to take a whole bunch of rapid breaths to make up for not breathing at all during the overly long windup. It was painful to watch. Two swings later, he was out.

Our next batter was a tall, lean, muscular man who moved with a physical authority that came from years of dominating the hoops. He was a basketball star before the Army got him. He exuded an aura of confidence as he walked up to the plate. He tapped home base with his bat a few times and pointed his bat where the ball would go.

He took a few practice swings, breathing out forcefully with each swing. As the pitcher took his long windup, our batter did a series of rapid changeups in his breathing pattern to stay in synch with the pitcher. As the pitcher threw the ball, our batter breathed out forcefully in perfect timing with his swing. He uncoiled in one fluid movement that began at his core. He hit the ball at the midpoint of his uncoiling and followed all the way through. He crushed the ball. It was a thing of beauty, poetry in motion.

The ball didn't seem to have an arc until it was long past the outfield fence. It took a good fifteen minutes for the other team to find the baseball, which went down into a gully a long way from the fence.

During the time the outfielders searched for the ball, I reflected on those two diametrically opposed breathing styles. Each was radically different, and yet each style perfectly matched the individual.

The shallow breather was timid, uncertain of himself. The deep abdominal breather exuded confidence. I started noticing how much breathing affects every aspect of a person's life. That was the day I fully committed to breathing abdominally.

Breathe, Then Act

Healthy, confident people breathe powerfully. When something startles them, their first reaction is to take big breaths. Breathing out strong interrupts unconscious patterns that are trying to take control. These people breathe out strong. Then they act.

Disempowered, fearful people breathe shallow, erratic breaths. When startled, they stop breathing. They hold their breath! When they start breathing again, they breathe very shallowly. A fearful state of mind takes over.

Living in a constant state of fear is stressful to the heart. In one of Jack Canfield's audiotape series, the coauthor of *Chicken Soup for the Soul* spoke of a study where they observed that all thirty-eight patients in the cardiac ICU ward of a major hospital were chest breathing. Chest breathing doesn't give you enough oxygen to adequately handle situations in your life. When you don't have enough energy to handle even normal stresses, all your fears become fire-breathing dragons. That causes you to live in highly stressful environments that lead to serious problems, like heart attacks.

Even breathing shallowly for a few minutes makes it difficult to plan out something you want. Courage and confidence—which must have big breaths to sustain—vanish. They just evaporate. Lack and doubt flood into the space created by the vacuum. All kinds of subtle and not-so-subtle fears move to the forefront of your mind. In this fear-based state, your mind's focus gets shifted away from your plans and dreams. Instead, all you see are the snags and obstacles.

After that Army baseball game I became mindful of checking in on my breath. Each time I noticed that I was breathing shallowly, I found that I had been doing so for a while. Then I took a "cleansing breath" or two. Those are fast, deep breaths. It doesn't matter whether they are through your mouth or nose. Then I went back to breathing out strong. That snapped me right out of the spell every time. Spells are any states of mind that take us out of the present moment.

Before I learned about abdominal breathing, I tended to get stuck in one of my unconscious spells at least a dozen times a day, and stay there for a long while.

Breathing out strong lifted me right out of low-grade spells like frustration, boredom, depression, or the anxieties that normally darkened my mood for hours. All of that cleared with a few cleansing breaths. You will be impressed at how well this works for you. You will also be impressed by how dramatically your self-esteem improves.

Any new habit you take on has a gestational period, like having a baby. The time it takes to birth a new habit is about the same amount of time that it takes to birth a baby. For the first nine months, every time you check in on yourself, you probably will be breathing shallowly. After about nine months—most of the time when you check—you will be breathing abdominally. Breathing out strong will give you the energy and courage to really *live*, to successfully meet and exceed life's challenges and difficulties.

Use every opportunity to breathe dynamically from your core. Every moment that you are breathing out strong makes your core musculature stronger and more stable, giving your low back greater stability. Your spirit is drawn down into its place of power, which is below your navel. All the analogous parts of your body and spirit line up so they can work together. That gives your spirit control of all aspects of your being. Your life starts feeling like *your* life, the way *you* want to live it.

- CHAPTER 38 -

Breathing Up Courage

Breathing out strong is your first gate to heaven on Earth. This is the way you breathed *before* you accepted any of life's traumas into your body. Breathing out forcefully from your core wakes you up to the present moment, where you stand at the very center of eternity with all possibility and all potential available to you.

The added oxygen provides enough fuel—and courage—to power up all your magnificent plans and splendid dreams. You ever more consciously become the lead actor in the unfolding drama of your life.

Notice *the focus is on breathing out*—not breathing in. Breathing in is passive, an autonomic function. It happens all by itself. If you breathe out shallowly, you will consistently breathe in shallowly. You always breathe in with the same intensity that you breathe out.

Breathing out strong strengthens your core and literally oxygenates your whole body. Feel your abdominal muscles work when you breathe out. Then you are really doing it right. This habit—the *First Habit*—will profoundly change your life. Each time you catch yourself breathing shallowly and resume breathing out strong, you wake up from a spell.

You step out of the quagmire of historical time: the past with its guilt, regrets and missed opportunities, or the future with its fears, worries, and anxieties. You step into the present moment—the eternal moment—where all potential and all possibilities are within your grasp.

Take a Deep Breath?

We have been taught to "take a deep breath," but that's just wrong. That is probably the main reason why most people don't breathe correctly.

Breathing out is your active breath. The first time you practice breathing, stand up. The best way to experience correct breathing is while standing—at least for the first few times you practice it.

Place your hand just below your navel. As you breathe out strong, feel your hand drawn inward toward your spine. As you relax, the in breath naturally pushes your hand outward. Keep feeling your belly draw your hand in (as you breathe out) and push it out (as you breathe in), out and in, out and in—the ancient rhythm of life.

Out and in—not in and out. *This* is how you are meant to breathe. Breathing out strong turns your diaphragm into a very effective bellows that forces oxygen all the way out to your fingertips and toes, and all the way out to that other extremity, your brain. Top athletes fully understand this way of breathing.

The next time you are at your computer and your brain fuzzes out, stand up, breathe out strong for about five forceful breaths, and do about fifteen gentle spinal twists. Feel the difference. You will be impressed.

When you breathe shallowly, life-giving oxygen barely gets out past your elbows or knees, much less to your fingertips and toes. That's why so many people have cold hands and feet. If your fingertips aren't getting enough oxygen, what do you think is happening to that other extremity, your brain? When you breathe shallowly, the energy of your life force is so minimal that you can hardly think. It keeps you from reaching for, or achieving, your heart's desires.

Breathing shallowly, your oxygen-depleted mind obsesses on obstacles and snags, all the ways you could be hurt or embarrassed if your dream were to fail. Meanwhile, your dreams get crowded further into the background—where they become "if only" wishes. Big breath fuels a big life. Little breath limits you to a little life.

Breathing out strong forces the greatest amount of carbon dioxide out of your lungs. Then your inbreath automatically draws in a full, deep breath. Breathing this way allows your diaphragm muscles to take in a big mixing bowl's worth of air with each breath. You fully oxygenate your entire body, including your brain and your life.

Your thinking sharpens. Your attention span becomes more focused. Your mental stamina allows you to embrace the big picture. You can wrap your mind around both the complex issues *and the details*. You have all the energy you need to live your dreams full on, making them happen. Breathing this way—anything is possible.

When you are breathing out strong, you are living powerfully on the earth. You breathe up enough power to imagine yourself in the dreams that usually stay in the background of your mind, just waiting for you to take them seriously.

Your muscles and nervous system are your body's largest consumers of oxygen. Mental and physical stamina requires a lot of oxygen. You *really* have to breathe out strong to fuel endurance. If you are only breathing in enough fuel to accomplish a small life, it is almost impossible to conceive of more.

Practice "breathing out strong" every time you think about it—when you are walking, standing in line, stopped in traffic or sitting at your desk. When you do, all your faculties come full on. You instantly become more aware.

You want to breathe out strong in more and more situations until *this* is the way you always breathe. The more you do, the better your entire body feels. If you commit to abdominal breathing, a year from now you will be experiencing twice as much energy as you are now.

Chest Breathing

Chest breathing is way worse than just shallow breathing. The incredible bellows of your diaphragm—which efficiently sends oxygen to every part of your body—is completely disengaged. It's not even working!

Ironically, a chest breather looks like they are really taking in big breaths. Often they are *really* breathing hard, struggling, yet *not* getting enough oxygen to make their body and mind feel safe and secure. This way of breathing ushers in fear and anxieties that can become overpowering. During stressful times, chest breathing can lead to panic attacks. The person is breathing so hard, and getting so little air that their mind can panic, which makes their breathing even less effective, like a vicious cycle.

People who chest breathe begin by taking a breath into their upper chest. *Their collarbones go up and down with each breath.* Oxygen can only get drawn down into about the third rib level. Since the lungs are bell shaped—small at the top and big at the bottom—chest breathing only takes in a tiny dessert bowl's worth of air. That is *the* puniest way to breathe.

Learning About Breathing

I first learned about breathing in an interesting way. I was in the Army, and went into the post library, which was tiny and outdated. I was looking for an action book when a book two bookshelves above me fell into my hands. I had heard about people's lives being changed by a book that mysteriously fell into their hand—and here it was.

It was a book on yoga, definitely not what I was looking for. But it did fall into my hands. I randomly opened it up to a page that said (from my memory) in all capital letters:

> UNTIL YOU LEARN TO BREATHE ABDOMINALLY,
> BREATHING IS THE MOST IMPORTANT DISCIPLINE
> YOU WILL EVER UNDERTAKE

It went on to show how the lungs were shaped like a bell, small at the top, big at the bottom, with the diaphragm (the wall-to-wall floor of the lungs) acting like a powerful bellows. Then it explained how chest breathing only activated a small portion of the lungs at the top of the bell. It went on to say that chest breather's collarbones went up and down with each breath.

I looked in the mirror and breathed my normal way. My collarbones went up and down with every breath. Dang! Shallow breathing was a puny way to breathe—and live—but the way I was breathing was way worse.

I began observing the way people around me breathed and how they acted. When people were breathing shallowly, especially chest breathing, I noticed that they focused more on what they couldn't do. There were always *excuses*. The more shallowly they breathed, the more reticent they were to take chances or to venture out of their "safe zone." Their fears controlled how they saw the world. I also saw this happening in me!

I could see that breathing shallowly nailed my feet to the ground because fear and anxiety held center stage. It dawned on me that when I did not have enough breath energy to complete something, I couldn't even *imagine* taking the courageous "first steps" on that journey. As my courage evaporated, fear took over as my advisor.

I noticed how breathing such a puny amount of air filled my life with fear. It showed up as shyness, not wanting to be noticed, especially not called on, concern about what others thought, not wanting to appear pushy, and thousands of subtle ways of holding back. All those fears stood in the way of the life I wanted to grab hold of.

A few cleansing breaths woke me right up, pulled me out of a spell—every time. I call them spells because low-grade feelings or disempowering thoughts take us out of the present moment. Usually I was worried, feeling inadequate, irritated by something or someone or lost in some distracting mental state instead of experiencing the present moment. Breathing shallowly lets our rational mind take over, and it immediately draws us into its vast library of stories that keep us from living in the moment.

In the absence of enough energy to accomplish your goals or dreams, courage withers. It just fades away. Fear, which is lack of courage, fills in the void. You have to breathe up enough courage to live the life of your dreams.

While I had no idea at that time how life affirming it would become, I began breathing abdominally. For the first few months, every time I checked in on myself, I was still chest breathing—or at best breathing shallowly—keeping me immersed in some unhelpful, disempowering mental state. It took about nine months before I was breathing out strong (as mentioned before, any new habit takes about nine months to integrate). Both my personal power and my energy levels have improved significantly every year since I made breathing out forcefully a habit so many years ago.

- CHAPTER 39 -

Fate or Opportunity?

Fate, in our society, is described as some sort of inevitable destiny. As we discussed in "Your Wellspring of Superhuman Strength," when you face a dire or even life-threatening situation, you actually have much more control in that situation than your brain *thinks* you have. Instead of focusing on the opportunity, your brain tends to look at all the times you failed in similar situations, and can now. When you say a resounding "no" to the dire fate your mind first presents, you expand your consciousness—and your opportunities—to successfully navigate that situation.

Imagine this scenario: A good friend and co-worker who is no longer with the company spaced out and did not perform a crucial step in a long-term process your department is responsible for. You just discovered his error, and realized that it's all going to go sideways. Lives could be at risk. Fingers could point at you. The promotion you were up for might evaporate if you become the fall guy, or fired.

You say NO! to the fate your mind is picturing. The adrenaline rush that follows gives you the crystal clarity to see the solution, and the steps that must be implemented to save the program. You immediately take all this to your executive director, show the problem the co-worker caused, and the way to guide the company out of the dilemma. All during that time, the clarity and profound depth of your perceptions saved the day.

In any dangerous situation—no matter whether the threat is to your life, or a threat to your job or a relationship—your brain's immediate response is to give you the dire outcome that will happen if you accept its version of reality. If you accept *that* at face value, quite often your mind goes blank and you feel like a victim, which is just another way of accepting "fate." That's usually where you leave your body, leaving you with only scant remembrance of details during the incident.

When you panic, your mind takes over and runs stories like, "This is happening too fast!" or "Uh oh, I'm screwed." The story becomes a command instructing your body that the situation is beyond its capacity, there's no way out, you are going to get hurt.

Your breath stops! You start breathing shallowly, shutting down your energy and courage, thus ensuring that your mind's version of reality *is* reality. The assumption that you can't handle the situation commands your body to fail, and sure enough, you get hurt.

There is a much better way. When you say an emphatic "NO!" to your mind's projection of a dire reality, you transform the situation from fate to opportunity. The instant you say "NO," time slows way down. Your entire bodymind goes into a full adrenaline hyperdrive. You see what needs to be done—and you do it! Your commitment and mental clarity allow you to handle the situation better than you *ever could* in normal consciousness.

Even years later you can vividly remember every second of the experience. You were fully present. These are some of your finest moments. You respond to situations like these with phenomenal clarity, strength and speed. The power that surges through your body is awesome. Your actions take you out of harm's way.

Isn't it interesting that without adequate breath, you experience fear or confusion when danger or difficulty comes? But when you breathe in enough oxygen, fear transforms into excitement. You breathe powerfully when you *commit* to doing what you have to do. You become your own hero in these adrenaline-charged moments.

Every day, you get into difficult situations. You may handle them well—or not so well. How you handle them depends on whether you breathe out strong, and *what* you commit to. If you commit to doing whatever it takes to get through the difficulty, you respond with great clarity and power. You seize the moment. You save the day!

I experienced an example of this when I was nineteen years old. I saw a woman drowning at Folsom Lake in northern California. I knew I could help her, took a big breath, and dove in. I had to swim about two hundred yards to reach her, then another two hundred yards to get her to shore. When I got her to shore, she was like a beached whale with me underneath her. She was a large woman, weighing over two hundred and fifty pounds, lying unconscious on top of me and painfully grinding me into the gravel beach.

There were about seventy-five people standing on the shore, and not one person put their foot in the water to help me. I yelled, "Will someone help me?" That seemed to break the trance they were in, the unconscious assumption that there was nothing they could do. Suddenly they all rushed to help me.

I am sure that most of those people on the shore had good intentions, that they sincerely wanted to help, but they were paralyzed. They were probably breathing shallowly, caught up in their own spell of inaction. As a result they did nothing. My yell for help broke the spell they were in.

I have been in several situations like this where everyone was stunned into inaction by a situation that was not like their normal lives. If you are not breathing up courage, any number of fears will come to the forefront of your reality. You wind up on the sidelines, not knowing what to do, doing nothing.

In moments of danger or extreme difficulty there are always two realities. The default "reality" is your brain's instantaneous analysis of the situation, fate. Based on past experiences, the brain thinks "what can *I possibly* do?" inferring that you can do nothing. When you say "no" to the disaster that will happen if you do nothing, what's left is opportunity. You become the hero in dangerous situations and the leading lady or man in all your everyday situations.

The Power of Breath

We take breathing for granted. After all, everyone breathes, right? Well, it's true that everyone must breathe enough air to not die. Unfortunately, *that* is about how much air most people breathe—just enough to not die.

Breathing is one of the largest factors affecting the quality of your life. And yet you can live your entire life without giving breathing a second thought. Your lungs represent your physical body's will to live, your right to be here. In your everyday reality, your lungs represent your right to pursue and enjoy the life of your dreams. All animals possess the will to live. Your right to exist is your animal spirit.

The life force of your animal spirit changes from moment to moment depending upon how much air you breathe (or don't breathe). The power of your animal spirit is a dynamic, constantly changing reality. You can be as awesome as a grizzly bear or as timid as a mouse.

A real-life example of the power of your animal spirit occurred to my wife on a camping trip. Without knowing why, she felt her breath suddenly catch in the top of her throat, a bolt of fear run down her spine. She felt as if a steel rod was running down her right leg, deep into the earth, freezing her foot to the ground. Just then, her friend yelled, "Look out! Rattlesnake!"

My wife said, "Where?" and looked outward. He said, "Right next to your leg!" Brain-numbing, freeze-your-feet-to-the-ground feeling turned to fear. The snake was coiled up, waving back and forth, its mouth about an inch from her right thigh.

In a moment of clarity she realized that had the snake meant her ill will, he would have already struck her. She breathed out the fear, took a deep breath and said, "Ho, snake brother, I mean you no harm." The snake stayed there for a few seconds, then dropped down peacefully and slithered away, causing her no harm.

You must breathe a lot of air if you want to live large, if you want to be the leading actor in the life of your dreams. Become aware of breathing out strong every time you start walking anywhere, going out to your car or standing in the checkout line. Who you are, beyond all of your stories, comes into sharp relief. Breathing out strong gives you the force of will to meet and exceed any obstacle—or accept any opportunity—that comes your way.

Since your mind needs a job to keep it out of trouble, *give it the job of making sure you are always breathing out strong.*

- CHAPTER 40 -

Developing Self-Esteem

As you make abdominal breathing a habit, you will probably catch yourself breathing shallowly about twenty times a day. Each time you breathe out strong, you wake up from a limiting or dysfunctional state of mind. Some of the things you wake up from can be old dysfunctional stories like "My life is difficult", "I'm not appreciated" or "I never get to do what I want."

You need not concern yourself about how many times a day you start breathing shallowly and fall asleep. We all fall asleep—dozens of times a day. *What's important is waking up*, and spending increasingly more of your time wide awake.

Each time that you wake up to the present moment replaces another old dysfunctional story with a more empowering one. Breathing enough energy to handle whatever is in front of you gives you that power. As you replace tired old stories with more empowering examples, your self-esteem grows.

Your self-esteem is like the reflection on the surface of a pond. The calmness or turbulence on the pond's surface is a reflection of your inner state of mind. Each time you wake up, you eliminate one more disempowering, anxious or fearful response pattern—one more wave. The surface of your lake calms, allowing you to see greater depths of your character and your own particular genius qualities. In this way, you grow your self-esteem.

Each situation you handle with awareness creates a new, more empowered default program. The next time you feel that same way, you have a better way to handle that feeling. As your self-esteem builds, so does your self-image. You develop greater personal power. With each success you spend more time being aware. Your mind chatter lessens, even ceases. You realize that you are *not* your old stories, that anything you have ever done pales in significance to who you are in this moment.

- CHAPTER 41 -

Finding Your Power

Hara is where your breath originates. In Japan, people are traditionally taught that *hara* is the epicenter of your awareness. In China, this same place of power is called the lower *tang Tien* (pronounced "dong she-in," but more like one word).

Hara is located just below your navel right in front of the fourth lumbar vertebra. Your diaphragm muscles connect to this vertebra. It's where your breath originates, and is your one-point center of balance and movement. Breathing out strong from hara strengthens—and connects you to—your core, the very core of your being.

Traditionally, people growing up in Japan have a number of sayings that focus their awareness into hara. If a boy is being problematic, his mother might tell him that he has black hara. That's like telling him that his soul essence has darkened.

If a child begs his father to get a dog, and his father asks, "Will you *always* remember to feed your dog?"—and he forgets after *promising*—the father might say, "You have weak hara." No Japanese person ever wants to be accused of having weak hara, because that also happens to be the definition of a liar. You can bet that's the last time the child ever forgets to feed the dog!

In Japan, if a man commits to helping you on a certain date, he might clench his fist in front of hara as he says, "I will be there." That's like saying "I commit my spirit to helping you on that date." In America you are more likely to hear, "Call me to remind me." That's a lot different, isn't it? Sadly, the results are different, too.

In Western cultures, we don't even have a name for our "one-point center" of awareness. Most Americans and Europeans have zero dialogue about where we should focus our consciousness. With the exception of health disciplines like yoga and Pilates, there is little awareness in our society about this extremely important part of our body.

Breathing out strong from hara draws your spirit fully down into your body. With your awareness in hara, you move with the whole body alertness of a cat. As you experience whole-body awareness, mental chatter falls away. You are present in this moment. You experience the pleasure of doing simple things, like you did as a child.

Finding the Center of Your Being

Your spirit has a dynamic focal point. It's about the size of a golf ball and is the most energetic point in your body. *The focal point of your spirit puts out more energy than your body can contain.* If you have not given it much thought, you probably have no idea where the focal point of your spirit resides. To discover where your spirit is presently focused within your body, pause for a few seconds:

- Close your eyes
- Go inside your body
- Notice where your awareness is drawn
- Notice the single place in your body where you feel the most energy

Most people breathe shallowly most of the time, which causes the focal point of their spirit to drift up to their forehead. When the energy is that intense in your forehead, it hyper-energizes your brain, influencing it to take control of your consciousness. That causes all your perceptions to be overwhelmingly mental. The result is, you *think* your reality. This is not good!

Breathing abdominally draws your spirit all the way down into hara, its home. Once your spirit is in hara, every part of your spirit aligns with the analogous parts of your bodymind. That gives your spirit firm control of your body—and your consciousness—much like an accomplished equestrian controls a spirited horse. Neither your spirit nor your physical body can ever function independently as well as they do together. Together they are magnificent.

When you have an epiphany or experience a deep truth, hara is the place in your body where you *get it*, where you *own* the truth. When you know something in your gut, then you've got it. Knowing something in hara, in your gut, is a quantum leap beyond thinking about it up there between your ears.

Hara is where your spirit lives when you are spiritually awake. It's the ancient heart place of your spirit. Every moment that you are breathing abdominally, the values and principles of your spirit control your thoughts.

Life improves dramatically. It keeps getting better each year, better than you ever dreamed in your wildest imagination.

Filling Your Lower Body With Energy

When you are breathing dynamically from hara, the powerful energies of your spirit fill your *entire* body to overflowing. As the energy expands downward, it pushes out through the energy centers at the balls of your feet. The chakras at the bottom of your feet are called "Bubbling Wells." When you are breathing out strong, your spirit energizes Bubbling Wells, making you feel as rooted as an oak tree—grounded.

Bubbling Wells chakras, when they are energized, greatly expand the field of awareness around your feet. You can *feel* where your feet are on a stair tread—even wearing thick-sole shoes—without ever having to look down at where your feet are.

When Bubbling Wells are energized, your awareness also expands to allow you to experience the emotional life of the trees and plants around you. Trees and plants have an emotional life as profound as your own. You get your hormones—which modulate your emotions—from plants, and from the animals that eat those plants.

Native Americans have traditionally shown more awareness of the elemental kingdom and how it interfaces with our own lives than the white settlers. The Hopi have a saying that teaches their children to respect their connection with the elemental world: "When you walk among the corn beings [which are sacred to them] you should make a prayer, say a poem or sing a song for *they* know more about you than you know about them." The whole elemental world welcomes your participation.

Getting Out of Your Head

When you breathe out from hara, the energies of your spirit expand upward—as well as downward—filling your whole torso, neck, and head full of energy. As your torso fills with energy, it's like blowing up an air mattress. When it's full of air, it requires less effort to stay erect. That's how your body feels when your spirit fills it full of energy, making it easier to maintain an exquisite posture. The abundant energy of your spirit, living in its place of power, creates a sense of lightness in your body.

When you breathe shallowly, on the other hand, you experience your torso as being limp and so heavy that it takes excessive effort to keep your body erect. Most people slump when they breathe shallowly.

Breathing out strong connects you to the entire spiritual kingdom, your guides, the angels and Creator. Life takes on much greater dimension and magnitude. You *get* that you are so much more than just your thoughts.

CHAPTER 42

How Posture Affects Breathing

Breathing dynamically requires good posture. There are "four rules of posture" that dramatically affect your breathing:

1. Breathe out strong from below your navel. This way of breathing strengthens your core musculature, including your diaphragm. You breathe up enough energy and courage to face all life's difficulty. Breathing out strong is also the first habit of spiritual awareness, connecting you profoundly to your spirit and the higher dimensions.
2. Keep your upper torso erect all of the time, no matter whether you are sitting, standing, walking up or down stairs or hills, or lifting anything. Let your neck and shoulders relax, while your breastbone (sternum) is always lifting upward. The more you can keep your upper torso erect, the greater your capacity to breathe powerfully.
3. First, let your neck be loose and free. Then, allow the back of your skull the freedom to float up to its "sweet spot" (where the least amount of effort is needed to maintain correct posture). Your forehead rocks gently forward. If you had a miner's lamp on your forehead, it would be shining on the ground 45 feet in front of you.
4. Keep your feet parallel whether you are standing or walking, lifting or sitting. This allows the two muscles that connect from hara to your diaphragm to function with equal strength.

These four rules will be discussed in greater detail in the posture section.

Taking in Ten Percent More Air

When your posture is anatomically correct, your lungs have the capacity to take in significantly more oxygen. If you want to dramatically increase your physical power or personal potential, there is an easy way to take in ten percent *more* oxygen. Ten percent more oxygen may not sound like much, but it feels like twice the power.

Years ago I test drove some Toyota Celicas. They had fuel-injected and non-fuel-injected models, so I drove both. The fuel-injected model felt like it had twice as much horsepower. When I said that to the salesman, he replied that the fuel-injected model only had seven to ten percent more horsepower depending on how high the engine was revving. Frankly, I found that difficult to believe. It felt like twice as much to me.

After he said that I test drove the fuel-injected model again. When I did, I observed that both models had about the same power at the lower rpms. But once the car accelerated beyond 3,500 rpms, the fuel-injected model felt twice as powerful. When accelerating quickly, the tachometer usually stays above 3,500 rpms, letting you really *feel* that power!

From that example, I began to understand how breathing in ten percent more oxygen feels twice as powerful—especially when you are playing hard, working hard, or facing intense mental or emotional challenges. When your performance is ten percent better than your best *at your peak*, the difference is awesome.

Here is how you can take in ten percent more air:

- Stand in good posture
- Breathe out strong
- Let your in breath fill your abdomen
- *After* your lower abdomen has taken in as much air as it can in abdominal breathing, let your upper chest expand upward

This is completely different from chest breathing, which *begins* with your collarbones lifting. In this enhanced way of breathing, your collarbones do not lift until the last phase of breathing in. This allows you to take in 10 percent more air. Note: You cannot breathe this way without good posture.

Ten percent more athletic prowess or ten percent more mental or emotional clarity is a *huge* difference.

Imagine Your Breath as a Powerful Wave

When you have a lot on your mind or feel stuck, you can do a walking meditation where you breathe air into your entire bodymind as if your breath were a powerful wave entering at hara. This meditation blows the cobwebs out of your mind and your body. It fills every part of your body with the power to accomplish whatever you are attempting.

You use *the power of your inbreath to focus attention* into places in your torso and head that feel dark, places where your attention has been lacking. Your attention dispels the darkness, blowing away all your fears, filling those places with such power that you begin to feel invincible.

As you breathe in, imagine the air coming into hara like a powerful wave of water. Imagine the wave's impact expanding into your pelvis like a dynamic wave of water would, expanding into your entire pelvis, filling all the dark places in your organs with the power of your attention. The dark places are all the places where your life force has been replaced by fears and limitations.

Feel each wave of inbreath progressively expanding, filling ever more of your torso, filling your bladder, large intestine, small intestine, kidneys and all your organs with light. Keep breathing this way until all your organs are full of light.

The waves come in and expand until all the darkness is filled with light. Since your entire bodymind is mostly energy and consciousness, the force of your attention disintegrates old limitations and blockages.

The light dissolves the darkness, replacing fear and limiting thoughts with the courage of your convictions.

Feel each wave expanding until it fills your neck and head, filling each part of your brain until your whole head feels clear and spacious.

As you clear the dark places with this walking meditation, you literally disintegrate the artificial limitations and fears imposed on you by society and your own limiting stories. The force of your attention dissolves shadow issues, limitations that would normally keep you from achieving your splendid dreams and goals.

During this meditation—as your breath is going out—imagine the energy pushing out through your fingertips and toes, out through the balls of your feet and the palms of your hands. By the end of the walk you will see the pathway of your life with much greater personal power and clarity.

The power of your attention fills all the dark places with excitement and enthusiasm, replacing all the fears and limitations with courage and conviction. You feel powerfully connected to your world. You *know* that you can handle the toughest problems life throws at you. I love this walking meditation. I do it often, especially when I feel stuck. I always come back feeling like nothing can stop me.

CHAPTER 43

How to Breathe While Playing Hard

When a friend and I were barely intermediate skiers, we ventured out onto the west face of KT-22 at Squaw Valley. The slope was frighteningly steep at the top, with snow up to our knees. With each intense fifty yards, the slope became steeper, so steep that I had a visceral perception that we were dropping into a great maw.

We were way past where we could turn back and clearly out of our depth, commenting on the fine mess we had gotten ourselves into when we heard great whooshing sounds coming down from above. It took a moment to figure out what the sounds were.

Long before we heard the clicking of his equipment, we heard huge, determined breaths. A skier was breathing powerfully and dropping about fifteen yards with each turn as he blew past us. His head was facing straight down the steep slope, his skis carving perfect side-to-side signatures. Less than a minute after he went past us we saw him ski up to the lift a half-mile away. Wow!

Considering how irregular and deep the snow was, and how unbelievably steep, we were in awe. We took more than twenty white-knuckled minutes to descend the remaining 1,500 vertical feet.

That scene branded into my mind. It took an enormous amount of skill to do what that guy did. It also took a tremendous amount of oxygen. He had to take huge breaths to ski *at his intensity* at that altitude.

Most of us live down at lower elevations where we do not need to breathe so intensely. When you first get up on a mountain, you're still used to breathing at lower elevations. On the top of a mountain the air is thinner. There's a lot less oxygen, so you have to breathe as quickly and deeply as you can to play at expert levels. Then skiing is a lot more fun.

If, however, you are still breathing as if you were closer to sea level, you have to keep stopping every one or two hundred yards to catch your breath. Just about the time you start to get your rhythm you are out of breath. You only get a few good turns in before you are out of gas. It feels like you don't get in enough turns to become skilled. Breathing shallowly makes everything more difficult.

One more skiing story to illustrate my point: When I was forty years old, I was skiing on a Thursday at Sugar Bowl. I rode up one lift with a young guy. Our skills were about equal, and we hit it off. We wound up skiing together for the rest of the day. Toward the end of the day, when we came to the top of the last mogul field, I had to stop and catch my breath while he kept going.

When I caught up with him at the lift, I remarked about his stamina. He said, "Do your legs burn?" I said, "Yes! They do." He said, "That's good. That means you are conditioning your legs." Then he asked if my legs seized up all the way around. They did. He said. "That's bad. That means you are breathing too shallowly."

I had really focused on breathing out strong for twelve years by that time. That day I got a lesson about breathing big in sports, noticing how intensely one has to breathe to play hard. Learning how to breathe adequately allows you to ski just about any run from top to bottom without having to stop. Then your skill levels start developing much more quickly.

When you are not conditioned, breath is the *biggest* factor in performance. Breathing in as much air as possible, and as deeply as possible, fuels both your nerves and your muscles. Oxygen: you've got to have it if you want to play hard. Breathing correctly gives you the energy to move beyond what used to be your upper limits. Every part of you gets excited when you have all the energy you need to play—and keep up. When you are excited, you cannot wait to get at it.

We Are the Otters of the Universe

If you are not a natural athlete—most of us are not—you have to put some effort into breathing enough air to play at higher levels of intensity. You have to focus your awareness on breathing *big*. You have to really breathe out strong or you may not be able to keep up with the others. When you can't keep up, it makes you feel like you are losing your prowess, holding everyone back. In your discouragement, you look for reasons to quit.

We are the otters of the universe. We are naturally playful, enjoying life to the fullest. But not being able to keep up makes us feel bad about ourselves. We look for reasons to quit doing what used to be so fun and exciting. That is pretty universal.

That is probably why many older people give up doing the things that used to give their life such pizazz. There may be legitimate reasons, like the fear of doing further damage to a badly injured knee. But the humiliation of not being able to keep up is the huge issue for most of us. *That* is often the reason we quit.

Most people give up progressively more of their life as they get older until the world they create isn't fun anymore. Then they die. That is *not* the way I want to create my world. How about you? We all just make our life up. Then we live it. You don't have to throw in the towel just because you are getting older. That is just old programming. I don't buy it.

When you breathe out strong, it is easy to imagine yourself getting to the top of that hill, successfully dealing with that difficult person, having that fun adventure, facing that fear. Breathe big. Live big. The less acceptable alternative is breathe small. Live small.

When you get scared, you might start breathing shallowly. That's a normal reaction, but it takes you out of the game. Take one or two cleansing breaths to break the old patterns. Then, start breathing out strong. As you break out of the pattern of fear, you discover that what had previously intimidated you may well be within your natural abilities.

Breathing out strong gives you the courage and conviction to dream big, to accomplish magnificent dreams—to keep taking your courageous "first steps" on the hero's journey.

SECOND HABIT

- CHAPTER 44 -

Stand Tall

Correct posture and breathing out strong empowers you. Together they *continually* improve the clarity of your consciousness for the rest of your life. Every cell gets powerfully energized. And every cell can communicate clearly with every other cell through all your powerful circulatory systems. All your energy systems can run full on—making all the wisdom of your bodymind accessible to you. These first two habits create a stable foundation. They provide enough *stable* energy to provide you with the confidence to courageously live the hero's journey.

The purpose of all postural considerations boils down to focusing your awareness in "hara" (just below your navel and at the front of your 4th lumbar vertebra). Dancers and martial artists move from this point, whether or not they know it as "hara." You cannot do spin moves, perform complex dance movements or have good balance without having your center of gravity at this point.

You want to learn these habits now. You don't think old people whose bad posture has them so debilitated just *started* moving that way, do you? No! They started moving in ways that gave up their prowess long ago. You are always getting better or worse, more powerful or puny. Time just adds your efforts up. How you feel right now—good or bad—is the end result of all your habits.

You don't have to struggle through life with a posture that makes you old before your time. You can enjoy a life that is fun and exciting, living each year in the upper realms where you have enough energy and stamina to attain the life of your dreams.

Chapter 36 introduced the four rules of posture because correct posture is essential for breathing powerfully. Let's go over them once more, this time in greater detail:

1. *Breathe out strong.* Feel your abdominal muscles work, which strengthens your core. Then feel your lower abdomen expand as your diaphragm fills your lungs full of air. You can let your chest expand upward at the *end* of the inbreath.

2. *Lift up your sternum,* letting your shoulders be relaxed and free. With your sternum lifting up, you do not squander your life force with excessive side-to-side motion while you are walking, or lead with your head out forward. These first two rules stabilize your core. They resolve at least 70 percent of what can go wrong in posture, gait, lifting, or going up and down hills or stairs.

3. Wiggle your neck and shoulders so they loosen up. My wife calls it "loosy goosy shoulders and neck." Then *let your head float up to its sweet spot* where it takes the minimum amount of energy to hold it erect. Your forehead rocks just slightly forward, so if you had a miner's lamp on your forehead, its light would shine on the ground about forty-five feet (15 meters) in front of you. Your ears should line up overtop of your shoulder socket.

4. *Keep your feet parallel* when you are walking or standing, even though it might not feel natural at first. This causes your inner (medial) muscles to develop, not only in your legs, but in your pelvis and up into the front and back of your low back vertebrae. This is very important, because the medial muscles enhance your prowess *in every sport.*

Walk Like This

If you go for a ten-minute walk in correct posture, you will literally walk most of the misalignments out of your spine and extremities. But if you walk around slumping with your feet toeing out, you walk all those pesky misalignments right back in.

When walking, land on the midpoint of your feet, not on your heels. Feel the arches of your feet expressing upward as you push off at the end of your stride. As the arches of your feet become more active in your gait, you tone up all the front and back muscles of your legs, torso, and neck. Walking this way makes your whole body feel incredibly alive and turned on. Little changes like this let you rediscover the pure joy you experienced as a child just going for a walk.

Notice how magical your body feels just walking out to your car. Begin to feel your feet all the way through their contact with the ground. When you walk up stairs with your sternum lifting up, feel the opposition as the ball of your foot pushes downward, while the back of your head pushes upward. Using your body correctly gives you a whole new world of sensations to enjoy. You experience an exquisite lightness of being in your gait.

The whole architecture of your body starts making sense. All your muscles and ligaments function more effortlessly. Every year your energy levels increase dramatically. As you move with whole-body awareness, you experience the grace of a cat with all your senses present in the moment. Whole body awareness, the awareness of your whole body in its totality, *is* spiritual awareness. It is mindfulness.

Just the act of sitting up straight or standing tall wakes you from a spell. It wakes you back to the present moment just like breathing out strong does. Both habits keep waking you up from the subtle spells you were not previously aware of being in. Once you break free of the slumping posture that reproduces all the old mental/emotional traumas from your past, you move—and experience life—like an authentic woman or man, free from society's conditioning, free from the limitations of your old stories about who you have been or what you can't do.

CHAPTER 45

Reclaiming the Magic You Felt as a Child

How you move in your body can feel magical, or slowly destroy you, plunging you ever deeper into a self-exiled world of drudgery and effort. As you learn to walk and move correctly, you recapture that magical feeling in your body, the pure joy of movement you experienced as a child. It is not gone forever.

Your everyday movements can take you there. It's like falling in love all over again.

Do you remember how exciting and fun it felt to do simple movements when you were a child? The thrill of deftly avoiding the dodge ball during recess? The joy of feeling you could run like the wind? The first time you rode your bicycle without your father running along beside you?

A fond childhood memory I have is fearlessly jumping barefoot over my mother's big old thorny pyracantha bush at the end of the day when the summer heat gave way to the magical twilight time. I remember feeling light as a feather, like the physical constraints that held me earthbound were loosened, and I could run like the wind.

As physical and emotional traumas built up over the years, I lost the magic of my body. As I healed my injuries, actively living the seven habits and the other recommendations in this book, I rediscovered the child-like wonder of doing simple movements with my body. Even a short walk brings me incredible joy.

How You Incarnate Trauma Into Your Body

Every trauma you accept into your body affects how you move through life. You take a hard fall off your bike. The person you love falls in love with your best friend. One by one, you collect mental, emotional, and physical traumas and incarnate them into your body. Your traumas take on a life of their own. Your posture and breathing become compromised. You lose the magic of walking. You surrender your childhood innocence. Most people think this is the natural effect of aging. It is not.

Each injury you have taken into your body alters the way you move. You stand and move in ways that accurately reflect your cumulative traumas. With every step you take, all the ways you allow your posture to slump re-create your entire history of trauma. Because "that's the way you walk," the traumas begin to seem like a permanent part of your makeup . You identify with them, give them names like "my bad knee," "my bum shoulder."

Each new trauma you take into your body causes you to give up a little more of your power. One step at a time, your current posture unconsciously reflects—*and re-creates*—all the traumas you have collected during your life.

You allow the injuries to become "so you" that you could easily believe they are a permanent part of your body. The injuries insinuate themselves into your belief systems, where they compromise your values and principles. You start to suspect that you don't deserve goodness, that life always brings pain and sorrow, and hundreds of other assumptions your injuries tend to project into the matrix of your life.

The more you internalize injuries by breathing shallowly or slumping, the more you start to believe that childhood innocence is naïve. After awhile, the temporary limitations to your life seem permanent. *This* is how you incarnate them.

Walking becomes a chore you have to do to get you to your destination. So you park as close as you can wherever you go and begrudge the short distances you have to walk. You take the elevator instead of walking one or two flights of stairs. Does anything seem wrong with this picture?

There is a better way. Just walking out to your car with an erect, fluid posture, or walking down a flight of stairs without having to look down at your feet becomes an adventure. You feel that sense of adventure in every cell in your body—like you did as a child. Every moment, every step you take, your own posture can be fun while simultaneously healing you. With each step you reprogram your body back to true. You heal yourself—or destroy yourself—one step at a time.

- CHAPTER 46 -

Circulation is Everything

Your spine is the core of your being. *Everything* works around it. Your body is mostly energy and consciousness. You have fourteen powerful circulatory systems that flow up and down your spine and up and down your arms and legs. They are completely dependent on the integrity your spine and skeleton provide. Without good posture, none of your body's exquisite functions work well. When you have good posture, every cell in your whole body can easily communicate with every other cell through all of your powerful circulatory systems.

Your spine reacts to the same laws of physics as a span bridge like the Golden Gate Bridge or the Brooklyn Bridge. Like the cables that suspend a bridge, ninety percent of the strength of your spine comes from its three primary curves, the concave curves of your neck and low back and the convex curve of your upper torso. If you lose ten percent of a primary curve, you lose 10% of its strength, and all the stresses increase by 10%. If the primary curve of your neck or low back goes ramrod straight (100% loss of curve), your stress is increased by 100%, even when you are sitting or lying down.

Any loss of your three primary curves translates into scoliosis (lateral curvature to the right or left). The spinal misalignments cause disruptions to the life force going into some of your organs. They cause one arm or leg to become weaker than the other, with all kinds of joint problems. Your whole body is thrown out of balance.

Even if the primary curves of your spinal column have been compromised, you can restore them to good health with correct posture, chiropractic care, massage and help from other holistic doctors. When all twenty-four vertebrae in your spine are moving fluidly and in harmony with each other, you naturally experience health and well-being through-out your entire body. You experience that health one step, one movement at a time.

Bad Posture Twangs Your Nerves

If you watched an x-ray video (video fluoroscopy) of your spinal column—while walking with incorrect posture—you would be appalled by the dysfunction. Just letting one foot toe out about five degrees and your head project a half inch forward *forces* a number of vertebrae in your neck, thoracic spine and low back to misalign, with every step! When they are misaligned, their pathological movement patterns are quite destructive. Faulty posture also causes a number of your extremity bones to misalign, with each step.

A misaligned vertebra usually only gets jammed up on one side. With one step the misaligned vertebra can move pretty well, but with every other step it can't. So it rebounds in the opposite direction. This is what chiropractors observe when they do motion palpation of your spine.

As you are walking, the direction where the misaligned vertebra can't move correctly causes it to snap back in an aberrant motion. To nerves exiting your spine at that level, the affect is like a heavy tree branch in a storm slapping the power line coming into your house. That twangs the nerves that come out where the vertebra is misaligned, sending disruptive power surges down that nerve.

Just as power surges fry circuits in your home electronics, in the body they cause organs, muscles and ligaments to similarly overheat, become inflamed, and function in an impaired manner. Power surges are every bit as disruptive to every part of your body as they are to your sensitive electronic equipment.

If these power surges are to the nerves that go to your stomach, liver or other organs, those organs suffer immensely. Spinal misalignments, caused by bad posture, cause most of your health problems.

Each misaligned vertebra also creates disruptions to all the powerful circulatory systems that pass by that particular vertebra. Depending on how you count them, you have fourteen powerful circulatory systems. Each circulatory system is uniquely different from the others, and all are completely essential to your health and well being. *All of them are disrupted in pathological ways by misalignments.* Most of your health-related problems are caused by, or greatly exacerbated by, spinal and extremity misalignments.

None of your misalignments are permanent, even if you have reproduced them one step at a time for many years. If you go for a twenty-minute walk with correct posture, you literally walk most of the misalignments out of your spinal column and out of your extremities.

Every step you take can be healing to your body. Imagine an African woman walking elegantly with a heavy weight balanced on her head, the undulating movements of her spine in perfect harmony with her gait—fluid and smooth. Feel these movements in your own body as you move. Become aware of the perfection of your own spine.

A motion picture x-ray of your spinal column while you are walking in correct posture has incredible beauty and symmetry to its motion. If you could somehow look from above, straight down into your spine while you were walking, all the combined movements of your vertebrae create a pattern that looks like a DNA helix. When you move in good posture, you truly are poetry in motion.

Walking correctly gets the knots out of your rope. Those pesky symptoms, which seem so permanent, turn out to be temporary. Go back to bad posture and you walk all of the misalignments—*and all of your symptoms*—back into your body.

Fortunately, the misalignments you cannot "walk out" respond quite well to chiropractic care. Doctors of Chiropractic are specialists at realigning your spine, which is an essential element of good health.

- CHAPTER 47 -

Your Body Language

Most of your communication with others is nonverbal. How you stand and move is a huge part of how you communicate with the world around you. Exciting people stand and move like they are excited by life. Depressed people stand and move, well, like they are depressed. It is really difficult to maintain a decent depression when you are standing in good posture. Posture is *that* powerful.

Your posture tells others how you want to be treated—how you want to be considered. It says, "This is how I see myself." Everyone responds to your posture, whether they are conscious of it or not. Consider what your posture says to everyone about you?

Good posture is elegant. It's like a strong clear voice. It garners respect. Every moment that you are in good posture, you are stronger and more flexible. Every cell operates at its fullest potential. You develop greater endurance. Simply going for a walk *in good posture* makes your whole body feel better. It's easier to work stuff out.

Elegant posture creates an aura of understated sophistication. In an interview, I heard Sophia Loren being asked the secret to her timeless beauty. Her immediate response was simply, "Posture." Elegant posture says "I occupy this space with my presence." When you walk around with your chest slumped it causes your head to fall down and jut forward. Your implied statement is, "Who I am or what I want is not relevant." Elegant posture is neither arrogant nor is it irrelevant.

When you see someone who is slumped down, your unconscious reaction is to discount that person in some way. Their posture does not attract respect. Your first impression—and subsequent judgment of that person—occurs long before you have time to think about it. How eager would you be to hire someone who slumped down and did not appear confident when you asked them pointed questions? Ask yourself: how much trust would you invest in that person? You do that unconsciously, whether you are aware of it or not.

People notice your posture. How you sit and stand, and whether or not you are present has profound effects on people's assessment of you. They respond to your facial expressions, the tone of your voice, and how open your posture is to them. Based on what they observe, they make instantaneous decisions about trusting you. Their assessment affects how they will respond to you, and how much energy and respect they will commit to you—usually below their conscious awareness.

When your posture looks good, you feel good. All your circulatory systems run wide open. Your life force expresses its fullest potential. Your body's innate intelligence has clear, open channels for all its communication throughout your entire body. Every cell can communicate clearly with every other cell and maintain homeostasis (the simple definition of health). You are feeling all your feelings and breathing enough energy to live the life of your dreams.

This clear, powerful communication creates a dynamic powerful state of health within your body, mind, and spirit. You are waking up and living more of your life wide awake. Your health shines through. Your self-esteem increases each year. Your bodymind processes all its impressions more efficiently. You make better decisions. All your parts work better. People notice.

- CHAPTER 48 -

Bad Posture Holds Pain and Suffering

Every incorrect posture is a primal way of giving our power away. We usually begin creating our postures in early childhood. Society conditions us to fear letting others see our light and beauty. It is easier to let them see our faults. That's called "fitting in."

The trouble is, slumping creates a mechanism that instantly brings all your old conditioning patterns to the forefront of your thoughts. Each faulty posture is a repository of unresolved feelings, actions, and beliefs.

The instant you slump, your mind transports you back to the earliest memory *this posture* holds a charge about. The slumping posture contains sensory/motor patterns of unresolved pain and suffering. Your mind instantly overlays those patterns onto what your eyes are looking at. Those patterns effectively overshadow the reality and beauty of this moment.

If this sounds familiar, it is, because slumping causes us to go unconscious the same way as breathing shallowly does.

I had a vivid experience of this a few years ago. I was building rock walls at my home to make terraces on the steep slope. I was doing everything in good posture.

I love having the time to work in my yard. I was having a good time that whole summer building rock walls to create walkways and gardens. For some reason—as I was pushing the wheelbarrow uphill to get another load of rocks—I let my chest slump down and my head go forward. The very next instant my mind projected how unfair it is that I have to work *so hard* at the office, and now here at home.

I threw the wheelbarrow down and busted out laughing. I asked out loud, "What was *that?*" Here I was doing something that I loved at my home, and had probably longed to have the time to do for lifetimes. All summer I had been breathing abdominally and doing all the rockwork with good posture. I love doing this kind of work. I only slumped for an instant, and my mind spun out such a dire story. What a great lesson!

These concepts are universal. Any way or anytime that you slump causes you to go unconscious. Some postures, like letting your chest collapse so that your head projects forward, are such common ways of giving your power away that they hold the history of not only *your* pain and suffering, but that of the entire culture you were born into.

You cannot stay in the present moment when your are slumping or breathing shallowly. Even when you are willfully doing your best to stay in the present moment, the slumping posture causes your mind to instantly project old memories that have unresolved emotional charge over the top of what you are doing. The projections take you out of the present moment, plunging you into some artificial construct of the past or the future, where you have no traction to manifest your heart's desires. The aliveness and potential of the present moment gets overshadowed.

The only place where you have any power is here and now. Archimedes said: "Give me a long enough lever, and a place to stand, and I can move the world." It is easy to forget about the *place to stand* when you are busy trying to move the world. The place to stand is here, now—present-time awareness. Correct posture has none of the stifling limitations of the past or fears of the future. There is only now.

- CHAPTER 49 -

Postural Awareness is Spiritual Awareness

Most people are not aware of doing things, they just do them: they do the dishes, but feel no real connection to the joyous meal that was eaten on those dishes. They are just trying to get through difficult situations, instead of truly experiencing all of the nuances of each moment. They drive to destinations, but are often so lost in thought that they hardly remember the journey. People want to skip past so many parts of their life that whole portions of their life are unmemorable. They are not really here.

The awareness of being aware brings you fully into the present moment. This moment—every moment—has such richness. There is so much enchantment in all of the moments that most of us are oblivious to. The eternity of each moment holds the promises of your hopes and dreams.

Every moment that you focus on what your heart loves creates the love you experience in the next moment. The more you love, the more loving your world becomes. You cannot change what is, but you *always* have the choice of how you relate to what is. One of the great Zen masters used to ask his students, "Is there anything in this moment you would change?"

As you return to your natural state, which is peace of mind, you return to the Garden of Eden. Actually, your spirit has never left the Garden. The Garden of Eden is now. It was now. It will always be now. *There is only now.* Everything else is illusory.

Heaven and hell exist right here on earth. One moment at a time, you choose to live in heaven—or hell. You can slump into that tired old posture, and instantly your brain takes over. In the time it takes to blink, you get swept out of the present moment and into one of your old stories. That's where all your pain and suffering exists. That's where your own personal hell exists, where it has always existed.

184

Although peace of mind is the natural state of your spirit, you have to be in the present moment to access it. Good posture and abdominal breathing continually draw you back to the present moment. When you are in the present moment, there is usually nothing you would change, so your spirit's peace of mind just naturally begins to push up to the surface of your consciousness like water bubbles up from a spring.

When you "get" that *this moment holds the potential of all your desires*, you can let go of the past, the future—and all your stories. Breathing out strong and moving through life in an elegant posture naturally brings your heart online where it directs your mind and enhances your life. You are the star of your own movie. After all, you are the one writing the script. As the director, you choose where the sets and locations are, and, one way or another, you create your own world. Then you live in it. There is nothing enlightened about being an extra, or a spectator in your own movie. And yet, that is what a lot of us do.

Many of us stand at the sidelines of life, so distracted by the stories our unruly mind generates that we don't *realize* that we can be a part of the action. I spent a lot of years standing on the sidelines thinking "someone" should do what I secretly wanted to do, but wasn't standing tall and breathing up the courage to do myself.

There are many other ways that help to bring your awareness back to the present moment. Some of the ways include appreciating the texture of what you are touching, experiencing pleasure in the warmth of the sun, noticing the sensuous pleasure of the wind's caress, or feeling the texture of warm soapy water on a dish you are rinsing—simply enjoying the process of what you are doing as if it were the only thing happening in the world.

Focusing your awareness on the simple sensory perceptions of mundane tasks brings your focus back to experiencing the present moment. All the wealth of the world is accessible in this moment. Spiritual awareness begins with whole body awareness, and how you interface with your environment.

CHAPTER 50

Pain Isn't Always What You Think it Is

When you have a breakthrough in consciousness that transforms your life in more loving, truthful, decisive ways of being in the world—that breakthrough causes your body to reject the neuromuscular patterns that reflect your old way of being. The old pattern no longer belongs in your body or your life. It doesn't fit anymore.

Your bodymind always resonates with its highest truth. Always. So, when you have the breakthrough, your bodymind must release the old pattern. As the old pattern releases, it moves out to the surface of your awareness. Your physical experience of releasing old neuromuscular patterns is translated into acute pain and dysfunction.

When patients come in with situations like this, they say, "This just *happened* to me." Even though they think it's a new injury, they can't come up with any way that they hurt themselves. It's usually painful enough to *be* a new injury. It takes education for them to understand that *this* just might be old stuff releasing.

For example, imagine you have a breakthrough where you finally feel safe enough to completely give your love to someone without secretly holding anything back. Within a very short period of time, your bodymind will release the old patterns that represented all the ways you previously withheld your love. If I were your doctor, I would likely see the following patterns in your body:

- Old sprains to the muscles that make energy for your heart and heart protector would surface, usually as intense pain. The origin and insertion of the muscles involved would need to be massaged out so they can resolve and heal.

- misalignments, often painful, to the 2nd and 3rd thoracic vertebrae and ribs where the nerves from your spine go to your heart and heart protector. There are usually misalignments to the lower lumbar vertebrae where the nerves go to the heart protector muscles (adductors, piriformis, multifidus and the three big buttocks muscles).
- inflammation to the meridians of the heart and heart protector

Until you have the breakthrough, none of that will be symptomatic or apparent, not even to a very competent doctor. The acute pain and dysfunction only surfaces *after* you experience a breakthrough, after you step out of old dysfunctional ways of being.

So, *you* have the breakthrough, then I, or some competent doctor comes along after the parade with the pooper-scooper. We realign your spine, or help you work out the kinks, and help your bodymind accommodate to the new, more efficient neuromuscular pattern. As your body begins to work more efficiently in the new consciousness you have stepped up to, the pain disappears.

We all have a great many old dysfunctional beliefs stored in our bodies as faulty postural patterns. They show up as ways we hold back from really living the life we desire. All the ways we slump or breathe shallowly are direct reflections of old disempowering beliefs, values, attitudes and assumptions we are hanging onto.

When we have a breakthrough that moves us into a more functional way of being, *that* changes everything. After the breakthrough, our body must release the old neuromuscular patterns, patterns that previously reproduced those old dysfunctional beliefs and values with every step we took. Releasing old neuromuscular patterns rewrites our DNA, transforming our beliefs and values in ways that reflect the new, more aware way of being.

As you learn to live your life at the upper realms—where life is a lot more fun and exciting—you will face a lot of healing crises. They are often exciting breakthroughs in consciousness, disguised as pain. Pain isn't always what you think it is.

- CHAPTER 51 -

The Miracle of Correct Posture

One summer many years ago, my girlfriend and I stopped in Florence, Oregon on a vacation and spent the night in a nice little motel on the beach. I woke up at first light, hurting in about a dozen places from old injuries I had lived with for years. I could not stay in bed one minute longer, so I went for a walk on the beach.

After walking for about a mile, I started really feeling sorry for myself because of all the pain from my old injuries. Suddenly I felt someone behind me! I looked back. I could see several miles and no one was there. What *was* there when I turned around were my tracks in the sand. They looked awful.

I doubled back about a hundred yards so I could study my tracks, as if I were tracking some other person. I had just begun learning about posture, and had recently studied the work of a Swiss chiropractor, Dr. F. W. H. Illi, who performed more than twenty thousand motion-picture X-ray studies of people walking on a treadmill. Now I could field test this knowledge.

Studying my own gait in the third person freed me up to be more discerning as I looked at this guy's tracks. His right foot toed out about twenty degrees. That made the right ankle wobble outward and then back inward both at the heel strike and again at the midstance of each right footstep. Then the ball of his foot twisted outward at the push-off phase of his gait obliterating the front two-thirds of each right footprint. All those wobbles and twist-off movements were making this guy's right knee perform a lot of movements a knee is not designed to do—with every step! His right knee *had* to be having a lot of pain. What a coincidence, so did mine!

188

Meanwhile the footprint of his left foot was perfectly intact. I could have made a uniform plaster cast of each one of the left footprints from that sandy beach.

As I wondered why he twisted his right foot laterally, I realized that letting his right foot toe out shortened the stride of his right leg by at least five-eighths of an inch. If he didn't make the twist-off movement with that foot, he would be walking in a big circle to the right. After a couple days of walking, this guy would end up right back where he started. Seeing that scene in my mind made me burst out laughing.

After studying my tracks, I decided to walk with both feet parallel. When I had walked for a hundred yards, I stopped and rechecked my footprints. My left foot was facing straight ahead, but my right foot was still toed out—just not as *far* as it was before. It was only toed out by about seven degrees. But, since it was still toed out, the right footprint still had the four troublesome wobbles and the nasty obliteration of two-thirds of each footprint.

I made both of my feet parallel while I was standing there looking down at them, then I stood up straight. That made my whole right leg feel stiff and unnatural, like it had a steel rod running down the outside of it. My right foot felt like it was pigeon-toed (toed inward) by about seven degrees—even though it was facing straight ahead.

Making my right foot track parallel felt weird—totally unnatural! Part of me thought "this *can't* be right." But I decided that no matter how unnatural my leg felt, by the grace of God, I was going to walk down that beach with my feet parallel.

Every hundred yards I rechecked my footprints until I was certain that my right foot had not reverted. Both footprints were perfect. I could have lifted a perfect plaster cast of either foot. Yes! Then I just walked, enjoying the magnificent sunrise and the sea.

After walking a couple miles, I stopped dead in my tracks. I suddenly realized that *all* my aches and pains had vanished. All of them! They were all gone. On a one-to-ten pain scale, I previously had ten areas that hurt constantly at seven or eight. The back of my right knee always ached.

For the previous ten years, in fact, I had been able to predict the ups and downs of weather with uncanny accuracy by where and how much my right knee hurt.

Now all my aches and pains were completely gone. Even all the minor symptoms I had lived with for years, like my constant stiff neck, a dull slight headache that was always there (and sometimes went nova), and my constant stomach discomfort. They were gone. When you are used to living with a lot of aches and pains, having them all disappear will definitely get your attention!

I had the realization that I literally walked all the misalignments out of my spine, just by walking with correct posture. When my spine realigned, all my organs and muscles recovered the energy they needed and all my symptoms disappeared. *That* got my attention. That moment on the beach was an epiphany.

That was the day I experienced, within my own body, *the miracle of correct posture*. I do not banter the word miracle about lightly. Yahoo!

Why Keep Your Feet Parallel?

There is a reason why boxers and high-level tennis players do not walk with their feet toed out like a duck. When your feet are splayed out, you give up too much prowess. The slight shifting of weight you must do before you can move increases the reaction time of all your movements. Your timing is always off—just by a split second. But that is enough to lose the game or sprain an ankle.

The essence of posture is to develop stable core musculature. You weaken your core when you let one or both feet toe out. *You strengthen your core by keeping your feet parallel—and breathing out strong.* Toeing a foot outward weakens the inner muscles and ligaments of not only that leg but into your pelvis and lower torso, both front and back. When a foot is toed out, you make it impossible for the medial (inner) muscles on that side to tone up. That forces the outer muscles to overwork, so they stay tighter.

When you strengthen the medial leg and pelvis muscles, it enhances your physical prowess in *every* sport and physical activity. As their strength and stamina increase, your lower body strength and balance improves. As you strengthen your core, your body starts trusting that you won't hurt it (by overdoing with bad posture). In return, it gives you more power and flexibility. *You must earn your body's trust.*

Now is a good time to check out your legs. Stand with your feet the width of your hips apart, and parallel. Bend down and feel the muscular tonus of your inner thigh muscles compared to your outer thigh muscles. Are your inner muscles as toned as the outer ones? They will be after about a year of walking with your feet parallel.

When one (or both) of your feet toe out, just your normal "acts of daily living" keep pulling your lower back and pelvic bones out of alignment. Your knees and ankles keep going out of alignment. The pain and dysfunction in your low back can become quite disabling.

Most people experience frequent low back pain. They sit, stand, and move in such unbalanced ways that it's inevitable. If you keep standing and moving in bad posture, your acts of daily living keep misaligning your bones. This is predictable.

When you make a habit of improving your posture each year, every part of your body continually remakes itself at ever-higher levels of organization. In the dance between "form and function," good posture continually *remodels* your bones into more efficient shapes year after year. Your entire musculo-skeletal system constantly improves. You dramatically see the effects of posture—good or bad—on x-rays.

Every minute of your life, approximately 300 million cells die—and are replaced. Every minute! As your posture improves each year, *remodeling is steadily transforming you to higher levels of organization.* As new cells are born you get to experience the magic of remodeling. Every year you look and feel better.

The marriage of form (your musculoskeletal system) and function (correct posture) is a dynamic and powerful process. It is ever changing. Good posture is transforming and empowering. On the other hand, every moment that you let gravity push you down into slumping postures causes your bones to break down further. They deteriorate into arthritic spurring. Vertebrae flatten out, discs degenerate. Every organ and system suffers. Your health inevitably worsens.

Since the only constant is transformation and change, good posture makes remodeling work *for you*. Correct posture and gait continually reshape your musculoskeletal form into the most efficient shape possible to handle *whatever* your life activities demand. Hard work can and should be healing. As a seventy-year-old adult, your spinal column and extremity bones can have the appearance—and the health—of a thirty-year-old. Good posture empowers every aspect of your life as you age.

Exceptions to Keeping Your Feet Parallel

Sometimes, when squatting down to lift something off the floor (like a sleeping baby), it is best to let your feet toe out, with your knees aiming the same direction as your toes. You can squat down over the baby, pull the baby up to your chest, lean forward until your nose is over your toes, and stand up elegantly. If your hips are free, and your knees are in relation with your toes, it is not as important that your feet are parallel.

When you are standing at the sink or the cutting board—and your lower back gets tired—you can let your feet toe out. That way, you can lean your knees into the cupboard, which relaxes your knees and lower back. What is important is that there is freedom in all your joints.

CHAPTER 52

Your Body's Fourteen Circulatory Systems

It is important to understand how your body functions. According to quantum physics, the matter of which you are made is 99.999% energy, and only 0.001% matter. In the marriage between form and function, you are almost entirely energy and consciousness. Poor posture compromises all your body's powerful energy systems.

Depending on how you count them, you have fourteen very powerful yet completely different circulatory systems that run up and down your spinal column, and up and down your arms, and up and down your legs. They include: your sympathetic and parasympathetic nervous systems; arteries and veins; the lymphatic system's flow of serous fluid that continually bathes all your cells, and its lymph nodes that filter out pathogens; acupuncture meridians that ultimately connect the nucleus of every cell to every other cell; your brain and brain stem that go down to your low back; and the cerebro-spinal fluid that nourishes the brain and brain stem.

On more subtle levels your feelings flow throughout your body, as does the more subtle energy of your spirit. Your attitudes and values are radiated out from your meridians to create a stable auric field (aura) around your body, which insulates you from having to feel everyone's pain or to have to listen to all their thoughts when they are near you.

You have subtle energy channels called "kundalini" channels that flow up and down your spinal column and the bones of your arms and legs. The kundalini channels connect all your chakras (higher sense organs of your most subtle body) together. As osteopathic doctors have discovered, there is a subtle "tide" of your body, another tide of your energy field, and the most subtle tide of your spirit. *All* these powerful circulatory systems are compromised when you slump. All of them. The effects are disastrous.

Bad posture—and the misalignments they create—wreaks havoc on *all* these powerful, but delicate circulatory systems. The kinks bad posture creates seriously disrupt all your feedback mechanisms. Your life force progressively dims down.

The simplest definition of health is: every cell communicating clearly with every other cell. Your body is a completely self-regulating system. But in order to self regulate, it needs continuous feedback to and from all its circulatory systems. That communication has to happen through *all* your circulatory systems in order to achieve homeostasis (balance). That means unobstructed flow through all your circulatory systems. *You need good posture.*

Vertebrae that are pathologically misaligned (subluxations) inflict major disruptions to all your precious life forces. The longer they are out of alignment, and the greater the misalignments are, the greater the disruption to your health. A healthy, aligned spinal column is the very best form of health insurance you can buy.

Chiropractors are the most highly-trained specialists in spinal alignment. If you want to live in the upper realms of your life (instead of down at the level of struggle and effort), it really helps to have your spinal column aligned on a regular basis.

If you want to live powerfully and in good health, I wholeheartedly recommend regular chiropractic care at least once a month, ideally once per week for your entire family. Chiropractors usually adjust their own families once a week because they know how critically important it is, and how powerfully it allows their family members to live their lives. Preventative health care is like the regular maintenance that prolongs the lifespan and efficiency of your automobile. You are investing in a lifetime of well being. It is absolutely life changing.

Most of the chiropractors I know do a lot more than simply realign misaligned vertebrae, although that is vitally important. If you are working at evolving, your chiropractor can help you with much more than just aches and pains. Most chiropractors help their patients with diet, exercise, and many other aspects that are vital to maintaining a healthy lifestyle.

CHAPTER 53

"Habits Make The Man"

An achievable goal is to make your posture better each year. That will enrich your entire life. Even a halfhearted effort delivers such wonderful rewards that soon you will want more.

Look at older people who are so alive and young at heart. They stand and sit erect. They eat more fresh vegetables and fruit. Their vibrant health and vigor is the result of healthy habits. Because they are healthier, they are more active and do fun things. Because they are excited about what they do, their lives are interesting. Although they may have lived a lot of years, they are not "old." Healthy habits begin now.

Sadly, older people who are vibrant and alive are not the norm. I want to see that changed. Every day more people are waking up to the fact that spiritual awareness begins with whole-body awareness, but currently most people's version of posture is just getting from point A to point B.

I have personally tried and discarded well over two hundred "health habits." They either took way too much time for what they delivered, or they were only marginally effective. There is a lot of noise out there, information that will not stand the test of time. The habits in this book are effective throughout the entire range from helping you when you are very injured, all the way to helping you to live in the upper realms of your life, and to compete at the highest levels. The habits in this book are like taproots. They firmly connect you to the *source* of your power.

The fruits of these habits are greater health and freedom every year from now on. Every year your life gets better. As you become proficient at each level of health, you are granted access to the next higher level. Each year you gain more mastery and achieve greater fulfillment. Age empowers you, and life is a lot more fun.

CHAPTER 54

Moving Like an Authentic Woman or Man

The way we move through life reflects all our societal conditioning. For our first 18 months we emulate mom. If mom's happy we are happy. If she's sad, we are sad. If she's mad we are mad. Then we go through the terrible 2s where we say "no!" to everything we are not. At three years of age we start emulating our friends. In our teenage years we pattern on ourselves. Those are the "I, me, me" years. Hopefully we get over them when we get into our twenties. All through those years, society is heavily socializing us into thousands of ways of giving away our power.

As stated earlier, in the average family the parents say "no" to their children in about three hundred ways per day, while only saying "yes" about five times. School and church reinforce this trend. All our friends are similarly conditioned by society. By the time we are seven years old, we have so thoroughly integrated all that conditioning that we don't need anyone to tell us "no." We say it to ourselves.

All the ways we move are a graphic representations of our conditioning. All the ways we are depressed causes us to slump down and move with our head dropped down and forward. Breathing shallowly spotlights all our fears and shortcomings.

There are so many examples of how movements get compromised by your conditioning: Your job can be so stressful that the tension is pulling your shoulders up to your ears. You are feeling kind of depressed so your chest slumps down, letting your head go way forward. Or you have been taught to pull your shoulders back, making your upper torso rigid, making your thinking just as rigid. Or you are just walking around with your feet toed out and your head out forward thinking *that* is normal. Stop! Whatever you are doing—stop!

Our greatest lessons are "unlearning." We must unlearn society's conditioning if we are to think and move in an authentic manner as the true authors of our lives. One of the tools I use is "inhibition."

Inhibition, which I learned from Alexander Posture Training, means stopping whatever you are doing or about to do. *Come to a full stop!*

Here is where you bring in the tools we have been talking about. Breathe out strong. Sit or stand tall with your breastbone lifting up. Feel your head float up to the sweet spot where it takes the least amount of effort to maintain good posture. Make your feet parallel. With these simple changes, you step out of all the old conditioning patterns. You can add about fifteen shoulder shrugs and spinal twists to get the tension out of your neck and shoulders.

With good posture, all your old stories just end. All the old conditioning loses its power over you. Your mind needs a job, or it obsesses on problems. Give it the job of making sure your posture is erect and you're breathing out strong. That keeps it too busy to be running its old stories. Long periods of time go by with hardly a thought.

When you are moving like you are in charge of your own reality, you are re-writing your DNA in more empowering ways for each situation you are experiencing.

Coming to a full stop—just for a brief moment—interrupts all your unconscious patterns, extricates you from any spell you might be in, and brings you back to the present moment. This is how you unlearn (release) old societal conditioning. Then you are free to move and think and function in an authentic manner as the author, director and star of your own unique world. You only have to pause for an instant to free yourself from patterns of "socialization."

How to Walk Up Stairs and Hills

Imagine you are standing at the bottom of a grand old spiral staircase. One of your friends on the balcony calls for you to come up. As you start up the stairs—stop! The way you are beginning to move most likely holds all your old conditioning patterns. You are probably leaning so far forward that by the time you get to the top of the stairs you are mentally/ emotionally discombobulated. When all your muscles and ligaments get out of balance, nothing makes sense—not just in your body but in all the ways you experience your entire world.

Most people lean so far forward going up a hill or stairs that their weight is as much as twelve inches in front of their kneecaps. That makes some muscles have to exert an inordinate amount of force to keep them from toppling forward. Other muscles become too flaccid. The unbalanced muscles create an uncomfortable disorientation to your "sense of self" that is so disconcerting that, if you are like most people, you would rather wait for the elevator, even for a single flight of stairs. That's how I used to feel, why I hated taking the stairs. Now I *love* the stairs.

Anytime you start up stairs, Stop! Breathe out strong. Stand up straight. Notice how far forward you had been leaning before you stopped.

Lift up your sternum. Relax your neck and shoulders. Feel the opposition of your feet pushing downward while your head floats up to its sweet spot. That's way different, isn't it? Now it feels magical walking up the stairs.

Correct posture while performing your mundane activities can turn your normal activities into joyful movements you experienced when you were a child. All your muscles feel balanced. The experience of "whole-body awareness" is exciting.

Walking Down Hills

As you walk downhill or on uneven ground, settle down into your pelvis with each step, keeping your head and upper torso erect. It is like you are starting to sit down with each step. You can really feel your body's weight settling into your legs with each step. That makes your gait really stable and fluid.

Very few people move through life with grace and dignity. If the ground is not perfectly flat, most people look down at their feet the whole way. This moves their center of gravity up around their neck. It's like they are walking down the hill with a heavy child on their shoulders, making them unbalanced and unstable.

Anytime you are looking down, you are top heavy. How could you not be with your center of gravity up around your neck? Then if your foot slips on loose soil or leaves, your posture is so precarious that you slide all over the place. It makes you feel unstable. You can easily fall on your buttocks or your back—bad form.

One day my wife, some friends, and I were hiking down a steep trail into the South Yuba River Canyon. I could hear them sliding around. Without looking back I said, "Quit looking at your feet." My wife asked, "How could you possibly know what I was doing? You weren't even looking." I said, "Because I can hear you sliding all over the place. Feel like your pelvis is starting to sit down with each step." Immediately they all quit slipping and sliding.

How wonderful it is to have loved ones that help us with our unconscious places. My wife tells me when I am starting to walk with my right foot toed out or letting my chest slump over. When we get tired, stressed out, or have a lot on our mind, it's easy to revert back to old postures that reflect our problems. That's when we go unconscious.

If you are negotiating stairs or hills every day and are looking down at your feet with every step, you may believe you have chronic knee problems. Instead, you may actually have a temporary gait problem where *each day, one step at a time, you are micro-traumatizing your knees.*

Walking downhill correctly removes the traumatic impact from your knees. Seemingly permanent knee problems begin to clear up. Sometimes you need to rub out the origin and insertion of sprained (weak/swollen) muscles or ligaments to heal them, and may have misalignments that need to be realigned so you can recover from these problems.

My knees used to be badly injured. A combination of chiropractic care, good posture, and massage techniques (directed at the origin and insertion of sprained muscles and ligaments) restored them and brought them back to normal healthy function. I love having my knees back in good working order.

When you are breathing out strong, your spirit settles down into hara, energizing the chakras at the balls of your feet called Bubbling Wells, which grants you a large field of awareness around your feet. You feel where your feet are, without having to look down at them, even with thick-soled shoes. You *know* where they are.

Walking downhill with an erect posture only lets you see the tips of your feet with your peripheral vision as they are landing. Your mind quickly learns to memorize the foot or two of the path right in front of you as you go. Memorizing that part of the hill as you go will be a new skill to learn, but it becomes natural very quickly. It is all right to look down when there are dangerous obstacles. You just don't want to be looking down at your feet the whole way down the hill or down the stairs.

When you keep your upper torso erect and feel like you are sitting down with each step, you are walking down the hill correctly. Then, if a foot slides, your balance is barely compromised. Your recovery of balance is immediate. You are "sure footed," no matter the terrain. Walking downhill in this manner settles you into a state of balance that is both safe and comfortable. When your mind is occupied with maintaining correct posture, it ceases its chatter.

Walk Down Stairs Without Looking at Your Feet

Most people look at their feet on every stair step, which is not graceful. Walking downstairs without having to look at your feet is exhilarating. It is also incredibly elegant. You have the power. This is the way heads of state and movie stars go down stairs when all eyes are upon them. Who teaches them that?

Walking down the stairs like this gives you the opportunity to overcome your fear of falling. When you are not looking at your feet, you get to face that fear. When you feel the fear, without giving it dialogue, its effect dissolves into nothingness. Feel the fear and do it anyway.

The key is breathing out strong from hara, which energizes bubbling wells chakras and lets you feel where each foot is as it lands, feeling the stair tread, and feeling alive. Your feet are experiencing full contact, the way an animal moves. You are gaining greater awareness and facing your fear of falling. The feeling of liberation is incredible.

When you can walk down an entire flight of stairs without having to look down at your feet, your body feels the thrill of it. It's exciting. This is another way you regain the simple pleasure, the magic you experienced as a child just doing simple movements.

CHAPTER 55

The Symphony of Your Movements

You "think" through your organs, but you also think through the muscles that make energy for your organs. With an erect, fluid posture, your movements become like a symphony. All your opposing muscles and interconnecting fasciae are toned up, working in concert, and contributing their harmonious sounds to the symphony your body makes as it is propelled through space.

When all of your muscles are joyfully participating together, it is so easy to think powerful thoughts about your life. Your bodymind has all the energy, stamina and clarity it needs to keep taking those courageous first steps. Your mind becomes so enchanted with its symphony of posture that it ceases its chatter. As a result, your spirit gets to play in the material world.

To paraphrase Isadora Duncan, whose inspirational work in the early twentieth century formed the basis of modern dance: I don't want to teach our children how to dance, I rather want to free their bodies so they can find their own dance within.

Settling Down into Your Bones: Gravity Wins

Until we learn better, most of us let gravity push us down. We walk heavily down into our bones, often leaning forward and exhibiting a lot of side-to-side movement where we sort of fall onto each foot. We land hard on our heels, letting our upper torso slump down and our head fall forward. Often our feet toe out, allowing the inner leg and lower torso muscles to go on welfare. The arches of our feet tend to flatten down over time, causing our great toes to misalign inward.

Walking heavily down into your feet creates misalignments in your spine and your extremity bones which worsen with age. Over time, x-rays show misaligned bones developing gnarly-looking arthritic changes. The slumping posture causes the shock-absorbing discs between each vertebra to dehydrate and lose more of their height each year, making you shorter as you age. Have you noticed how most old people shrink? This need not happen to you.

When you walk with that heavy posture, letting gravity push you down into your bones, all your normal activities are tiring instead of energizing. Doing hard work with destructive postures causes everything to break down, and old age gets blamed.

Feel the Arches of Your Feet As You Walk

Feel the arches of your feet flexing upward with each step, like your feet are shortening. This is different than your toes gripping the earth. There is an exercise that strengthens the arch of your feet called "short foot exercise." In this exercise, you practice flexing the arches of your feet so it feels like your feet are shortening, while your toes stay relaxed. It's like gripping a towel with your feet, but with your toes relaxed. If your feet are really flat, this exercise may be more difficult but the results are very beneficial.

When you walk with your arches flexing upward, it enlivens all of your front/back muscles. *They all tone up*—not just in your lower legs—but also in your upper legs, pelvis, upper torso and neck—even the muscles up into your head. With each magical step you can feel a whole-body aliveness. *All* your muscles tone up and participate together in a joyous symphony. Walking takes on whole new levels of pleasure and excitement.

As you are walking in this magical way, the enhanced tonus of all your muscles working together propels you forward without dissipating your energy into wasteful side-to-side movements. You dramatically improve your balance. The more you walk with your arches flexing upward, the better your balance becomes—at any age. Deteriorating balance is not "the aging process." It's just poor posture.

Whole-body awareness is spiritual awareness. It is mindfulness. All your muscles working together in harmony enhance the clarity of your consciousness significantly. Your self-esteem is enhanced. You progressively become the promise of yourself.

Try an experiment: First, walk heavily down into your bones, letting your weight fall into your feet. Notice how you sort of *fall* into wasteful side-to-side movements with your gait. Often your posture is slumping. If you pay attention to how you are feeling when you walk like this, you will notice that your feelings are considerably less than joyous.

In the next part of the experiment: go for a walk where you are lifting up into the arches of your feet. Feel the heightened awareness you feel in your entire body. Experience the aliveness of all your muscles as they tone up, all the way up the front and back of your legs, the front and back of your pelvis and torso, and even up to the crown of your head. Your whole musculoskeletal system is participating, working in harmony. You feel like you are propelled along by the purity of your design.

Your whole body feels alive to this moment. In this awakened state, you have a more intimate awareness of the space that is all around you. Your whole body feels spacious. You experience the profound sensation of knowing the entirety of your body in the same instant. There is no other moment but this moment. The totality of whole-body awareness completely occupies your brain.

Breathing out forcefully lets you feel your core muscles working. Your feet are parallel. All the muscles in your whole body are joyously participating. Your body is propelled through space, pushed along by a force unknown, yet vaguely familiar, floating in the childlike joy of pure movement. You can really get in the zone—like the magic you felt as a child—feeling the thrill of an "alive" body.

It is easy to forget how magical this is. *It is so, so easy to forget.* Keep remembering how good this feels. As you keep returning to this way of moving through life, you integrate more of your own power, grace and elegance. The bonus: every year your balance is more enhanced. Can you imagine yourself living like this for your whole life, becoming progressively more powerful each year as you age?

- CHAPTER 56 -

Is Your Belt-Line Horizontal?

Years ago, I was watching a major golf tournament on television. All the front-runners had great posture. I was impressed that every golfer had their beltlines perfectly horizontal to the ground—all but one. When he stood or walked, his posture was so swaybacked that his belt buckle aimed at the ground a few feet in front of him.

As I was wondering how a professional golfer could be in the front running with such obviously bad posture, the commentators said, "How good it is to see him in the top running." They were saying, "When he's hot, he's exciting to watch. The trouble is that he's inconsistent."

When you stand swayback, your hip sockets sway out over your toes instead of aligning over your lateral malleolus, the big knob that's right above your ankles. Standing swayback makes your core musculature weak, and that stresses your lower-back muscles. It limits your movements and causes low back pain and dysfunction.

Mastery of golf, or mastery of any highly-competitive sport for that matter, requires near-perfect posture. Talent will only take you so far. To get to the level of mastery, you must develop the fundamentals. Abdominal breathing and correct posture are essential fundamentals.

Breathing shallowly weakens your core musculature. It sets you up to become swaybacked, which tips your pelvis and causes your belt-line to aim at the ground right in front of you. A lot of people stand like this, with back problems to prove it.

You may not aspire to be a world-class athlete, but having better posture every year will give you more enjoyment in everything you do. You want to feel your abdominal muscles work as you breathe out strong. *That strengthens your core.* Then just walking out to your car, let you recapture the pure pleasure of being alive you had as a child.

The "big idea" is that correct posture does not require greater effort, just greater awareness. It's all about being mindful. When your muscles are working in harmony, the tension releases. The job of whole body awareness keeps your mind occupied so it is not focusing on all the problems out there. As long most people are unconscious, there will always be ignorance and stupidity going on. That is not what you want your mind to be focusing on. With bad posture, that is exactly what it does.

As you stand and move in correct posture, all things improve with time. Arthritis naturally begins clearing up. Your bones continuously remodel into their most effective shape. Every part of your body keeps transforming to ever-higher levels of organization and efficiency. The life force of all your circulatory systems runs more powerfully. Age is much kinder to you.

Your body is constantly changing, transforming. Use that transformation to enhance your health and well being and experience greater personal power. Let time be your friend.

CHAPTER 57

Improving Your Balance

Correct posture gives your sense of balance impeccable feedback. Half of your balance comes from the semicircular canals of your inner ears. The other half comes from a vast plexus of sensory nerves that give feedback from the tonus (how flaccid or toned the muscles are) of your legs, torso, arms, and neck. Muscles that have a healthy tonus give impeccable feedback through your nerves when you start to go off-balance in one direction or another. These two systems, working together, give you an integrated sense of balance.

None of your body functions ever stay the same. They are all getting better or worse. Your balance continually improves as your posture improves, no matter your age; but incorrect posture causes your balance to continuously and progressively deteriorate. Bad posture progressively compromises the feedback mechanisms of your balance system. It's one of those "the worse it goes, the worse it gets" scenarios.

Bad posture creates unbalanced feedback from your ligaments and muscles. Weak muscles—muscles that underperform when you slump—do not make enough nerve energy. This forces opposing muscles to work too hard. Overworked muscles put out too much nerve energy.

It is important to understand that your body's innate intelligence *always* does the best it can. However, bad posture creates a steadily worsening feedback situation. Muscles that are forced to work too hard constantly fire off too many impulses, which really freaks out your nervous system. Your central nervous system cannot tolerate nerves constantly making that much noise. That would be like someone following you around yelling all the time.

The nervous system is forced to dampen the "hot" nerve feedback coming from your overly-tight muscles in order to give you some peace of mind. As a result, your central nervous system dumbs down, and that's not just your balance. Your awareness and courage also deteriorates—slowly, insidiously, influencing you to be more trepidatious, more fearful, less turned on to life.

In this condition, when you start to fall, your "dampened" neuro-muscular feedback system fails to recognize that you are falling until you have listed too far. Then it overcompensates in its attempt to prevent you from falling. That causes movements to become jerky and progressively unsteady. Your thinking becomes just as unsteady. Although it is common to see elderly people move and think like this, this is not old age. It is the simple progression of bad posture, and can be changed at any time.

When you get to senior citizen status, loss of balance becomes a serious issue, often tragic. After years of bad posture, your balance becomes steadily more precarious. Older people begin to fall more often. They don't bounce nearly as well as they did when they were kids. Bones break more easily. They mend slowly, if at all.

Surgeries to repair broken bones in the elderly, the time they are laid up, and a much slower recovery create very serious immune challenges. Many never really recover—not a desirable way to end your life.

Your life force will diminish as you age, but by your seventies you only need give up about 10 percent of the strength and agility you had when you were 18 years of age. This is the way your body is designed to age. Bad posture turns aging into something ugly. I'm not buying into that. How about you?

Many elderly people have thrown in the towel. For them, change is not possible. Isn't it ironic that healthy people are always looking for ways to be healthier, and those who need help the most are usually the least likely to seek it?

Fortunately, there have been many large studies that prove "old dogs can learn new tricks." It is just as easy to learn new things when you are older as it was when you were young. Young people (of all ages) know that anything they commit to is possible. Learning anything is called synaptogenesis. Anytime you are learning *anything*, your nervous system develops new synapses and whole new neural pathways to perform that. When you practice good posture, your body develops whole new neural pathways to improve your balance—at any age.

As soon as you start having better posture and a better gait, your neuromuscular feedback system immediately begins to respond and balance returns. The better your posture, the better your balance. Courage and confidence develop at the same time.

- CHAPTER 58 -

How Bad Posture Creates Arthritis

As we have discussed before, incorrect posture causes many of your bones to go out of alignment. All bones react to a law called "the piezo-electric effect," which is the physics of crystals and how they develop polarities. Your bones are made up of crystalline materials and function as crystals, so here is how it works:

When a bone misaligns, the part of the bone that gets jammed against another creates a "negative force field." The unequal pressures cause misaligned bones to develop positive and negative force fields, like a magnet. The aberrant force fields play havoc with a number of positively charged minerals—especially calcium.

Calcium, with its *positive* electrical charge, starts filling up the *negative* force field to balance the electrical charge. On X-rays the calcium infiltration is easy to see. A short time after the misalignment occurs, the calcium infiltration looks like a cloud that fills in the negative force field where the misaligned bones jam into each other. Over time, the cloudy areas become denser, coalescing into calcium spurs.

Calcium infiltration into tissues around a misaligned bone is irritating, like sand getting into your shoes or bathing suit. With every movement, the buildup of calcium irritates all the muscles and nerves it infiltrates. This causes inflammation and pain. If the misalignment continues because you keep moving with the same old bad posture, the calcium forms gnarly-looking arthritic spurs on misaligned vertebrae and bones.

The longer you have bad posture, the worse the spurs will get. The muscles, nerves, and other soft tissue around arthritic joints become increasingly painful. You lose your range of motion. Again, old age, or hard physical labor gets blamed.

There is good news, however: As soon as you start having good posture and walking with a correct gait, you walk the misalignments out of your spine and extremities. The aberrant force fields immediately fade away. The spurs and arthritic buildup start to disappear. But if you return to bad posture and incorrect gait, your arthritis comes back.

Your bones are continuously changing their shape. With good posture, all your bones are continuously organizing into their most efficient shapes for the movements you are performing, even as you age. With bad posture those same bones flatten out into progressively less glamorous, less efficient shapes. They develop arthritic spurs and get worse with age. Time just adds them up.

In addition to correcting your posture, there are two simple exercises you can do to clear arthritic build-up out of your body:

1. **Spinal twists**. You can break up old entrenched neurological feedback patterns by doing "spinal twists." Bring your elbows up level, with your hands at your shoulder sockets. Twist your neck left and right, letting your torso follow for 15 repetitions each direction. Do the spinal twists anytime you feel stress building up anywhere in your spine. *Warning:* Don't twist as far as you can. Stop comfortably short of full range of motion. Doing them *gently and often* works much better.

2. **Shoulder circles**. When you do about fifteen shoulder circles, keep your hands close to your shoulder sockets so you do them gently enough to not make any creaking noises. Then shake your hands out (like swimmers do before competition), where your upper arms quickly rotate clockwise and counter-clockwise. This enhances circulation and clears away a day's worth of arthritis from your shoulders, arms and hands.

If you do these energizing exercises four or five times a day, you are getting rid of four or five day's worth of arthritic buildup *every day*, and greatly increasing the life force getting into each of your cells. Anytime you feel stress building up, repeat the exercises. With good posture, shoulder shrugs, and the spinal twists, you rebuild the discs between your vertebrae, which reverses height loss.

CHAPTER 59

The Best Way to do Things

·*Goal Orientation vs. Process Orientation*·

Years ago one of my best friends, Ed, said, "There are two ways to do any big project. Most people just want to get the job done, which is rarely fun and always takes longer than you think. *Process orientation is always better.* And it's a lot more fun. When you compare the two, process orientation consistently gets the job done twice as fast."

Imagine a big chore, some "have-to-do" project like spring-cleaning your house, or re-organizing your garage or shop. In goal orientation, you consider that the job will take X amount of time, and you begin. The trouble is, in the real world, it takes X amount of time plus about 50 percent more than you anticipated. The job is a chore. It is something you *have to do* before you can do what you want to do. Generally, you do not joyously anticipate doing a big project that has been weighing heavily on your mind, like clearing out years of clutter or spring-cleaning your house, right?

Now consider the same previously dreaded job in "process orientation." Instead of focusing on how long it will take to get the job done, you focus on:

- Feeling happy
- Having a good time
- Breathing out strong and having good posture while performing each and every aspect of the project

It takes about five minutes to do a complete walkthrough, visualizing yourself doing each part of the whole project in a joyous and efficient manner.

You can do your mental walk-through while drinking your morning tea or coffee, observing yourself performing each aspect of the project. During the entire project you are *focusing entirely on the process*—not the goal.

In the visualization, anytime you observe yourself moving or lifting incorrectly—rewind the video, like a movie—and run it again, lifting and moving correctly this time. Keep rerunning each scene, as many times as it takes, until you imagine yourself happily doing each portion of the job in good posture, breathing out strong, with good ergonomics and a joyous heart.

Having a good time during the whole project is crucial. If you start getting stressed out, back the video up and ask yourself, "Why am I uptight?" That is when you get revelations about your own unique process, insights that were completely unconscious to you before.

One of my realizations was that I *always* stress out at the midpoint of *every* project. At that point, I am focusing on how much I still have left to do. I realized that I needed to look at what I had already accomplished by the midpoint of the project. When I did, I saw how much I had done, and how quickly I had done it. I could see that I had done way more by the midpoint than I ever thought I could. I was impressed. The earlier uptight feeling was replaced by a deep sense of satisfaction and fulfillment.

When you finish the walk-through visualization you are ready to begin. The five minutes you spend visualizing the process gets repaid many times over. Your bodymind uses that time to very efficiently organize every aspect of the project, so you barely take an extra step. The organization is so thorough, your attitude so upbeat, and you are so in the zone that you get done way ahead of the anticipated schedule.

In *process orientation* every part of your bodymind and spirit gets to participate. When you are breathing out strong, with your upper torso erect, you really get to experience the stability of your core musculature. After you are done, your body feels buffed. The whole process is joyous. The job feels sacred, and every part of the project reflects that sacred feeling back to you—even when you reflect on it later.

Do the math about the time the project takes, but also consider the value of your moods during that time. Any project that you do in goal orientation takes longer than you anticipated—usually about 50% longer. The job doesn't feel like it is going to win you any awards. You are usually not thrilled by the outcome. It's something you *have* to do. The lack of organization causes you to keep going back for something you forgot, and spending a lot of time in less-than-stellar moods.

Process orientation gets your projects done a good 50% sooner than you antici-pate—and it's always more fun. Your body is healthier. You get to perform the whole project in a wonderful mood, alive to the present moment. Often your spirit glimpses how *this* is the answer to all your longing for as far back as you can fathom. For example: the house you may be cleaning may be the home you always dreamed of owning. And here you are making it sacred. I often hear my wife singing to herself as she cleans. Afterward, our home feels sacred.

You feel the warm glow of happiness and joy for hours after the project is finished. You are all done, and you still have plenty of time— and energy—to stand back and admire your job. Process orientation is definitely the way to go.

There is a delightful Buddhist saying, "Before enlightenment, chop wood, carry water. After enlightenment, chop wood, carry water." When everything is done as if *this moment* is what your whole life was destined for, then all life becomes profound. Every moment is sacred. This is the life you are meant to live. You live your life in the upper limits of what is possible. And your upper limits keep expanding, presenting you with ever greater possibilities and higher potentials. Your life fulfills its promise. You discover that you are the one you have always sought outside yourself. You always were.

CHAPTER 60

Posture Review

Before you do anything, get out of your car, walk up stairs, get up from sitting down, whatever you are about to do, *stop!*

- Stop whatever you were starting to do—just for an instant—which interrupts all your old conditioning patterns. This always brings you back to the present moment.
- Breathe out strong, so you feel your abdominal muscles working. Then allow your lungs to fill with air.
- Stand up straight.
- Lift your sternum (breastplate), letting your shoulders fall free.
- Let your neck and shoulders loosen up. Once they are loose, let your head float up into its sweet spot, where it takes minimal effort to hold it erect. Your neck feels free. Your ear canal lines up right over your shoulder.
- Keep your feet parallel, your weight landing on the mid-point of your foot as you walk.

You are now doing whatever you're doing with greater awareness—leaving old baggage behind—experiencing more joy. You feel more alive, experiencing the magic of the present moment.

Review of Walking

When you start walking anywhere, breathe out strong from below your navel. Lift up your sternum. Free up the tension from your neck and shoulders so your head can float up into its sweet spot.

Keep your feet parallel, with your gait landing at the midpoint of your foot. Let yourself experience full contact with the earth throughout the gait cycle.

Experience the arches of your feet expressing upward—bringing all your muscles into a heightened state of whole-body awareness. Feel the experience of your body being propelled along, elegantly, in harmony with the universe.

Experience your aliveness, with no other moment but this moment. Simply going for a twenty-minute walk realigns your body, mind and spirit. Eons of cultural conditioning fall away, allowing you to move from your authentic self.

When going around a corner, let your head lean slightly, almost imperceptibly into the direction of the turn and your whole body delightfully follows. Ah, this feels so magical.

Review of Lifting

It's all the little things that heal you—or kill you—so *lift everything as if it were as heavy as you can possibly lift.* If you make this a lifetime habit, the more you lift the healthier your back becomes. Then, hard work heals and restores you instead of injuring you.

90 percent of your injuries come from incorrectly picking up objects from below your knees or above your shoulders. Some come from lifting in an awkward position, like jerking groceries out of the trunk of a car. It usually takes less than a minute out of your day to prevent all these injuries.

Keep your upper torso erect when lifting anything. Feel the weight settle down into your legs, which frees up your lower back.

When lifting anything from the floor or ground, take a few seconds to get a prop, like a chair, and place it next to what you are planning to lift. Go down onto one knee and lift the heavy object onto the prop. Then, keeping your torso erect, lift with your legs. Your legs are powerful. Let them do the lifting, not your arms or your back.

To get something out of the trunk of the car, take a brief moment to slide it toward you. Work it into a position where it is easier to pick up. Use leverage, so you never "jerk things up" that are heavy or cumbersome. Stop for a moment and visualize lifting anything heavy or cumbersome correctly. Then pick it up.

Lifting anything over your head usually traumatizes your lower back. So, when you have to put something up high, like up in a cupboard, get a chair to stand on so you are not lifting heavy things over your head.

Preventing injuries generally takes a minute or two out of an entire day. That minute save days, weeks—or even a lifetime of pain and disability. Many of your injuries are cumulative micro-traumas, caused by lifting things incorrectly for years, even though they might not be that heavy. Remember, lift everything as if it were as heavy as you can possibly lift. That way, the harder you work, the healthier you get.

Review of Getting Up from Sitting

Before getting up from a sitting position, scoot your buttocks to the front of the chair. Lean forward until you feel your whole weight come onto the balls of your feet. As your nose goes over your toes, let your forehead bob down and then arc upward as you push downward through the balls of your feet. Feel the opposition of your feet pushing downward while your torso and head gently push upward. This is getting out of a chair with absolute economy of movement.

Sitting down is also a two-step operation. Sit down at the forward edge of the chair. Your torso stays erect. If the chair were not there, your movement would continue down into a squatting position, like a monkey, instead of falling on your buttocks. Then, scoot back until the chair supports your back. Sitting with your torso erect and relaxed, all the parts of your bodymind communicate clearly with each other. You feel more settled.

Review of Walking Down Stairs

Breathe out strong, settling your spirit into hara, its place of power. This creates a "field of awareness" around your feet that is usually about the size of a snowshoe. The heightened awareness lets you experience exactly where your foot is without having to look down. Breathing out strong, you can feel precisely where your foot is on the stair tread, even through thick-soled shoes.

Lift up your sternum as you walk down stairs. Let your shoulders and neck be free and relaxed. Let yourself experience any fear of falling that comes up. As you feel the fear, it transforms into excitement.

With each step your pelvis settles downward—as if you are starting to sit down. When you are not looking at your feet with every step, you get to observe the world beyond the stair treads. Walking down stairs without having to look at your feet is elegant and quite exciting.

THIRD HABIT

- CHAPTER 61 -

Feel Your Feelings

You must learn to feel all your feelings if you want to live a fully-empowered life. Your feelings open you up to the wonder and glory of your higher realms of consciousness, opening up so much more of life.

Feeling your feelings also opens you to the wisdom of your spirit. Spiritual energy and emotional energy are the most alike. It's just that the energy of your feelings is denser, like water, while the energy of your spirit is more ethereal, lighter in nature. Both energies are similarly expansive and fill all the space. You hone your intuition by feeling your feelings, and trusting their validity, especially your first feelings about an event you just heard about or a person you just met.

Intuition and imagination are faculties of your bodymind. They operate at much higher frequencies than your brain can access, with its twenty-four frames-per-second speed limit. Intuition and imagination can operate into the hundreds of frames per second. So, you have seven senses, but your brain only accesses five.

You often discern the feelings of other people around you as your own feelings. You can feel it when someone hates you—like the temperature just dropped 10 degrees. Brrrh! Did someone leave the door open? You can feel when someone is trying to manipulate you. When you pay attention to your feelings, you can feel the truth of what has been said—or the lie. You can also feel the integrity—or lack of integrity—of your own thoughts, or words as you speak them. You learn as much about yourself as you do about others.

Actions, words and thoughts only convey a small portion of the information available in any situation. If that's all you are paying attention to, you miss out on all the good stuff. The feelings and bodily sensations you experience—while actions are happening or words are spoken—convey much more understanding and wisdom. Your intuition only works if you are paying attention to the feelings that come up. Feeling your feelings opens you up to the higher dimensions, making your life so much richer.

When your brain is in charge of your consciousness it only pays attention to two dimensions (thoughts and physical action) out of your seven dimensions. It tends to discount feelings as if they were just weeds along the path. The problem is: the instant you fail to feel the feelings that come up, you are drawn into the unconscious state.

Your mind's unconscious response is to make up stories about the feelings that come up. The stories are so familiar because your brain has generated them so many times in the past. The familiarity of this way of thinking is so seductive, so beguiling. And *that* is how most of your friends handle their feelings too, so, in a way it feels normal.

Most people only think about why they feel a certain way. They don't actually *feel* the feelings that come up. They don't go inside and fully experience the feeling. For instance, they might say, "I am so disappointed in George," but they don't actually go inside and experience the feeling of disappointment. Thinking or talking about old hurts pushes them deeper into the bodymind, where they become your shadow issues, your blind spots.

Ignoring your feelings as if they were just weeds in the background scenery to what you are seeing and thinking is spiritual unconsciousness. In this state, your brain can easily think the world *it sees* is the real world. And yet, the information you get from feeling your feelings, and then reflecting on them is more valuable—by multiples of hundreds—than all the physical and mental information combined.

Handling Uncomfortable Feelings

When I find myself in any kind of situation where I feel uncomfortable, I begin to simply *feel* all the feelings that come up. Sometimes the emotional environment is so intense and awkward that I feel very uncomfortable.

I have gone places where I had to feel one uncomfortable feeling after another for a half hour to forty-five minutes before they all cleared. As soon as I become free of the disempowering feelings—feelings that were rampant in that place—I have a delightful time. After such encounters I have had people say to me, "You always seem so comfortable wherever you are."

When you find yourself in situations where you feel uncomfortable, the solution is to just keep feeling all the feelings that cause discomfort—until they are gone. Sometimes it only takes a few minutes, but sometimes it takes quite a while. When they are resolved, you get to enjoy all that situation has to offer.

When things are happening, or people are talking to you, become aware of the feelings that are coming up. The feelings lend context, the backstory, to what others are saying. Feeling the awkward feelings allows you to understand people's motivations, and it all starts to make sense.

When you feel all the feelings that come up, and reflect on them, your understanding of what is happening beneath the surface expands. You begin to hear, really hear what the other person is saying. It's like a window into their soul when you listen not just with your ears, but also with your feelings and your heart.

You also learn a lot about your *own* values and beliefs by paying attention to what you are feeling. When you become aware of a feeling—especially if the feeling goes against your core values or beliefs—ask yourself leading questions, like "is that how I want to create my world?" or "what would a person believe that would cause them to feel this way?" When you ask profound questions, your spirit answers. Questioning your feelings, like an ardent reporter would, pulls the depth of your spirit's wisdom to the surface.

Such questioning opens a pathway for the mysteries of life to reveal themselves. Your spiritual wisdom goes untapped if you don't have a vehicle for bringing that wisdom up to the level of your consciousness. Feeling, then questioning why those feelings came up is one of the vehicles.

During an office visit, one of my self-employed patients told me she was mortified when she realized she was experiencing big-time envy of her daughter's success with her new business. I asked my patient if her own business was exciting and successful? She emphatically said, "Yes!" I had her feel the envy, without dialogue. Then I had her ask herself a couple questions and listen to the answers.

The first question was: Why did her daughter's success elicit envy? The answer my patient got was, she, the mom, was at a part of a process where she had done all she could, and had to wait for another person to do their portion before she could go forward. While waiting, she had jumped ahead—thinking about all the things she wanted to do in the future—flying around like Peter Pan, "I'm going to do this, I'm going to do that," none of which she could actually do until she had finished the project at hand.

Thinking about all the future things she wanted to do—*but couldn't*—made her feel stuck. Her epiphany was, "Oh my! I go into my mind and do the Peter Pan scenario *so often* that it always seems like I am stuck. Thinking this way *always* makes me feel stuck, and then I get bored."

Next, I said, "Ask yourself, how do I get out of feeling stuck and bored?" The answer she got was "I need to keep focused on the project at hand until it is running smoothly instead of flying around like Peter Pan." Because she inwardly *knew* she wished her daughter all the success in the world, her enlightenment came from challenging and questioning the feeling of envy about her daughter's success. Years later she said, "I have not felt stuck or bored once since we did that exercise."

- CHAPTER 62 -

The Nature of Unconscious States

As we know by now, our brain retains a vast library of everything we have ever seen, heard, felt, tasted, smelled, or done. A smell or a texture can bring an old forgotten memory vividly into our awareness. Many of the memories are positive.

The smell of a peanut butter and jelly sandwich has vividly transported me back to walking to kindergarten in Napa, California. I open the paper bag and the sandwich my mother prepared for me smells so wonderful. The smell of lilacs in bloom, and also the blossoming of pyracantha come right along with that lovely memory.

We all have positive memories like that. Our mind also whisks us back to negative memories that resonate with a *feeling* we just ignored. The negative feelings are what we call "baggage."

Often we have a lot of negative baggage attached to particular feelings. They drag us out of the present and back into the uncomfortable, unresolved issue that is associated with those particular feelings. The feelings come up, we don't feel them, and bam! we're back to acting out like the five-year-old who was so humiliated, or the seven-year-old who does not fit in. We usually acted out badly in those scenes.

When something triggers a memory that has a lot of unresolved negative feelings, like being completely humiliated—and you do not pause to *feel* the humiliation—you immediately regress to the emotional age you were when you were originally humiliated. How you reacted *back then* becomes your coping mechanism for this current situation.

Suddenly, you start to breathe shallowly. Your rational mind takes control, transports you into a spell, and your whole body reverts to a posture that accurately reflects the way you felt at that earlier time. The whole gestalt of that unresolved memory floods in on you. A "spell" is the best definition of these emotional states.

Each unconscious state we fall into is triggered the instant we start breathing shallowly, slump, or don't actually "feel" a negative feeling that comes up. The triggering emotions can be subtle, like worry, frustration, insecurity or boredom. The trigger can also be a body sensation such as tension in your chest or gut, pain behind your eyes, or the feeling of extreme tiredness when something difficult comes up. Those are actually feelings, too.

When a feeling comes up and you do not pause to feel it, your brain instantly takes over. It creates a story that *rationalizes* all the reasons why it's all right for you to "act out" like you do. That's why the brain is called the rational mind. If you believed, for example that the original humiliation was too painful to experience, you may have converted it to a feeling you were more comfortable with, like anger. So your mind weaves a story that rationalizes why it is totally acceptable for you to act angrily. To your brain, your actions seem normal, even justified.

As long as your brain is in charge, it reacts to every conceivable situation with its "stories." It weaves one plausible story after another, encounter after encounter for days, weeks or even years. All the stories are woven linearly in the world of time, predicting how the future will turn out, based on what happened in the past.

As long as our brain is in charge, our lives are confined to, and limited by the artificial world of time, which is best defined as being in a "spell."

Shadow Issues

Over your lifetime, your brain has created many hundreds of thousands of these stories. When you breathe shallowly, slump, or fail to feel the feeling that comes up, your mind takes over. It generates one of its stories, and they seem so "normal" that you don't realize you are in one of these spells. Psychologists call them "shadow issues" because they do not exist in present time. They pull you into the shadowy realms of the past, or some *imagined* future your mind suspects will happen.

Each shadow issue was created at a time when you were in an emotionally painful or stressful situation, and—for one reason or another—you did not actually feel the feelings that came up. From then on your mind makes up "stories" anytime that feeling comes up.

Now, whenever a situation comes up that elicits that unresolved feeling, your mind takes you back to the earliest story that justifies your thoughts, actions and beliefs you had back then. And *that* gets superimposed over the present moment.

Most of your shadow issues are from childhood or traumatic periods. Once you fall into one of these spells, your coping skills are reduced to the emotional age of that incident. For example, you may be making an executive presentation in a high-powered meeting and someone's pointed question makes you feel vulnerable. If you do not pause to feel the vulnerable feeling (it only takes a second to feel the feeling), your unconscious mind immediately takes control. It takes you out of the present moment by superimposing the earlier unsuccessful time when your feelings of vulnerability caused a situation to go bad. If that moment happened when you were seven years old, your coping skills revert to being a seven-year-old child who didn't handle feeling vulnerable very well. Odds are that you will not handle this executive presentation very well either. Oops.

On a positive note, if you *stop for an instant* and simply feel the vulnerable feeling, it dissolves within a second or two. In the next microsecond, you are fully present, totally in control of the situation. You feel more alive and powerful than ever. You handle the situation brilliantly.

The bonus is, this new, more successful way you have handled feeling vulnerable deletes *and replaces* the old shadow issue from when you were a child. Each time you feel a negative feeling, how you handle the situation replaces yet another shadow issue with a more conscious default program. Each success builds your self-esteem and your personal sense of power.

How We Transcend Shadow Issues

The beauty of your innate healing mechanism is that you are compelled to return to all your tired old shadow issues *no matter how many times it takes* until you resolve them. You are nudged toward healing by having your painful issues thrown back into your face until you handle them in present-time awareness. Pain is your friend.

Shadow issues affect all the ways you think and move. They influence your values, beliefs and principles. They show up as the flaws in your logic and all the ways you space out or "get an attitude." They contain all the unresolved (unfelt) fears that inhibit your magnificent plans and dreams. They are your blind spots.

In every sport, shadow issues show up as the microseconds when your awareness spaces out. They are all the flaws in your techniques. They show up in your baseball swing as the place when you space out—just for a microsecond—and lose visual contact with the ball. They are the unstable portions of your golf swing or the part of your tennis serve where you lose your focus.

The same process happens with your logic. Often with a patient, I will have them go over their logic regarding an area where I see them spacing out. Intelligent people self-correct. When they get to the exact place where the flaw is in their logic, they often see that they have it wrong.

If you did not feel the painful feeling from a traumatic event of your past, a current situation that elicits the same feeling will superimpose the thoughts, beliefs and attitudes from that old unresolved story over the current situation. This is how shadow issues distort your perceptions of the situation you are in currently. The logic from that unresolved time in your past rarely represents the truth in *this* situation.

Your spirit and soul bring you most of your lessons. One of your soul's jobs is to keep pushing your unresolved shadow issues to the surface of your awareness until there are no more to resolve. That is one of your soul's primal duties, one it never shirks. You can count on this. Your soul will continue performing this duty for your entire life. This innate trait is *not* going away, so you may as well accept it and use it for positive gain.

Your shadow issues are as familiar as an old coat. They are, however, almost always uncomfortable and usually downright painful. But they are so familiar that you are lulled back into them more quietly than a whisper. You so insidiously become the eight year old who can't do anything right, the seven year old who does not fit in.

This process occurs dozens of times a day. Each time they occur, you have the opportunity to replace yet another shadow issue with a more empowering thought form. Once you get stuck in one of your old shadow issues, you are in a spell. Your rational mind may have gotten stuck on that particular shadow issue 786 times in the past. You can be stuck in one spell after another, day after day, without ever coming up for air. Until you feel the feelings, you will remain stuck.

Many of your shadow issues came down your family line. Many of them are part of the culture into which you were born. But the buck stops with you. *You* can break these age-old patterns. You heal them one at a time. As an added bonus, as you break your own old patterns and remodel your behavior, it helps others around you break their old patterns. Your love shines through. In the presence of a loving person, it is easy to see that love is the answer.

Without a discipline to extricate yourself from one of these spells, you are seldom aware that you have slipped into an unconscious state. The spells are as subtle as falling asleep.

We are conditioned by history to think and believe in ways that give our power away. In the present moment, any story about how the world has held us back is just that—a story. Every moment has more potential than *any* of our old limiting stories.

Here's a recap of how your stories take control of your life:

• The moment you ignore a feeling that comes up, you start breathing shallowly.

- In the next microsecond your rational mind projects you back to the earliest time you felt that way. Along with breathing shallowly, you assume the posture you had at that time. The whole experience floods in on you. It can seem so believable when you are in it. That's why they are called shadow issues. They are your blind spots.
- Your brain weaves a story that justifies why you are stuffing down the feeling. The story often blames others for how you feel.
- Your brain deftly projects "the story" over the top of the current scene. The story completely changes the context of what is happening, but it is so familiar that—when you are under its spell—it seems normal to you.
- The more unconscious you are, the more completely your old stories will dictate what you think and believe, and how you act.
- Technically you are not in present time and space. The spell has transported you into the past or some fantasized future. The story obscures and overshadows all the good that is happening in the present moment. The stories are the cause of your pain and suffering.

All this from not *feeling* your feelings.

CHAPTER 63

Changing Old Painful Thought Patterns

For a lot of people, family holidays can be pressure cookers that stress individuals into acting out old painful patterns. You are fine until *the precise moment* when a family member negates you or pushes one of your hot buttons. If you are not aware enough to feel the feelings that come up, your breath stops, and then goes shallow.

Family members can be so good at triggering your shadow issues. They instinctively know where all your hot buttons are. You find yourself reacting in painful old ways, getting suckered into *oh, so familiar* patterns around your family.

Family gatherings and other high-pressure situations are great times to practice breathing abdominally—and feeling the feelings that invariably come up. You need to be particularly aware of your breath and feelings in situations where you have a history of painful encounters or acting out.

The focus required to breathe out strong and feel the feelings that come up may seem daunting at first. But a *lifetime* of pain and suffering— from which your brain is incapable of extricating itself—is much worse. Instead of falling into your old dysfunctional loops and being part of the problem, your rock-solid awareness liberates you and all those around you. Your presence becomes a healing agent at family functions.

You need to understand that when you walk into a situation where there are hidden agendas—your breathing takes a direct hit. If you don't pause—and feel that feeling—you instantly revert to shallow breathing. You so insidiously get suckered into the dysfunction. As you become more aware of breathing abdominally, you start noticing more quickly when your breathing goes shallow. You become more successful in situations where you used to lose it.

On a wonderful note, when you walk into a room where everyone is fully conscious, loving, and not running any hidden agendas, your whole being comes up a notch. You feel safe to speak your truth. Your creativity is enhanced. Your mind and feelings soar. You feel wonderfully alive. You are safe and loved.

This is the kind of world you want to live in. As you take the necessary steps to master your shadow issues, your life begins transforming into that magical loving world.

CHAPTER 64

"Thinking" Your Feelings Only Makes Them Worse

The way we have always dealt with unpleasant feelings is to *think* about them and *talk* about them with our friends. Let's take the example of anger: Until we wake up, we tend to think about all the things the other person does that makes us angry. Our mind spins out story after story about what that person did, what we *suspect* they will do. The brain runs infinite scenarios about how we will respond. Those thoughts act like grappling hooks, binding that person's karma to us, inextricably linking us, even if that is the last person we would ever want to be connected to.

The more we "think" about why we are angry, the more the anger builds up inside us. We build a tempest in a teapot. As unfelt feelings build up, so does pressure—and pain. The buildup of unfelt feelings causes most of the physical pain any of us experience.

As a reminder, on a one-to-ten pain scale, physical pain rarely exceeds a four or five for any extended period of time. Anytime your pain builds up beyond a six or seven, you can bet that 60 or 70 percent of it is emotional. One of the ways you can tell it's emotional is that the pain just steadily builds. The pressure that builds up in your body from unfelt feelings causes pain that is considerably more intense than pain that is purely physical.

You cannot live a long, healthy life while hanging onto old anger, hurts or worry. And worry isn't any less harmful to your body than anger. Even low-grade feelings you would consider minor, like frustration, seriously diminish your longevity.

Every cell in your body takes what you think personally. When you are thinking angry thoughts toward someone, all your cells firmly believe that you are angry with them. Muscle testing confirms this. The whole time you are "thinking" about how disappointed you are in someone, all your cells believe *they personally let you down, that you are disappointed in them.*

233

The way this plays out is that you find yourself acting out in ways you never would have scripted, like overeating or lashing out at your loved ones when they had nothing to do with your disappointment or anger.

Your brain is a great servant to your heart—actually it's fabulous. But, like any servant, it needs a job description. Lacking clearly-defined duties, it starts focusing on all the problems of the world. Give your mind the job of always making sure you are standing tall, breathing out strong and feeling your feelings. These habits extricate you from the unconscious hallucinations. As you wake up, you "get" that this moment is fulfilling your deepest desires.

For example, imagine that you are cleaning the house—your beautiful home—the home you always fantasized having. The contentment, which your spirit is continually immersed in, is permeating all that you are experiencing, making your house feel sacred as you clean it. The peacefulness of your spirit is bubbling up into your consciousness like an underground spring. You are having a good time.

Then, for whatever reason, you unconsciously slump into some tired old posture. Your mind immediately starts spinning out stories about the unresolved feelings contained in that slumping posture. The brain takes you into your old conditioning. The old unresolved feelings in that posture drive stories like: how hard you have to work, how unappreciated you are doing all that hard work, how demeaning housework is, and how *you* have to do all the housework.

The transformation—from how wonderful it is to have a beautiful home to clean to how unappreciated you are—is so slick. You wouldn't even notice the seduction if you weren't aware that you started breathing shallowly, slumping or feeling unappreciated.

Your new realization might be "I am fulfilling one of my most profound desires by having this beautiful home—my home—to clean." *This* rewrites your DNA. Actually, you are rewriting your DNA every moment. You can rewrite it by living wide awake, focusing on and truly living your heart's desires, or unconsciously rewrite it the same old way it was by complaining about all your woes.

- CHAPTER 65 -

Set a Goal and Fear Immediately Comes Up

As soon as you commit to a goal, fears *always* come up. Always! If you do not feel those fears, the fear-based thoughts your mind generates turn into monsters. They can become like fire-breathing dragons you can't get past. They effectively distract you from your goal.

Anytime you desire something but don't go inside and feel the fears that invariably come up, the fear usually wins out. The thoughts, driven by the unfelt fears, keep building in intensity—like monsters—until you can see no way around them. That is why *you must feel all the negativity that invariably comes up.* If you ignore a pervasive fear, it is like turning your back on a junkyard dog. The unresolved fear will come up behind you and bite you on the backside.

A fear you do not feel keeps building in intensity, causing your mind to spin stories that progressively escalate. Under that onslaught, courage wilts. Your earlier bravado fades away until your heart's desire starts to seem like a bad idea. And yet another desire goes unfulfilled.

Some fears are so great that you must develop strategies to successfully overcome them. When fears take up residence in your awareness, you need to fully experience them. You may also need to create affirmations or visualizations that confront the fears head-on.

When I took my California state board exam to be a chiropractor, I was scared. I had been drafted into the Army in 1967, just two weeks into my senior year. Four years later I came back and finished my last year. The board exam was testing basic science knowledge that was four to seven years old in my memory.

Worse, the politics of the new board was like being a left-wing democrat, and having all your examiners be ultra-right-wing republicans, or visa versa. That combination really had me worried, so I developed a complex affirmation to overcome those fears:

- Doctors who heal people do just that.
- Those who can't, or do not want to be healers, do other things like becoming board examiners.
- So without bragging I will probably heal more people in my lifetime than all of those examiners put together.
- Because of that, none of them have the right to stand in my way.

Every time I felt frightened—which was at least twenty times a day leading up to the test—I felt the feelings and went over that long complex affirmation. By the time I took the test I was so pumped up that I averaged 87.7 percent on the written portion of the exams.

Most fears can simply be felt, which successfully dissolves them. Fears that keep building in intensity, that are deeper and more persistent may require affirmations, visualizations, beliefs, or attitudes that successfully confront them.

Keep ripening your plans and ideas. That is crucial. That allows your entire bodymind to joyously participate in the creation process. It is also crucial to feel all the fears that keep surfacing until there are no more. With them out of the way you can concentrate on accomplishing your heart's desires. You must keep confronting and slaying the dragons if your cherished plans and dreams are to come to fruition and your kingdom is to remain safe.

Each time you go inside and feel the fear, every part of your body gets more pumped up. By the time the feared event comes to pass, you are so energized that you are invincible. Nothing can stop you. Don't let your brain run dialogues about all the ways you could fail. That's not its job. *Your mind needs to stay on point* by reminding you to keep up the seven habits, like breathing up all the courage you need to overcome your fears. That's how you succeed.

The Dance We All Do

Everyone is telepathic. Everyone. On a meta-conscious level we all have awareness of thoughts and feelings that pass between us. This is a dance that happens. We need to develop more awareness about how our thoughts and feelings impact others.

Think of your more complex thoughts as "thought forms." As your mind starts building a thought, the form of the thought starts enclosing feelings until you have built a thought form. It can have good or bad feelings enclosed within its framework.

Every thought form causes a reciprocal thought from others as a response. I find myself thinking about someone I haven't communicated with for months, and suddenly they call, seemingly out of the blue. I think about you, and you respond with a thought back to me. If I cherish you, you tend to cherish me back. If I think an angry thought form toward you, you tend to respond with either an angry, resentful or self-depreciating thought form back to me.

While you are thinking or talking negatively about someone, that person will tend to act out. They act out when they are around you, or even if your name is mentioned. But they do not necessarily act out *toward you*. You think they are a jerk, and they act like a jerk, especially when you are around. Isn't that interesting?

It's so much better if you feel any negative feelings you may have about them. That causes the wall—made up of negative feelings about them—to dissolve. Feeling all the feelings has the added benefit of dissolving negative attachments, which are like grappling hooks that bind that person to you.

It is not only important how we treat others when we are in their presence. We also need to assume more responsibility about how we treat them when they are *not* in our presence. This includes how we talk about them and think about them.

You have to remember, it's all energy—a dance you are having with others. There are no "one-way thoughts." Part of being impeccable is assuming that everyone responds to your thoughts *as if they hear you.* In some part of their consciousness, they do.

Fourth Habit

- Chapter 66 -

Shake It Off like a Cat

The Fourth Habit that will change your life is *shake it off like a cat*. The world of cats is fascinating. Cats who spend their time out of doors are like psychic kung fu masters. With their consciousness focused laser-like in the now, cats do not squander their life force by allowing their precious attention to dwell on injuries of the past. They never *linger in self-pity* by limping, gimping, or favoring an injury.

Cats heal very fast. Their focus is on reflecting the highest quality of being a cat. Rudyard Kipling summed it up best: "I am the cat who walks by himself and all places are alike to me."

When I was a teenager I saw a young cat get caught up in a friend's feet. My friend was in a big hurry, moving way too fast in the house. The cat got tangled up in his feet and slammed *hard* against a wall. The cat's reaction to being kicked into a wall was incredible. He got up, shook it off, and walked away as though "that never happened." No limping. No favoring the trauma. Only one second later, and the cat had already put the trauma behind him.

That incident made a profound impression on me. I didn't fully comprehend the lesson of it until many years later. Now I understand that cats rarely show residual trauma in their bodies after the traumatic

239

moment is past. For a cat, the past is past, even if "the past" only happened a few seconds ago. I have come to understand that cats live fully in the present moment.

When you shake off *any* trauma—whether physical, mental, emotional or a traumatic event that negates your values or beliefs—and walk away like "that never happened," you step fully into the present moment, powerful and alive. You are reflecting the highest quality of a spiritual being living in a human body. You move like you are the hero of your own story.

How We Lock Trauma Into the Body

Dogs are not quite as bad as humans about favoring an injury, but they are far worse than cats. They react more like people when they get hurt. They show it. Most dogs will milk a trauma for all it's worth. A dog will limp around for days garnering sympathy for its pain. At least for a while, the trauma becomes part of its gait, an integral part of its movements. Luckily for dogs, their attention span is not as long as ours. They soon forget. After a while they drop the limp.

After a physical injury you are often battered and bruised. It's often hard not to limp or favor the injury. But, as much as humanly possible, you need to walk away from all your traumas in perfect posture, breathing out strong and feeling all your feelings. Right after an injury, you may have to make smaller movements or not walk as fast as you normally would to keep from limping or favoring the injury. As your body trusts you—*and you must earn your body's trust*—it will quickly give you more. It will heal much faster if you do not favor injuries in any way.

When you limp, every step you take creates "sensory/motor feedback loops," which are neuromuscular patterns that create an altered, more pathetic "reality" within your consciousness. With every step, "the limp" recreates the whole gestalt (all the unfelt feelings, negative thoughts, and beliefs from the time of the trauma). And with every step the limp projects *that* over your current situation. Ouch!

Years later you may be stepping into a beautiful day shared with dear friends, but the limp brings along all your baggage from the time long ago when the limp began. The sensory/motor feedback loop created by limping overlays the beautiful day with a background story from that time, for example, "how difficult life is."

In the unconscious state, you tend to make subtle shifts in posture or gait to move away from tension, aches, and pains. You shift your weight onto your "good leg." You let your torso slump down, causing your head to drop down and forward. That causes your unconscious mind to overlay all the difficulties from those earlier times over the top of whatever you are experiencing. The old stories overshadow the joy of *this* moment. They suck the life out of it.

Each faulty posture contains vast amounts of pain and suffering, stored in your consciousness as sensory/motor feedback loops. These loops whisk your mind away from the present moment. You are not really here now. Technically, you are in an artificial construct made up of some past or future projection.

The sensory/motor feedback loops—created by the aberrant postures—creates backstories that "seem appropriate" to what your eyes are focusing on. It can seem so real. You can so easily believe *this* is reality.

On the physical plane alone, the secondary complications from favoring an injury create disruptions to all your body's physiological functions that are far worse than the original trauma. With each step, the limp or slump misaligns a number of vertebrae and skeletal bones, severely inhibiting all your powerful circulatory systems at those levels. The spinal subluxations and misalignments to your other skeletal bones compromise all of your movements. After a while the misalignment patterns seem permanent.

Reaction times in all your movements become progressively compromised. Each postural fault causes its own split-second delay before you can make a proper movement or correction. They make you just off balance enough to be vulnerable to further trauma.

Worse, any bony misalignment starts developing bone spurs and arthritic changes. Over time your health deteriorates. Favoring injuries is just a *bad idea*—on every level.

Lessons of a Hollywood Stuntman

When I was a young chiropractor, a Hollywood stuntman retired and moved to my town. He had a long career falling off horses, falling off buildings, wrecking cars, and doing whatever was too dangerous for the actors to do themselves.

One day I saw him in town, and he said, "I have an appointment to see you tomorrow." I said, "Great!" I really liked him and looked forward to our visit. In the middle of that night though, I woke up in a full sweat. In my imagination I was afraid that he would be so injured that there would be nothing I could do for him. I worried that he might be held together with duct tape and baling wire.

When he arrived at my office the next day, he handed me his most recent X-rays. "Standard procedure," he said as he handed them to me. I put his X-rays up on the view box. Remarkably, his spine looked good. Actually, his spine looked a whole lot better than most people a third his age.

He had been a stuntman since he was nineteen. He was then in his late sixties, yet his spinal column looked like it belonged to a healthy young man. As I was working on him, I could not fathom how he had an entire career in such a traumatic profession and yet present such a healthy spine. I asked him how he had done it. He replied:

> "In the Industry, when we do a gag [industry-speak for
> a stunt], my team sets up every aspect of the stunt very
> carefully in advance. If I am to crash a car into a brick wall,
> my team constructs the wall of bricks that weigh less than
> a third of what normal bricks weigh. The bricks are stacked

with a light mortar that has no cement in it. As the crew sets up the gag, they try to think of everything.

"But sometimes things go wrong. The car might hit so hard that my rib cage slams into the armrest, and I crack a couple of ribs. I groan for a few labored breaths. Then I remember that there are over three hundred people on the back lot tour watching the gag. I take a couple breaths to get myself together. Then I look up and wave at the crowd. They cheer. As I get out of the car, it may take a few steps to get the limp out. Then I walk off to the trailer like nothing happened.

"My crew saw what happened. They were quite aware of how long it took for me to look up and wave. Back at the trailer, they help me take off my shirt and tape up my ribs. Then we do triage to decide whether to take me to the chiropractor, the physical therapist, or the orthopedist. I grab my X-rays out of the filing cabinet, and off we go."

From that conversation, I understood that being a stuntman taught him to act like a cat. No matter what happened, he always walked away as if the injury *never happened*. The couple of breaths he took before he looked up and waved at the crowd interrupted him from a pattern of focusing his attention on the injury. The breaths brought him back to present-time awareness. *It was a gag.*

You want to walk away from all your traumas, whether physical, mental, emotional or even spiritual as if "that never happened." Winston Churchill said, "Success is going from one failure to another with no loss of enthusiasm." That's shaking it off like a cat.

FIFTH HABIT

- CHAPTER 67 -

Trust Your Gut

Your spirit is not confined in any way by time or space. To your spirit *everything* is happening here and now. The moment you imagine doing something, your spirit is standing there, experiencing that event. Your first feeling is your spirit's preview of how you will feel if you physically do what you were thinking about.

Your first feeling is akin to what people call "gut instinct." It is your spirit informing you of what you are about to encounter. Your first feeling previews whether you are going to enjoy an experience, or are in harm's way. The feeling only lasts a second or two—then it's gone. If you are not paying attention, you completely miss it.

When you are traveling in some exotic place, your gut instinct can keep you safe and out of harm's way, especially when you don't understand the language or the culture. We all have stories where our gut instinct led us out of situations that later went bad.

I went to an all-day musical concert in the 1970s in Stockton, California at Billy Hebert Field. It was held inside a baseball field with a very high fence fully enclosing it. When we arrived, I got a really bad feeling going through the narrow turnstiles that led into the field. I remember it felt like a severe bottleneck that would take way too long to evacuate if there were a panic.

Later in the afternoon the bad feeling in my gut returned and started building. I started getting a tension headache. I told my date I was getting a bad feeling, and asked her if she didn't mind leaving soon. She said she was fine with leaving now. Just as we were leaving, a Hell's Angels motorcycle gang rode up. They spread their blankets on the lawn right next to the baseball field. The hair went up on my neck.

One of my friends later told me that right after we left, the Stockton police showed up in mass, wearing full tactical riot gear. When the Hell's Angels refused to leave (actually they flipped the cops off), the police lobbed tear gas canisters at them. The slight breeze pushed the thick fog of tear gas into the baseball stadium that was packed completely full of people, including a large number of women and children.

Everyone inside was choking and gagging, but they were packed together so tightly, they were unable to get out due to the narrow turnstiles. People in the upper stands started throwing beer bottles at the police, injuring numerous police officers. The whole thing turned into a full-blown riot. Trusting my gut got us out of that hellish situation just before it happened.

Your first feeling works with people as well as experiences. When you first meet someone, your spirit is instantly taking in the full measure of that person. It fully experiences them in that moment. Your first impression of them is your spirit's preview of how you will feel about that person later, if you choose to have further interactions with them.

I used to have a girlfriend who had a silver wolf named Sitka, who was the best judge of character I ever met. The day after Sitka died, I went to the Herb Shop in Nevada City to have an espresso. I was reflecting on Sitka's life, and wondering how she *always* discerned the good people from the bad.

Just then a stranger walked past the window and I found myself hating his guts. That was weird because I don't *hate* anyone. Luckily I had the clarity of mind to ask "What was I thinking just before he walked past the window?" I realized I had been wondering how Sitka was always such a great judge of character.

The stranger came into the Herb Shop, walked right up to me, and said, "You're John Mayfield, right?" I said I was, and without any foreplay he said, "I do acupuncture, and I would like to do a trade, where you work on me and I work on you." I said, "I have an acupuncture doctor in my office and we work on each other. We also do rounds on mutual patients. So, I am not open to a trade right now." I could actually hear Sitka softly growling in my ear from beyond the veil, still looking out for me, my own spirit keeper, warning me about this guy.

A few months later he abruptly left town, leaving a trail of uncompleted trades, shoddy workmanship, and owing people money. My first feeling warned me ahead of time. Then I *got* how Sitka could be such a good judge of character. She *never* talked herself out of her first feeling about a new person she just met. She was a good teacher. She taught me to trust my gut.

You need to start noticing all your first impressions. Make it your habit. This is one of the ways you grow spiritually. The first feelings you have from one situation to the next gives you access to the wisdom of your spirit. This is how your intuition develops and matures. You become quite insightful and face life with enhanced awareness. The wisdom helps you control your own destiny.

It's just as important to notice first impressions that are good. There is always the balance. When you get a warm happy feeling about an upcoming event or someone you just met, that's your gut instinct telling you that this is going to be good.

When I have two choices of roads to take, one at a time I imagine taking each road and see how it feels. As I travel that road in my imagination, if there is a blockage or something bad happens on that road, I cannot visualize myself getting past the blockage. In that situation I take the other road. Later, on the news, it turns out there was a major accident, and the road was closed so a med-evac helicopter could take injured people away from the scene. I have also had some wonderful adventures as a result of this way of choosing.

Become aware of all your first feelings. Respect them. Trust your gut. It provides you with enhanced wisdom about what's going on in your life.

One of my firm rules is: I do not allow my rational mind to talk me out of a first feeling—*about anything*. Every time I have, I have paid dearly. I have pleasantly observed that every year I am aware of my first feelings on ever more subtle levels. I am still learning, so I often notice—after things went wrong—that I *knew* they would go wrong, but I did it anyway. But I am getting better all the time, and so can you. It's quite enchanting.

You can commission your mind to investigate *why* you had that first feeling, but *never to talk you out of it*. Then you get to observe the mysteries of life that used to pass you by. Ignore your first feelings at your own peril.

Sixth Habit

- Chapter 68 -

Be Decisive

The foundation of your life is a triangle, with each point supporting—or detracting from—the other two. Each point of the triangle represents a dynamic quality of your character that needs to be honed and developed throughout this lifetime:

- Cherish yourself, others and *all* life.
- Be truthful without malice. Be honorable and true to your word. Do what you say you will do.
- Be decisive, especially about all the little things. Do not procrastinate. Stand up for what you believe.

For this entire lifetime, this triangle either makes your life magical and enchanting or plunges you into a frustrated lifetime of thwarted ambitions and dead-end journeys. Cherishing, being truthful and decisive are absolutely crucial to living a truly rewarding life. Your job is to keep these three points of the triangle in a state of balance. It is like standing on a three-way balance board and keeping each point level throughout all of the varied circumstances in your life.

The good news is that you *get* to decide everything in your life. The bad news is you *must* decide everything in your life. Any part of your life where you fail to make your own decisions, someone else makes them for you, and that rarely turns out the way you want.

Make decisions about all considerations in your life, both large and small. Do what you say you will do. Keep your promises to yourself and others. Declare what you believe in. Have the courage to stand up for your principles. Commit to what your heart believes in.

It's time to step up. We all need your contribution. When you are decisive about all the little things, the big picture of your life becomes crystal clear. If you want your life to stand for something, be decisive.

You build character when you commit to your principles, values, and beliefs; when you say a resounding "yes' to whatever life sends your way. Being decisive is every bit as crucial to your character as being honorable and cherishing others. *Being decisive, especially about all the little things, will change your life.*

Each time you come to a point where you need to make a decision, and you fail to make that decision, your mind is forced to run scenarios on all the possible options of that decision. Then if you are indecisive about another issue, and then another, your mind must continually process all the possible scenarios.

If you are indecisive about five or six issues, all those indecisions take up so much bandwidth that they slow your mind's processing speed to a crawl. You can hardly think. Indecision acts like a virus in your computer-like mind.

That would be like putting a four-way stop sign at the intersection of two busy freeways. Imagine that at rush hour, all that traffic backing up for miles, all that frustration. That's how your thought processes are affected when you have a lot of undecided issues. When you have a lot of things on your mind and you leave a lot of them undecided, the clarity of your thinking becomes impaired, leaving you overwhelmed.

Once you make the decision, the dance ends. Your mind can be still. Then you experience spaciousness in your mind, creating space for inspiration. You have the freedom to contemplate other things that may be more important.

Many people are quite decisive about big issues in their lives, while letting the "little issues" pile up. They assume little issues don't matter. A wife might ask her husband, "What do you want for dinner tonight?" If he answers, "I don't know," or "Whatever you make is OK," all the meal planning and shopping decisions fall to her.

She ends up feeling frustrated, having no idea what her husband actually wants to eat. If he does not like what she has cooked, she experiences anger or resentment, and wonders why she even bothered. The emotional undertow from little indecisions like this creates seemingly unrelated outbursts that seriously disrupt your life.

When I really *got* that being decisive about the little things was so important, I began to make that a conscious practice. One day shortly afterward, my wife asked me what I wanted for dinner. I went inside and asked myself "what would I like?" The first thing that came to mind was a delicious stir fry she makes, with snow peas, red onions and a good cut of sirloin over basmati rice. When I said that she said, "All we have is chicken."

I silently laughed to myself and wondered why she even asked. But on Friday night when I came home she had gone to four stores to find snow peas. She was so happy and pleased with herself to be cooking my favorite meal. Our loved ones want to do loving things for us, but are usually not psychic about the little things—like what we want to eat— *unless we tell them.*

If you are indecisive about the little things, the big picture of your life will always be fuzzy. The clarity of your thinking can be like television in the early days, when there was so much "snow" it was really hard to see the picture. Indecisions keep you wrong-footed. They sap your life force.

Years can go by while you putter around on the sidelines of life. The only reason this doesn't seem totally weird is because most of the people around us are doing the same thing. But that does not make it right.

Furthermore, indecision cheapens your love. It demeans your truth. Everything is up for renegotiation. You don't stand for anything. Waiting for something to happen and then responding to it may appear suave and debonair from the outside, but life is passing you by. If you really love something and believe in it, why aren't you totally committed to it?

When all the members of a family or team at work are keeping this triangle in balance, the fruit of their actions multiply exponentially. It's like multiplying the combined numbers of their members by the third power. Each person's contribution enhances the contribution of all the others. For your entire lifetime, focusing your attention on cherishing, being truthful and decisive improves every part of your life.

The Power of Commitment

There is a poem by W. H. Murray that hung on a wall right next to my adjusting table for fourteen years. I read it about twenty times every day at work. It affected my life quite profoundly:

Commitment

"Until one is committed, there is hesitancy, the chance to draw back, always ineffectiveness. Concerning all acts of initiative (and creation), there is one elementary truth, the ignorance of which kills countless ideas and splendid plans: that the moment one definitely commits oneself, then providence moves too.

All sorts of things occur to help one that never otherwise would have occurred. A whole stream of events issues from the decision, raising in one's favor all manner of unforeseen incidents and meetings and material assistance, which no man could have dreamed would have come his way.

I have come to have a newfound respect for one of Goethe's couplets:

'Whatever you can do, or dream you can, begin it. Boldness has genius, power, and magic in it. Begin it now.'"

Over the years, as I continued to read this poem, a deep understanding of the underlying principles of creation began ripening in my mind. I began to see clearly that *commitment is the access code to the universe*. Without commitment, you are stuck. You just sit there with all possibility and all potential surrounding you. You just sit there, not moving.

The universe is like an interactive computer game where all your desires—and fears—are manifested as you move through the game's maze. When you commit to something you want to do, the doors of opportunity in your present situation begin to close off to you. The doors of opportunity open for you in the direction you commit to. Your life is mysteriously propelled in *that* direction.

Until you make that commitment, those opportunities do not present themselves. Without commitment, very little changes in your life. As you become more decisive, *especially about the little things*, you experience significant changes in your life. You progressively fulfill more of your hopes and dreams.

Because you are a spiritual being living in a universe that has spiritual rules, all manner of unforeseen things occur as the direct result of your commitment. The entire spiritual kingdom conspires to help you.

The Gift, the Teacher, and the Mystery

When you commit, your life takes on a trajectory, a definite direction of movement. This is important because when you arrive at the intersections of your life the spiritual world provides the mystery, the teacher, and the gift. They are *always* there at the intersection points of your life's lessons.

At the intersections of your life the teacher may be someone who angered you so much that you stormed around getting things done that your heart wanted you to do all along—but you would *not* have done it if you hadn't been so blasted angry.

The gift can be someone who later becomes a friend. It can be realizing how fortunate you are to be involved in a situation as rich and rewarding as this.

The mystery that is there at every major intersection of your life can be an epiphany or a breakthrough in your understanding that carries over into many other avenues of your life.

But there is a timing to life. You make a commitment, and that starts everything going. The spiritual world starts setting things up for you so that when you get to the projected intersection, everything is all set up for you to have a rewarding experience.

But if you procrastinate—or second-guess yourself so that you delay moving in your previously committed-to direction—the lesson, gift and teacher are there, but you are not! And you may not even have a clue about the opportunity you missed.

When you rail against the lessons that occur—which are direct results of decisions you have made—it can be just as bad. You may get to the intersection on time, but if you are railing against the lesson, thinking "this should not be happening to me," you are probably so distracted by your own protestations that you don't even notice that the gift, teacher and mystery were right there.

So, next time a lesson comes up, say "yes" to it. Don't delay. If you start paying attention, you will see that there, just beyond your normal depth of perception, is the mystery, the teacher, and the gift. Start looking for them. You will see what I'm talking about.

After you die and are in the next world, you sit down with a reviewer and review your life—one day at a time—from the last day to the first day of your lifetime. You have two tablets that look like blueprints. When you look at where two lines intersect, a scene opens up for you to see.

From the one tablet you see what the universe held out for you to experience, which was usually quite magnificent. From the other tablet you see what you actually allowed yourself to experience. You also experience how your actions affected other people in that scene and the unintended consequences of your actions—both good and bad. Often you limit your choices because of baggage you are carrying, like projecting "I don't deserve it," or "nothing ever works out for me."

Say "yes" to the lessons that appear to come at you. Your spirit and the spiritual kingdom are always pushing you toward higher limits of what you can believe and what you have previously allowed yourself to experience. The more you say "yes" to life's lessons, and the more decisive you are, the faster you progress and the higher you go in this life.

When I *got* this lesson, I would walk around the house saying, "Yes. *Yes*. YES!" I would shout out "Yes" when we got in the car to go somewhere. My wife would laugh at me, but later she told me she was inwardly more pleased than amused. Life is so much richer when you just say "yes."

- CHAPTER 69 -

Cherish Others

The purpose of life is to cherish others, ourselves, and the world around us. That's what we are here to learn. When we love everyone and everything, and let them love us back, we come into harmony with all creation. Then our life makes sense. All life is about choices. Moment by moment, we have the sovereign power to choose where we focus our precious attention.

There are no victims. There is no injustice. But we can fritter away huge portions of our lives focusing on stories about injustice and victimization, feeling controlled or wanting to make others do what *we think is right*. We can be angry with others, worry about them, try to fix them, or any number of other dramas. Or, we can simply love them for who they are.

Any negative feeling you have about another person becomes a wall, a barrier that separates them from you. When you simply *feel* the negative feelings you have toward that person, the wall between you and them dissolves. The barrier ceases to exist. Once the wall is dissolved, your heart naturally loves them. No matter how traumatized you have become, your heart never loses its child-like innocence. It always chooses love.

You come into harmony with all life every time you bring your attention back to what you love. Life is short. You are *wasting* every moment that you spend focusing on what's wrong in the world. Your life has so much more value when you focus your precious attention on what you love. Only then are you are making the world a better place.

Every moment you are focusing on what you love, your heart is providing insights into how to make your world a more loving place. Cherishing others creates thousands of times more healing to the world than thinking about or protesting what is bad or wrong.

In relationships, you can always choose to focus on your inner core values, which begin with how much you cherish your loved ones. Or you can focus on worries, problems, or on building a case about what that person said, or what you suspect they will do. When you remember that you really love people, you are much less susceptible to bickering and dwelling on their faults.

When you focus on what you love and love what you have, you are in harmony with the values of your heart. Your face and eyes brighten. Your mind lights up. There is a lightness to your step. You find yourself humming or singing to yourself. You laugh more. You are filled with enthusiasm for life. Others can hear it in the tone of your voice. Enthusiasm, by the way, comes from the Greek words *Theos* (God) and *ism* (condition of). The condition of having God within. I like that.

Choosing to love is one of the seven habits that change your life. Love yourself. Love others—especially the difficult ones—and focus your attention on loving your splendid plans and dreams. Everything else is a distraction.

The Dalai Lama, who is one of the brightest spiritual lights on the planet at this time, has said numerous times, "The purpose of life is to cherish others." He has also said, "When I cherish others, they tend to cherish me back. When they cherish me back, it makes me feel so good inside that I cherish others for purely selfish reasons." If your heart could speak, this is surely what it would say.

The Dalai Lama is a living example of how your heart can be the emperor of your consciousness while living on Earth. He loves *everyone,* even the Chinese leaders who had millions of his people killed or tortured. It is easy to love someone who is nice to you. It takes considerably more courage and insight to love someone who treats you badly. But *they* are your greatest teachers.

When you forgive others, you change the present moment in a more loving way, which transforms the future. Forgiveness also changes the past. When you feel all the negative feelings that drive toxic thoughts about another—thoughts that previously seemed so all-fired important—all your reasons for thinking toxic thoughts about them fade into obscurity. Meanwhile the deeper, more meaningful qualities of that person become the most prominent features in your relationship with them.

In that moment they change. And—more importantly—*you* change. You both transform into the best versions of yourself. You have rewritten your DNA. You have allowed that person to rewrite their DNA, and everything changes.

Loving others takes courage. It is not for the faint of heart. As you let go of old hurts and issues that used to consume your thoughts, you create a more loving world in which your plans and dreams flourish. *Consistently choosing to love is the real revolution.*

CHAPTER 70

Mastery

When I studied martial arts, my sensei (teacher), in a private moment, told me about the first time he had to spar with his eighty-nine-year-old master. His master was a five-foot-two Korean. My teacher was in his thirties, six-foot-two and powerfully built. Fighting a little old man went against every instinct.

The master leaped up, stepped lithely through the ropes of a regular boxing ring, and none of the ropes showed any evidence that he had stepped through them. My sensei thought, "I can do that." He leaped up, deftly placed his foot, and moved with catlike grace through the ropes. From inside the ring he looked back at the ropes. They were all waving up and down. *That* should have told him something.

Then the master wanted my teacher to fight him. My teacher did not want to hurt a little old man, so he pulled his punches. The master said, "You not very fast." Moments later he said, "You not very strong." The match was frustrating.

At lunch one of the other teachers said, "I see on the schedule you fought the master today." My teacher said, "If you *call it* that!" The other teacher belly laughed and said, "You don't *ever* have to worry about hurting him. I go out there and throw everything I've got at him. The best I can ever do with a punch or kick is brush the edge of his gi (his martial arts tunic) or the top of his hair. He makes no more movement than is absolutely necessary. He easily deflects all my blows. And at the end of the match, he is not sweating at all. I, on the other hand, can wring the sweat out of my gi. Then he critiques my technique, skill levels and strength."

At that time I had focused on abdominal breathing for several years. In one magical month, I started doing karate, began to learn about correct posture, and was introduced to exercises that effectively realign the spine. At that time, the whole process of becoming a master seemed *far* beyond anything I could aspire to.

Most people do not decisively commit to their own unique plans and dreams. They fritter away large portions of their life, waiting around for some mystical "sign" to occur in the heavens, for some heavenly host to give them permission to commit the power of their attention to the sacredness of their own ambitions. That is completely backward to how life really works.

Now I see that mastery begins with committing to a simple step— and then another. It is amazing how much one person will accomplish in their lifetime if he or she keeps decisively putting one foot in front of the other, and trains their unruly mind to single-mindedly focus on their own plans and dreams. Mastery naturally develops.

Life is a paradox. If you want more freedom, be more disciplined. Look around at people you know who have figured out how to be free. Notice how disciplined they are. At the opposite polarity, observe people who have not developed discipline in their lives. Notice how life seems to entangle and encumber them every way they turn. True freedom is not mysterious. It follows simple laws.

As you make the decision to incorporate the habits in this book into your life, your prowess will continue to build on all levels. As you focus on breathing out strong and having good posture, your self-esteem and energy levels will both double every year for many years. So will the clarity of your logic and the power of your mind. Feeling your feelings and trusting your gut opens whole new vistas and expands your life in extraordinary ways. Your spirit is able to guide you past all the minefields in life.

Every part of your bodymind becomes more powerful every year— even if you are not participating zealously. *All your efforts are rewarded tenfold.* You get so much return for so little effort. When you see how much you gain from even halfheartedly participating, you will be motivated to participate on progressively greater levels. It all starts with baby steps.

The more time you spend living into the seven habits in this book, and bringing your consciousness into harmony with the "five elements," the faster and greater your upper limits expand. You step out of the realm of pain and suffering and enter the rarified upper realms of existence. There, life is so much more fun and exciting. As a bonus, age continually empowers you.

Your awareness can be likened to the headlights of your car shining into the darkness. You can only see as far as your headlights illuminate. As you live into these seven habits, your light and your power shine further into the night of your yet undiscovered world. This is like having a whole array of super halogen lights that exponentially expand your wisdom and perception.

You are an immortal being of great power and magnificence—living in a physical body—a spirit having a human experience. When you *get* that you are an immortal being of great beauty and power, your life becomes richer and more rewarding.

- CHAPTER 71 -

Conclusion

This magnificent human body of yours is so elegant. Mindfulness of its simple operating rules consistently rewards your efforts by multiples of ten. The understandings in this book, even though they are so simple, take your whole life to master. That may seem like a daunting journey, but all along the way you are fulfilling your heart's desires while empowering your bodymind, which is impressive.

I have lived with these principles, taught them to my patients over the years, honed them, worked out the rough edges. I have watched as patients have implemented these simple changes, seen how their lives have changed, subtle at first, until the chaos of their lives has transformed into lives well lived. The concepts work. The rewards are worth the effort.

Earth is a perfect free-will world. We can do anything we want with this lifetime we have been granted. We can waste it or we can focus our precious attention on what our hearts desire. The good done by one person who keeps redirecting his or her focus back to what their heart desires has more real power in the world than the efforts of thousands of people who rail against what's wrong.

Love is the real revolution, and one person does make the difference. What you do—when you are focused on what you love, doing what your own heart desires and doing what makes you feel most alive—is ultimately what will change the world.

This is a book I hope you will read over and over. Each time you read it you will notice different issues that require your attention. Your life will change, and you will like who you are becoming. I wish you a life of fulfillment, and all the love and blessings this incredible world has to offer.

GLOSSARY

Chakras: You have seven main chakras and a number of lesser ones. Chakras are the organs of your most subtle body. They are etheric antennae. The more loving, truthful, and decisive you are, the more they open, the faster they spin and the more beautiful and radiant the rainbow-like colors they display. The energy your chakras spin out is encoded with all your thoughts, attitudes, values, and beliefs. They are amplified by your love—or fear. Since your spirit puts out more energy than your body can contain, the energy spinning out from your chakras and acupuncture points trails out behind you like the wake of a ship.

The Seven Chakras:

- The first—in the perineum at the bottom of your body—is about knowing you are unconditionally loved. When this chakra is healthy you know that you will always have enough to eat, a place to live and be able to survive and care for your loved ones in the physical world.
- The second—below your navel—is your sexual energy, your passion for life. When you are passionate about life you start developing charisma. The highest octave of sexual energy is compassion. When this chakra is healthy, you believe that you fit in, that you are an integral part of every aspect of life, beginning with your family, school and including any group you are in any way affiliated with.
- The third—your solar plexus—is where you manifest your own power into the world, your work, your plans and dreams. It blossoms as you feel nurtured, develop firm boundaries and give yourself permission to have the sweetness of life. This chakra is about knowing that you are safe. The two greatest sins of us two-leggeds is not feeling safe and loved.

- The fourth—your heart chakra—is in charge of your consciousness. Your heart focuses its precious attention on cherishing everyone, everything and letting them cherish you back. The more you focus on what you love, the more loving your world becomes. Every part of your body and every part of your world depends on and flourishes under the warmth, unconditional love and guidance your heart provides.

- The fifth—your throat chakra—develops fully as you learn to speak your truth clearly and succinctly, and express your creativity. Not having a creative outlet clogs up your throat chakra as much as not speaking your truth.

- The sixth—sometimes called the third eye—represents how well you perceive the eternal truths between all dualities (male or female, good or bad, republican or democrat, etc.) of the physical universe. This chakra also represents your ability to perceive—and stand in— the eternal moment that exists between past and future.

- The seventh chakra—the crown of your head—connects you with Creator and the entire angelic kingdom. It also connects you with the akashic records, which is an invisible database of everything that occurs within the Earth, an archive of all past and potential future experiences. We use this information to determine how to deal with current experiences. Meditating on this chakra can take you into the upper heavenly worlds.

Cleansing Breaths: One or two fast deep breaths interrupt unconscious patterns, pulling you out of a spell, bringing you back to present-time awareness.

Hara: In Japanese culture your "one point center" is traditionally called *hara*. Its location is just below your navel. It is the absolute midpoint between your upper body and your lower body. Breathing from hara is the first law of breathing, as well as the first law of posture—and spiritual awareness. The purpose of all postural considerations boils down to focusing your awareness in hara.

The Five Qualities of Your Spirit: Respect, trust, wisdom, power in the manifest world, and all oneness (knowing that you belong). These are qualities you *have*, not qualities that you must earn. You do have to flesh them out though.

The Four Posture Rules:
1. *Breathe out* strong from below your navel.
2. *Lift up your sternum*, and let your neck and shoulders be relaxed and free. The first two rules stabilize your core, and resolve about 70 percent of what can go wrong in posture, gait, lifting, or walking up and down hills or stairs.
3. *Let your head float up to its sweet spot*, where it takes minimal energy to hold it erect. Your ear canal lines up directly over the top of your shoulders.
4. *Keep your feet parallel* no matter whether you are walking, standing, or sitting. Your gait lands on the midpoint of your feet (not on your heels) as you walk. Feel your arches expressing upward as you push off at the end of your stride.

Meridians: Meridians are ductless energy channels. You have twelve main pairs of meridians on either side of your body, plus the midline vessels and accessory meridians. Not shown on acupuncture charts are ever-smaller vessels coming off the main meridians until you have a vessel terminating in the nucleus of every cell in your body. The meridians form up before your organs, muscles or bones. They form the template that every part of your entire body forms up around.

The fluid in your meridians looks like water, but has a high specific gravity (like oil), which allows the meridians to push out and maintain an easily palpable and stable auric field. The aura around your body insulates you from having to experience the pain and thoughts of everyone around you. This insulating quality lets you experience your own autonomous life.

The Seven Habits That Change Your Life:

- *Breathe Out Strong:* Breathing from your core is absolutely essential for reclaiming awareness and power.
- *Stand Tall:* The Second Habit is to improve your posture and gait each year.
- *Shake It Off like a Cat:* Walk away from injuries like a cat, like "that *never* happened."
- *Feel Your Feelings:* Feeling your feelings is the key to true self mastery. It is the next great frontier.
- *Trust Your Gut:* Your first feeling is your spirit's exact preview of a person you just met, or an event you are invited to.
- *Be Decisive:* Being decisive is every bit as crucial to your character as cherishing others, telling the truth, and being honorable. Say yes, commit to the lessons that come at you.
- *Cherish Others:* The purpose of life is to cherish others, yourself, and your plans and dreams.

The Seven Dimensions of your bodymind:

- *Physical:* This first dimension, or realm, gives your spirit and soul access to the adventures of physical activities like sports, exploring this amazing world, the sensuousness of eating food, and making love.
- *Etheric:* Your etheric body is your energy double. It holds your pain body, all your unresolved feelings. When you hold a blouse or shirt in front of you to see how it affects the "color" in your face, you are focusing on your etheric body. Eating high quality food, getting

adequate sleep, breathing fresh air, and spending time in nature reflects directly into your etheric body. When you are healthy, the color in your face is radiant.

- *Mental:* This third dimension is ruled by the brain and nervous system. It allows your spirit and soul to comprehend life through all our sciences, philosophies, politics, religions, and all of the ways we communicate with each other.

- *Emotional:* The fourth dimension is expressed through the blood vascular system, and ruled by our kidney/bladder system. Spiritual energy and emotional energy are the most alike. Feeling your feelings and questioning them like an ardent reporter gives you access to the wisdom of your spirit.

- *Causal:* The fifth dimension is ruled by your meridians, which constantly project your attitudes and values out into your energy field where everyone can feel, or in some way experience them.

- In the sixth dimension, which is not generally named, your endocrine glands (like the thyroid, adrenal, and pituitary) translate the wisdom of the spiritual kingdom into language your mind can understand by secreting hormones into your bloodstream. Hormones give your emotions stability. For example, your uterus or prostate gland allows you to experience what life is like in a woman or man's body. The thyroid hormones give you the stability to speak your truth, and express your creativity. Your hormones give purpose to your feelings.

- The seventh dimension is ruled by your chakras, which are spinning vortexes. As you become more spiritually evolved, they spin faster, which gives them the appearance of growing more petals, like the petals around a flower. Chakras function like large sprinkler heads that radiate your thoughts and beliefs outward into the world where they somehow become the "reality" you experience.

BIBLIOGRAPHY

Health & Nutrition

Dr. Abravanel's Body Type Program for Health, Fitness and Nutrition. Abravanel, E. D. Bantam Books, 1985.

Immaculate Deception; A New Look at Childbirth in America. Arms, Suzanne. Houghton Mifflin, 1975.

Heal Thyself, Bach Flower Remedies. Bach, E. Keats Publishing, 1977.

Heart Attack Rareness in Thyroid-Treated Patients. Barnes, B., and C. Charles C. Thomas, 1972.

Hypothyroidism: The Unsuspected Illness. Barnes, Broda O., M.D., and Lawrence Galton. Harper, 1976.

Government Reform Committee Hearing on Vaccines and Autism, April 6, 2000. Burton, Dan, U.S. Representative. (www.cspan.org).

Babies Remember Birth. Chamberlain, David, Ph.D. Jeremy P. Tarcher, 1988.

The Mind of Your Newborn Baby. Chamberlain, David. North Atlantic Books, 1998.

Portraits of Homeopathic Medicines, Psychophysical Analysisw of Selected Constitutional Types. Coulter, Catherine R. North Atlantic Books, 1986.

Portraits of Homeopathic Medicine, Psychophysical Analysis of Selected Constitutional Types, Vol. 2. Coulter, Catherine R. North Atlantic Books, 1988.

Divided Legacy: The Conflict Between Homeopathy and the American Medical Association. Coulter, Harris L. North Atlantic Books, 1973.

A Shot in the Dark. Coulter, Harris L., and Barbara Loe Fisher. Avery Trade, 1991.

"Wugi Qigong and the Essence of Taiji Quan: The Teachings of Grandmaster Cai Song Fang." Diepersloot, Jan. Mount Diablo Taiji Quan Center, 2nd ed., 1989.

Coming to Life, A Companion Piece to the Self-Exploration Process. Doak, James. Grass Valley, CA: Blue Dolphin Publishing, 1987.

Nourishing Traditions. Fallon, Sally, with Mary G. Enig, Ph.D. Washington, DC: New Trends Publishing, rev. 2nd ed., 1999.

Organon of the Medical Art. Hahnemann, Samuel. Edited and annotated by Wenda Brewster O'Reilly, Ph.D.; based on a translation by Steven Decker. Palo Alto, CA: Birdcage Press, 1996.

On Intelligence: How a New Understanding of the Brain Will Lead to the Creation of Truly Intelligent Machines. Hawkins, Jeff, and Sandra Blakeslee. New York: Times Books, 2004.

You Can Heal Your Life. Hay, Louise L. Carlsbad, CA: Hay House, Inc., 1984.

Clean: The Revolutionary Program to Restore the Body's Natural Ability to Heal Itself. Junger, Alejandro, M. D. New York, New York: HarperCollins Pub. 2012

Wisdom in the Body, The Craniosacral Approach to Essential Health. Kern, Michael. Berkeley: North Atlantic Books, 2001, 2005.

Birth Without Violence. Leboyer, Frederick, M.D. Rochester, VT: Healing Arts Press, 2002.

Who Dies? An Investigation of Conscious Living and Conscious Dying. Levine, Stephen. Garden City, NY: Anchor Books, 1982.

Heal Your Mind, Rewire Your Brain. Lind-Kyle, Pat. Santa Rosa, CA: Energy Psychology Press, 2009.

Class Notes: Palmer College of Chiropractic. Mayfield, John, D.C. (1964-1967 and 1971-1972).

Born to Run. McDougall, Christopher. New York: Alfred A. Knopf, 2009.

Your Health, Your Choice: Your Complete Personal Guide to Wellness, Nutrition & Disease Prevention. Morter, M. Ted, Jr., M.A., and Robert L. Brown, Ph.D. Lifetime Books, 1995. This book explains the acid/base balance in healthy nutrition.

What Every Parent Should Know About Childhood Immunization. Murphy, Jamie. Boston: Earth Healing Products, 1993.

The Sanctity of Human Blood: Vaccination Is Not Immunization. O'Shea, Tim. San Jose, CA: New West, 1999.

The 100 Year Lifestyle. Plasker, Eric. Avon, MA: Adams Media Corporation, 2007.

Applied Kinesiology: Synopsis. Walther, David S. Pueblo, CO: Systems DC, 2ⁿᵈ ed., 1988.

The Essential Calvin and Hobbes. Watterson, Bill. Kansas City, MO: Andrews and McMeel Publishing, 1988.

The Practice of Personal Transformation: A Jungian Approach. Williams, Strephon Kaplan. Berkeley: Journey Press, 1984.

The Five Elements (Basis of Acupuncture)

Traditional Acupuncture, The Law of the Five Elements. Connelly, Dianne M., Ph.D., M.Ac. (UK). Columbia, MO: The Center for Traditional Acupuncture Inc., 1979.

Grasping the Wind. Ellis, Andrew; Nigel Wiseman and Ken Boss. Brookline, MA: Paradigm Publications, 1989.

Plant Spirit Medicine: A Journey into the Healing Wisdom of Plants. Cowan, Eliot. Updated New Edition. Boulder, CO: Sounds True, 2014. (Also included in the Quantum Physics section.)

"On the Kyungrak System." Kim, Bong Han. Pyongyang, North Korea: Medical Science Press, 1963. http://primosystem.wikispaces.com/ Kim+Bong+Han+Paper+in+1963. Dr. Kim, a North Korean researcher, first proved the existence of acupuncture meridians (in the above paper). In further research projects I read, he showed that the acupuncture meridians form up completely while we are still embryos, and that our organs and bones and muscles form up around the matrix that is first developed by our acupuncture vessels. Further he showed that meridians connect to the nucleus of every cell.

Body Intelligence: How to "Think" Outside Your Brain and Connect to Your Multi-Dimensional Self. Mayfield, John, D.C. Grass Valley CA: Nubalance Pub. Co. 2008

The Illuminated Heart: Perspectives on East-West Psychology and Thought. McKeen, Jock and Wong, Bennet. Gabriola Island, BC: The Haven Press, 2012

Classical Five-Element Acupuncture: The Five Elements and the Officials. Worsley, J. R. Taos, NM: Redwing Book Co., vol. III, 1998. Dr. Worsley introduced the five elements into most of the non-Asian societies.

Relationship Issues

The Seven Habits of Highly Effective People: Restoring the Character Ethic. Covey, Stephen R. New York: Simon & Schuster, 1989.

The Aquarian Conspiracy: Personal and Social Transformation in the 1980s. Ferguson, Marilyn. Los Angeles: Jeremy P. Tarcher, 1980.

The Art of Loving. Fromm, Erich. New York: Bantam Books, 1963.

The Prophet. Gibran, Kahlil. New York: Alfred A. Knopf, 1923.

Centering and the Art of Intimacy. Hendricks, Gay, Ph.D., and Kathlyn Hendricks, Ph.D. Upper Saddle River, NJ: Prentice Hall, 1987.

Conscious Loving: The Journey to Co-Commitment. Hendricks, Gay, Ph.D., and Kathlyn Hendricks, Ph.D. New York: Bantam Books, 1992.

The Corporate Mystic: A Guidebook for Visionaries with Their Feet on the Ground. Hendricks, Gay, Ph.D., and Kathlyn Hendricks, Ph.D. New York: Bantam Books, Bantam trade pbk. ed., 1997.

Rumi: Gazing at the Beloved: The Radical Practice of Beholding the Divine. Johnson, Will. Rochester, VT: Inner Traditions, 2003.

Modern Man in Search of a Soul. Jung, C. G. New York: Harcourt Harvest, 1933.

Relax Focus Succeed. Palachuk, Karl W., and Ben Gay III. Sacramento: Great Little Book Publishing, 2010; and Kindle eBook.

The Enneagram in Love and Work: Understanding Your Intimate and Business Relationships. Palmer, Helen. San Francisco: Harper San Francisco, 1995.

Magical Child: Rediscovering Nature's Plan for Our Children. Pearce, Joseph Chilton. New York: Bantam Books, 6th ed., 1986.

Gestalt Therapy Verbatim. Perls, Frederick S. Moab, UT: Real People Press, 1969.

The Stress of Life. Selye, Hans. New York: McGraw-Hill, 1965.

Quantum Physics & the Physics of Our Subtle Bodies

The Body Electric: Electromagnetism and the Foundation of Life. Becker, Robert O., M.D., and Gary Seldon. New York: William Morrow and Company, 1985.

Wholeness and the Implicate Order. Bohm, David. Boston: Routledge & Kegan Paul, 1980.

The Tao of Physics: An Exploration of the Parallels Between Modern Physics and Eastern Mysticism. Capra, Fritjof. Boston: Shambala Publications, Inc., 25th ed., 1975.

The Turning Point: Science, Society, and the Rising Culture. Capra, Fritjof. New York: Bantam Books, 1982.

The Heartmath Solution. Childre, Doc, and Howard Martin with Donna Beech. New York: HarperCollins Publishers, 1999.

Plant Spirit Medicine: A Journey into the Healing Wisdom of Plants. Cowan, Eliot. Updated New Edition. Boulder, CO: Sounds True, 2014 (Also included in the Five Elements section.)

The Subtle Body: An Encyclopedia of Your Energetic Anatomy, illustrated. Dale, Cyndi. Boulder, CO: Sounds True, Incorporated, 2009.

Albert Einstein, Out of My Later Years. Einstein, Albert. New York: Wings Books, 1993.

Vibrational Medicine: New Choices for Healing Ourselves. Gerber, Richard, M.D. Rochester, VT: Bear & Company, updated ed., 1996.

The Elegant Universe: Superstrings, Hidden Dimensions, and the Quest for the Ultimate Theory. Greene, Brian. New York: W. W. Norton & Co., Inc., 1999.

"Photography and Visual Observation by Means of High-Frequency Currents." Kirlian, Semyon Davidovich, and V. Kirlian. Alma-Ata, Kazakh, USSR: Kazakh State Institute, 1950. Also reported in the Journal of Scientific and Applied Photography, Vol. 6, No. 6. (Showed the first photographs of the etheric body.)

The Kirlian Aura: Photographing the Galaxies of Life. Krippner, Stanley (ed.), and Daniel Rubin (ed.). New York: Anchor Books, 1974.

The Awakening of Kundalini. Krishna, Gopi. New York: E. P. Dutton & Company, 1975

Acupuncture Points, Images and Functions. Lade, Arnie. Seattle: Eastland Press, 1989.

The Chakras. Leadbetter, Charles Webster. Wheaton, IL: Theosophical Publishing House, 1927; Quest Book reprint, 1977.

The Biology of Belief: Unleashing the Power of Consciousness, Matter, and Miracles. Lipton, Bruce H. Felton, CA: Mountain of Love/Elite Books, 2005.

The Farther Reaches of Human Nature. Maslow, Abraham H. New York: Viking Press, 1971.

Toward a Psychology of Being. Maslow, Abraham. New York: Van Nostrand, 1968.

Prodigal Genius: The Life of Nikola Tesla. O'Neill, John J. New York: David McKay, 1971.

Anatomy of the Spirit: The Seven Stages of Power and Healing. Myss, Caroline. New York: Three Rivers Press, 1996.

Psychic Discoveries Behind the Iron Curtain. Ostrander, Sheila, and Lynn Schroeder. New York: Bantam Books, 1970.

The Biology of Transcendence: A Blueprint of the Human Spirit. Pearce, Joseph Chilton. Rochester, VT: Park Street Press, 2002.

Holistic Medicine from Stress to Optimal Health. Pelletier, Kenneth R., Ph.D. New York: Delacorte Press, 1979.

Mind As Healer, Mind As Slayer. Pelletier, Kenneth R., Ph.D. McHenry, IL: Delta, 1977.

Brain and Perception: Holonomy and Structure in Figural Processing. Pibram, Karl H. Hillsdale, NJ: Lawrence Erlbaum Associates, 1991. I read six more of his monographs, which explained memory, and how our anatomical brain and holographic mind interface.

Character Analysis. Reich, Wilhelm. Rangely, ME: Orgone Institute Press, 1949.

The Global Brain: Speculations on the Evolutionary Leap to Planetary Consciousness. Russell, Peter. Los Angeles: Jeremy P. Tarcher, 1983.

Spirituality

I Come as a Brother: A Remembrance of Illusions. Bartholomew. Taos, NM. High Mesa Foundation, 1985.

The Three Years. Bock, E. London: Christian Community Press, 1955.

The Gods of Eden. Bramely, William. New York: Avon Books, 1993.

Spiritual Economics: The Principles and Process of True Prosperity. Butterworth, Eric. Unity Village, MO: Unity Books, 1993.

The Hero with a Thousand Faces: The Collected Works of Joseph Campbell. Campbell, Joseph. Novato, CA: New World Library; 3rd ed., 2008.

Starseed: The Third Millennium: Living in the Posthistoric World. Carey, Ken. New York: HarperCollins Publishers, 1991.

Many Mansions: The Edgar Cayce Story on Reincarnation. Cerminara, Gina. New York: New American Library, 1950.

Start Where You Are: A Guide to Compassionate Living. Chödrön, Pema. Boston MA: Shambhala Publications, 1981.

Testimony of Light. Greaves, Helen. London: Neville Spearman Publishers, 1973; later published by Jeremy P. Tarcher, 2009. This is the most thorough and complete of five books I read about life on the other side of the veil.

The Law of Attraction: The Basics of the Teachings of Abraham. Hicks, Esther, and Jerry. Carlsbad, CA: Hay House, 2006.

Lifetimes: True Accounts of Reincarnation. Lenz, Frederick, Ph.D. New York: Fawcett Books, 1979.

Journey of Souls: Case Studies of Life Between Lives. Newton, Michael, Ph.D. St. Paul, MN: Llewellyn Publications, 2002.

Beyond Belief: The Secret Gospel of Thomas. Pagels, Elaine. New York: Random House, 2005.

The Spiritual Value of Gem Stones. Richardson, Wally, and Lenora Huett. Marina Del Ray, CA: DeVorss & Co., 1980.

A Course in Miracles. Schucman, Helen, Ph.D., and William Thetford, Ph.D. Mill Valley, CA: Foundation for Inner Peace, 1975.

Voluntary Controls: Exercises for Creative Meditation and for Activating the Potential of the Chakras. Schwarz, Jack. New York: E. P. Dutton, 1978.

Beholding the Nature of Reality: Possibility of Spiritual Community. Schwarzkoph, Friedemann, Ph.D. Fair Oaks, CA: Rudolf Steiner College Press, 1997.

The Spiritual Writings of B. J. Palmer. Senzon, Simon A. Asheville, NC: S. A. Senzon, 2004.

How to Know Higher Worlds: A Modern Path of Initiation. Steiner, Rudolf. Translated by Christopher Bamford. Hudson, NY: Anthroposophic Press, 1940.

The Influences of Lucifer and Ahriman. Steiner, Rudolf. Canada: Steiner Book Center, 1919.

Knowledge of the Higher Worlds and Its Attainment. Steiner, Rudolf. London: Steiner Press, 1969.

Learning to See into the Spiritual World. Steiner, Rudolf. New York: Anthroposophic Press, 1990.

Energy Fields and the Human Body: Frontiers of Consciousness. Tiller, William A. Edited by J. White. New York: Avon Books, 1974.

The Power of Now: A Guide to Spiritual Enlightenment. Tolle, Eckhart. Novato, CA: New World Library, 2004.

Shaman, Healer, Sage: How to Heal Yourself and Others with the Energy Medicine of the Americas. Villoldo, Alberto, Ph.D. New York: Harmony Books, 2000.

Miscellaneous

Writing Creative Nonfiction: Fiction Techniques for Crafting Great Nonfiction. Cheney, Theodore A. Rees. Berkeley: Ten Speed Press, 1987.

The Art Spirit. Henri, Robert. Philadelphia /New York: J. B. Lippincott Co., 1980.

Zen in the Art of Archery. Herrigel, Eugen. New York: Pantheon Books, 1953.

The Alphabet Versus the Goddess: The Conflict Between Word and Image. Schlain, Leonard. New York: Penguin Books, 1991.

The 12th Planet: Book I of the Earth Chronicles. Sitchin, Zecharia. New York: HarperCollins Books, 2007.

INDEX